A Second Exodus

BRANDEIS SERIES IN AMERICAN JEWISH HISTORY, CULTURE, AND LIFE

Jonathan D. Sarna, Editor
Sylvia Barack Fishman, Associate Editor

A Second Exodus

THE AMERICAN MOVEMENT
TO FREE SOVIET JEWS

Murray Friedman and Albert D. Chernin, editors

BRANDEIS UNIVERSITY PRESS
Published by University Press of New England / Hanover and London

Brandeis University Press

Published by University Press of New England, Hanover NH 03755

© 1999 by Brandeis University Press

Printed in the United States of America   5 4 3 2 1

CIP data appear at the end of the book

This book has been partially underwritten by a grant from the Myer and Rosaline Feinstein Center for American Jewish History, Temple University.

Contents

I. OVERVIEW

II. IMPACT OF STRATEGIC PRESSURES

III. HARMONY AND STRIFE

Abbreviations

AIPAC: American Israel Public Affairs Committee
AJCommittee: American Jewish Committee
AJCongress: American Jewish Congress
AJCSJ: American Jewish Conference on Soviet Jewry
BACSJ: Bay Area Council for Soviet Jews
CJF: Council of Jewish Federations and Welfare Funds
CRIF: Representative Conference of the Jews of France
CSCE: Conference on Security and Cooperation in Europe
CSSJ: California Students for Soviet Jewry
FSU: former Soviet Union
GNYCSJ: Greater New York Conference on Soviet Jewry
HIAS: Hebrew Immigrant Aid Society
JCRC: Jewish Community Relations Council
JDC: American Jewish Joint Distribution Committee
JDL: Jewish Defense League
MFM status: most-favored-nation status
NACSJ: National Advisory Council on Soviet Jewry
NCRAC: National Community Relations Advisory Council
NCSJ: National Conference on Soviet Jewry
NGOs: non-governmental organizations
NJCRAC: National Jewish Community Relations Advisory Council
OVIR (Soviet immigration agency)
POCs: Prisoners of Conscience
SJEIC: Soviet Jewry Education and Information Centre
SJM: Soviet Jewish movement
SSSJ: Student Struggle for Soviet Jewry
UCSJ: Union of Councils on Soviet Jewry
UJA: United Jewish Appeal
USSR: Union of Soviet Socialist Republics
WJC: World Jewish Congress

A Second Exodus

Introduction

The Jewish Community Comes of Age

In 1984, together with a number of Jews from Philadelphia, I traveled to the Soviet Union to meet with Soviet refuseniks to express solidarity with them in their efforts to leave the country. We "tourists" and those Soviet citizens we met with were deeply distrusted by Soviet authorities. The act of becoming a refusenik resulted in severe penalties and dangers to Soviet Jews, including loss of their jobs and in some cases imprisonment.

When it became known to Soviet dissidents in Moscow that I was an American historian, I was asked to lecture to a group gathered at the home of Boris Klotz (who is now a citizen of Israel). I chose as my topic the role of the United States and American Jewry in the rescue of Jews during World War II. The evening stands out for me with special vividness. The shades and curtains were tightly drawn in the Klotz living room. Some fifty Soviet Jews crowded into the tight quarters. As I spoke, my words were simultaneously translated into Russian. When I finished, there were questions. One affected me very deeply: "Will American Jews forget us?" I recall saying that I thought we would not. I described the efforts under way in the United States—indeed, throughout the world—on their behalf, including, of course, our own visit.

American and world Jewry did not forget. More than a million Jews have come out of the Soviet Union since the movement began, and for much of this time against the strong opposition of the authorities there. This has to be seen as one of the great exoduses in Jewish history. The means for bringing this emigration about was the Soviet Jewry movement (SJM), a mobilization of Jews and their friends throughout the world to bring pressure on the Communist regime and force the authorities there, as the Bible proclaims, to "let my people go." These pressures, as the essays in this volume indicate, came from many directions and were marked by creative imagination, enormous skill, and above all with consistency over forty years. In the process, the American Jewish community matured. From a series of disparate and contending groups—"a cacophony of voices" in Henry Feingold's telling phrase—that during World War II was unable to mount a major campaign to rescue their coreligionists from the horrors of the Nazi onslaught, Jews formed themselves into a community able to bring about a positive resolution.[1]

There was another important and little noted effect of the SJM. The Soviet Union was made up of a variety of nationality groups, many of whom were restless and sought release from Soviet oppression. The fact that in releasing Soviet Jewish citizens, the ruling authorities felt constrained to yield to worldwide human rights protests (including that of their own citizens) may have weakened the system and played a role in the ultimate destruction of the Soviet Union.

As might be expected, there are a number of surprises in this story. The first is that the SJM began not in the United States but in Israel, as Nehemiah Levanon's and several other essays here make clear. During the war, Soviet authorities enlisted all elements of the population, including its Jewish citizens, to repel the invaders. After the war, however, Soviet authorities embarked upon a campaign of repression (described here by Albert D. Chernin), a systematic anti-Semitism that grew increasingly harsh.

While it never reached the proportions of the Nazi horrors, harassment and murders of Jews took place regularly. The 1948 murder of S. M. Mikhoels, a leading personality in Soviet theatrical life and leader of the wartime Jewish Anti-Fascist Committee, at the orders of Stalin, marked the onset of what has been called the "shvartze yoren," the black years. During the last years of Stalin's reign, the Soviet Union embarked upon a campaign to wipe out every vestige of Jewish cultural and religious life. During this time, except for an occasional report by the American Jewish Committee and others, Soviet Jewry was cut off from the world's Jewish community.

Levanon, who directed the Israeli effort through the Liaison Bureau—the "Office Without a Name"—describes here the start of the campaign in 1952, beginning with a meeting in Tel Aviv of Soviet Jews who had come to Israel in the 1920s. The decision was made at the highest level of the Israeli government to initiate contact with their endangered brethren: Emissaries would be sent into the Soviet Union to awaken there a sense of Jewishness and solidarity with the Jewish state. Surrounded by hostile Arab neighbors bent on its destruction, Israel was anxious also to encourage immigration to strengthen it in the battles that lay ahead.

The bureau, also known as the Lishkat HaKeshar, set out to arouse world Jewry and others to the threat that existed. Working with Israeli diplomats like Meir Rosenne, stationed at that time in New York City, it helped to create a Jewish Minority Research organization under Moshe Decter, a brilliant organizer and activist, to mobilize support for Soviet

Jewry. Decter helped to organize major conferences involving such notables as Martin Luther King, Jr., Supreme Court Justice William O. Douglas, Leonard Bernstein, and the Reverend Theodore M. Hesburgh in the 1960s. At the same time, other factors (described in Chernin's essay in this volume) had led to the formation of the American Conference on Soviet Jewry, the first overall body of major Jewish groups working on behalf of Soviet Jewry. The Lishkat, of course, had to maintain a low profile, and its activities are not widely known today. Prior to the Six-Day War, the Jewish state had diplomatic relations with the Soviet Union and undertook activities in support of Soviet Jews (as described in Nehemiah Levanon's essay). However, Israel did not want attention drawn to those activities.

Except for elements linked to the Jewish Labor Committee, the Yiddish *Forward* and the *New Leader*, a small but influential publication associated with David Dubinsky's International Ladies' Garment Workers' Union, American Jews were slow to come into this effort. Eager to put behind them their own "schvartze yoren," including the memory of the Holocaust, they were more focused on their upward climb in American life. Indeed, the postwar years were the "golden age" of American Jewry. As historian Howard Sachar has suggested, Jews were concerned about defining Judaism in American terms. At best, they were prepared to support the establishment and sustenance of the State of Israel, but mainly as a refuge for the remnants of European Jewry. During this period, Jews were eager to take their place alongside other Americans, and to overcome remaining barriers and threats (like McCarthyism) that appeared to loom large at this time.[2]

The Jewish community and a significant segment of the intelligentsia of this period, it must be recalled, was also a community of the Left. The "real" socialist experiment (that is, the Soviet Union) was still being hailed by some in this country and abroad. Beatrice and Sidney Webb in England declared in their book *The Truth About the Soviet Union* that Stalin was not a dictator, but President Franklin D. Roosevelt was. Historian Arthur Schlesinger, Jr. called the Webbs and their cohorts "doughface Progressives," but there were still some Jews in the late 1940s and 1950s who viewed the Soviet Union as the place where poverty was being eliminated, unemployment did not exist, and "the workers of brain and arm controlled their destinies." Influential publications like the *New Republic* and the *Nation* for the most part faithfully followed the Communist Party line. The year 1948 saw the formation of the Progressive Party, which nominated former vice president and secretary of commerce Henry Wallace to challenge the cold war policies of Harry Truman.[3] Even where the policies of the far left did not predominate, liberal domestic issues, and especially the excitement and hopefulness of the civil rights movement led by Martin Luther King, Jr. engaged much of the energies of Jews in the 1950s and early 1960s.

While Israel, through its early organizational efforts both in the Soviet Union and the United States, may be said to have been the starting point of the SJM, by the early 1960s, a significant, grassroots movement was getting under way. The Cleveland Council on Soviet Anti-Semitism was created in 1963 and became the genesis of a broader group, the Union of Councils of Soviet Jewry (UCSJ). In addition, a British activist, Jacob Birnbaum, who had emigrated to the United States, was instrumental in the creation of the Student Struggle for Soviet Jewry (SSSJ), which began organizing student protests, mainly in New York.

In addition, by 1969, Rabbi Meir Kahane's Jewish Defense League, which had gained public attention by its efforts to defend poorer Jews in racially troubled areas, began to shift its energies to anti-Soviet efforts. Contemptuous of what it saw as the slowness of establishment bodies to move, Kahane and his compatriots were not above using violence, including bombings of Soviet agencies in this country such as Aeroflot and AMTORG, as well as Sol Hurok Productions, killing one person in the latter case and injuring fourteen others.

The Soviet Jewry movement, in short, reflected certain philosophical and ideological divisions already extant in the Jewish community (establishment versus nonestablishment, universalists versus particularists) as well as long-standing debates over tactics (behind-the-scenes versus mass protests and, of course, the role of Israel in Jewish life). While each of the different Soviet Jewry organizations came to believe that it was primarily responsible for the movement's success, we can safely conclude that the organizations together, with their various strategies and activities, did more than any one of them could have done alone.

The dissenting groups bore some resemblance to the revisionist Zionist Peter Bergson group in this country during World War II, which recognized early on the threat to Jews abroad and advocated more militant measures to meet that threat. These groups exerted pressure on Jewish establishment bodies to move the SJM to a higher level of priority, and ultimately led to the formation of the National Conference on Soviet Jewry in 1971.

The SJM developed against the backdrop of the cold war. During this time President Nixon and his national security adviser, later secretary of state, Henry Kissinger, sought détente with the Soviet Union. Their aim was to avoid the danger of nuclear devastation while seeking simultaneously to contain Soviet expansionism. This double goal posed exquisite problems for Jewish communal leaders, particularly leading Republicans like Max Fisher and Jacob Stein of the President's Conference of Major Jewish Organizations: the latter sought to support Soviet Jews who wished to leave, but came under enormous pressure not to compromise the search for accommodation with the Soviets. President Nixon and Kissinger argued vehemently to Fisher and others that the Jackson-Vanik legislation (discussed in this volume) to trade off commercial advantages for liberalized Soviet emigration policies would not do the job; that tying Soviet emigration policies to arms control and other issues would be more effective. Initially, Fisher and other establishment leaders closely involved with the administration accepted the argument and sought to gain acceptance for it within the SJM.[4] The leadership of the National Conference on Soviet Jewry, however, vigorously rejected it.

How to handle rescuing Jews *and* cooperating with governmental powers was a test Jewish political and communal leaders had faced and failed during the 1930s and World War II. Historian Henry Feingold writes of such earlier figures as Justice Felix Frankfurter, Judge Sam Rosenman, and the American Jewish Congress's Rabbi Stephen Wise "as peculiarly ill-suited to discharge the responsibility history and kinship assigned" to them.[5] Caught up in a liberal, universalist social agenda most of their lives, many of the Jews around Roosevelt were secular Jews who "did not feel empassioned by what was being done to their brethren in Europe." They had "laid aside their Jewish identity as part of the transaction for social status. . . . They no longer felt themselves Jewish at all and could not identify with European Jewry."[6] Henry Morgenthau, Jr., Roosevelt's secretary of the treasury, was an exception, and his intervention with FDR led to perhaps the sole bright note in this country's relationship to European Jews during the war: the War Refugee Board.

Subsequent generations of Jews, however, embraced the movement wholeheartedly. As one examines the evolution of the Jackson-Vanik amendment in essays here by William Korey and Marshall I. Goldman, one cannot help being impressed with the extraordinary activism of Jewish political leadership (and especially their Jewish aides on Capitol Hill) as they responded to the SJM. Indeed, the idea behind Jackson-Vanik was originally projected in 1972 by Bertram Podell, a two-term Jewish House Democrat from Brooklyn, who showed it to lobbyist I. L. Kenen of the American Israel Public Affairs Committee (AIPAC). Podell soon dropped out of history; two years later, he would be defeated in a reelection bid. The idea was nonetheless continued by Richard Perle, a brilliant defense expert whose interest in Soviet Jews had been activated by a visit to Israel arranged by Levanon, and who was now a key member of Jackson's staff, and Mark Talisman, a member of Vanik's staff. Perle worked closely with Morris Amitay, chief of staff for Senator Abraham Ribicoff of Connecticut. The popular support for Jackson-Vanik ultimately could not be withstood by Fisher and others who earlier had lined up with Nixon. The campaign for the amendment was the first of a number of Jewish legislative initiatives that "transformed the Jewish lobby" into a Washington powerhouse in the 1970s and the years ahead.[7]

Passage of the legislation in late December 1974 and early January 1975 went beyond the immediate interests and concerns of the Jewish

community. It was the first major piece of international human rights legislation ever passed in the United States. As such, it was a manifestation
of and helped to broaden this country's interest in human rights violations throughout the world. Jackson-Vanik led inexorably, as William
Korey points out here, to the Helsinki Final Act, signed in 1975 by thirty-
five European and North American countries, including the United States
and the Soviet Union. This rapidly moved the issue of human rights to the
center of international diplomacy. In follow-up conferences, especially
the Vienna conference extending from 1986 to 1989, and coinciding with
Mikhail Gorbachev's policy of glasnost and openness, the right to leave a
country—free emigration—was assured.

The world Jewish community, of course, used the Helsinki Final Act
and the meetings of the Conference on Security and Cooperation in Europe (CSCE), created by the act, as major instruments to promote human
rights and emigration of large numbers of Soviet Jews to Israel, the
United States, and other countries. The fulfillment of Helsinki's "freer
movement of peoples," however, as Korey notes, had extraordinary and
unexpected consequences. For instance, thousands of East Germans vacationing in Hungary in September 1989, several months after the Vienna
document was approved, decided to move to West Germany. This mass
emigration weakened the East German government, and set in motion
the crumbling of the Berlin Wall and ultimately the Soviet Union itself.

There is no mistaking, of course, the overriding sense of guilt
American Jews felt following World War II that clearly was at work in
the extraordinary efforts they mounted on behalf of Soviet Jews. They
were determined to learn from this experience and "never again" remain
silent when their brethren were endangered. Christian leaders, such as
Sen. Henry Jackson and Chairman Wilbur Mills of the House Ways and
Means Committee, also displayed this new determination. Sister Ann
Gillen of Rosemont, who headed the Interfaith Coalition operating out
of Chicago for many years, found her true vocation in the SJM. Of course,
legislators are not immune to political considerations; nonetheless, they
were also influenced in large measure by the "lessons" of the Holocaust.

I do not suggest that there was not much hesitation, acrimony, and
backing and filing on the tactics employed within the SJM, as this volume
amply attests. Early activist groups like the UCSJ and the SSSJ never fully
made peace with Jewish establishment bodies—or even, for that matter,
with the Israeli bureau, which they felt did not provide them with adequate information. In turn, the latter often felt the nonestablishment
groups were sometimes irresponsible. Ultimately, however, the "cacophony of voices" Feingold describes in the days of President Roosevelt gave
way to a unity of purpose among Jews at all levels—particularly after the
Six-Day and Yom Kippur wars in 1967 and 1973, which heightened the
sense of identity felt by most Jews. Jewish leaders increasingly came to

take their role as Jews seriously, even as they discharged their broader political and civic responsibilities. It is in this sense that the SJM, along with broad-based support for Israel, marks the coming of age of the American Jewish community.

It is the great and imperishable achievement of the SJM that it played a critical role in bringing out 1.3 million Soviet Jews. Less understood, perhaps, is what it did for American Jews. As Howard Sachar writes, it "functioned as a vital emotional compensation" and provided "a new focus of communal purpose."[8] The visits of thousands of American Jews to Soviet refuseniks, the deep ties that developed between the individuals involved, along with protest activities in their infinite forms in this country helped to heighten the sense of Jewish identity and consolidate an American Jewish community well along on its path to assimilation. Many would find their exposure to it, as one SJM leader told me, "the most meaningful experience" of their life. Simultaneously, the interest and expressions of solidarity exhibited by world Jewry, alongside the Six-Day War and harassment by Soviet authorities, heightened the sense of Jewish identity among Soviet Jews.

The SJM was a product of its time and place. It was affected by the civil rights and other activist student movements that were developing simultaneously. A sampling of SSSJ activists showed that some 51 percent had taken part in some measure in the antiwar movement, 28 percent in civil rights activities, and 26 percent in campus activism.[9] The moral consciousness and tactics of the civil rights movement—demonstrations, protest marches, involvement of Christian clergy—were skillfully pressed into service by Jewish agencies involved in the SJM, who recruited, not surprisingly, such figures as Martin Luther King, Jr., Bayard Rustin, and A. Philip Randolph. And as the civil rights movement wound down beginning in the latter part of the 1960s, succeeded by a form of black nationalism that permitted little room for Jewish involvement, Jewish energy and utopian sensibilities often found a new outlet in the SJM.

Of course, the emotional energies and involvement of virtually every element of American Jewish life in the SJM brought in its wake newer and broader issues. What was to be the place of Israel and American Jews in the leadership of American and world Jewry? The role of American Jewry in the SJM, at least initially, was a "subordinate one." It was the government of Israel, Howard Sachar writes, "that conceived, launched, and executed the campaign to establish a relationship" with the third largest Jewish population in the world.[10] Following the first World Conference on Soviet Jewry in Brussels in 1971, an international body emerged that led to Jewish communities throughout the free world, including Israel, jointly planning the campaign for Soviet Jewry. The Liaison Bureau and Israel's continued involvement would remain a quiet but unmistakable force in the SJM over the years. It was especially important with establishment leadership. The fact remained, however, that this leadership was forced to embrace new tactics and thought arising in the communities and from nonestablishment elements. The American Jewish community had moved beyond Israel and evolved into the prime force in the SJM.[11]

With this growing assertiveness also came a new and sobering change in the U.S.-Israel Jewish relationship with regard to Israel and a greater willingness on the part of American Jews, save in matters involving security, to challenge the Jewish state. This came to a head in what Steven F. Windmueller calls in his essay here "The 'Noshrim' War." Between 1967 and 1980, some 160,000 Soviet Jews had gone to Israel and 90,000 to the United States. However, between 1980 and 1988, some 23,000 settled in Israel and 35,000 came to the United States. As the numbers of Soviet Jews coming out grew and sought increasingly to emigrate to the United States rather than Israel—in contrast with the earlier exodus of Zionist-oriented Soviet Jews to the Jewish state—the question arose as to what posture U.S. Jews should take. Should the SJM be a Zionist or human rights movement?[12]

The Israelis, originally supported by key leadership of the Council of Jewish Federations, pushed hard to have U.S. Jewish communal bodies like the Hebrew Immigrant Aid Society (HIAS) put pressure on Soviet Jews to select Israel, and they had the support of such leaders as Max Fisher.[13] Other elements, including the Union of Councils, the American Jewish Committee, the National Jewish Community Relations Council (NJCRAC), and a number of local communities opted for "freedom of choice." After all, the parents and grandparents of American Jews had come here of their free wills. Why should Soviet Jews be denied the same right?

Ultimately, the matter was resolved with the "triumph of Jewish federation (domestically oriented) leadership over United Jewish Appeal (Israel-oriented) leadership."[14] The debates, perhaps influenced also by growing dissatisfaction among American Jews with the right-wing government of Menachem Begin, engaged every element of Jewish communal life. It represented, as Windmueller notes here, the first issue of conflict for a broad range of Jewish interests and institutions in both Israel and the United States. In subsequent years, other issues such as "Who is a Jew?" and the role of the Orthodox rabbinate in Israel in matters of marriage and conversion would roil the waters of the two centers of Jewish life.[15]

There were other issues the two societies would have to face growing out of the success of the SJM. How would the increasingly large number of Soviet Jews be integrated? Economic dislocation was only the beginning of the problem, in some respects the easiest aspect of it. Soviet Jews had been cut off from Jewish life since the Russian Revolution. Once in the United States, they did not fit easily into the Jewish community. Few were religious; indeed, as Nora Levin writes, most Jews came "with a negative sense of their Jewishness and even fear of it because of the handicap it placed on them in the Soviet Union. Still, studies showed they wanted to be seen as American Jews and identified with the State of Israel."[16] They would have to learn about bonds with Jews and their Jewish past.

To be sure, Jews had been outsiders even in Russia and had learned to do what they had to in order to survive. Reports soon began to appear in newspapers and magazines following their arrival here about criminal activities on the part of a small number.[17] The habit of working around "the system" that some brought here was often irritating to the children and grandchildren of Eastern European Jews (whose own families had sometimes been looked down upon by earlier and more assimilated Jewish immigrants). There is reason to believe, however, that as with other earlier immigrants, these problems would decline as the group, and especially their children, learned to adjust to American life. In any case, whatever the strains, local federations and their component agencies assumed responsibility for them.[18]

The arrival of so many Soviet Jews in Israel and the United States has affected Jewish life in these countries. The May 1996 election in Israel witnessed the overnight rise in political power of the Russian émigré community. It won seven seats in the narrowly divided Knesset and two cabinet posts by members of Natan Sharansky's Israel Ba'aliyah Party in the Likud-led coalition.[19] This rise in power has attracted much attention. Less noticed, however, has been the impact of the 350,000 Soviet Jews in the Jewish community in the United States. Between 1975 and 1988, some 81,000 moved here in a "first wave." A second wave of almost 200,000 arrived between 1989 and 1994. By 1997, an official of HIAS reports, a quarter of New York City's Jews were born in the Soviet Union. Whole neighborhoods like Sheepshead Bay and Brighton Beach in New York, and West Hollywood, Santa Monica, and the San Fernando Valley in Los Angeles have been transformed.[20]

This political transformation, at first glance, appears to be exclusively rightward. The *Jewish Forward* has reported that the second wave began voting in 1995 after the six-year naturalization process, along with their predecessors here, for more conservative political candidates. One of their reasons for becoming citizens, a resettlement expert in Brooklyn told the *Forward*'s Douglas Feiden, was to vote for Ronald Reagan. They still view Russia as an "evil empire," especially for Jews, and continue to see themselves as voting against the Soviet Union. "The rightward trend in Russian émigré voting patterns may be unleashing a new force in American politics," Feiden declares, "similar to the fervid conservatism that refugees from Castro's Cuba brought to Southern Florida."[21] Such a judgment, however, may be premature. A HIAS official reports also the deep resentment among Soviet Jews at Republicans who helped push through recent "welfare reforms" that limit or wipe out benefits to many of these newcomers. It is still too early to develop any firm conclusions about the place of Soviet Jews in our society. It is only a few brief years ago that they were knocking on the doors of their Soviet masters, asking for permission to leave.

Indeed, the SJM and its successful outcome is so near to us in time, there has been little opportunity for historians to study this extraordinary episode. The Myer and Rosaline Feinstein Center for American Jewish History, operating in cooperation with the Philadelphia Chapter of the American Jewish Committee, has set out to remedy this. With a grant from the Pew Charitable Trusts, my colleague Albert D. Chernin and I invited many of the major figures who took part in this movement, along with several scholars, to present papers and discuss the movement from their various perspectives at the national headquarters of the American Jewish Committee on 15 and 16 June 1995. This book is composed of essays prepared by these individuals, including some we commissioned subsequently in order to fill out the story. I am especially grateful to Al Erlick, former editor of the *Jewish Exponent* in Philadelphia, for editing and helping us assemble these essays.

It is hardly surprising that there are sharp differences expressed here— just as there were in the movement itself—and we make no effort to resolve these here. Rather, we lay the groundwork for further investigation. Many questions remain. Because the SJM began, at least in this country, as a grassroots movement, we need to know more about its development in various communities. (A study of the Philadelphia experience sponsored by the Feinstein Center is currently under way, but we need to know more about Cleveland and other cities.) What about the SJM and the broader struggle for human rights in the Soviet Union? A decision was made at a critical point among SJM leadership—it was challenged by Sharansky and Alan M. Dershowitz, among others—to dissociate the issue of release of Soviet Jews from broader human rights efforts in the Soviet Union. Dershowitz has even suggested that there was an "understanding" between the Israelis and the Soviet government in which Israel would concern itself only with refuseniks and Prisoners of Zion.[22] The advocacy campaign was determined that the demands appear to the Soviet Union as narrow and modest, in contrast to the pressures mounted by other Soviet dissidents who justifiably called for the overhaul of the Soviet system. The former feared that commingling the issues would severely endanger the cause of Soviet Jewry.

What were the ethical and moral issues and the harsh realities of the politics of rescue involved in such a dichotomy? What were the psychological forces involved in the role played by *shtadlunim*-type leaders (community elders) like Max Fisher, caught between their role as advocates for their people and maintaining their ties with government leaders like Nixon and Kissinger? We need to take a closer look, too, at the impact of the civil rights revolution and its transformation into a race revolution, as well as the strategies and tactics and, perhaps even more important, the psychology of the SJM.

Much of Jewish history has been a record of helplessness, tragedy, and recrimination. American Jews still debate whether they could have done more to rescue their endangered brethren during World War II. It is time perhaps to replace an older image of Jews as "losers" with one of Jews as occasional "winners," and of a society that looks on indifferently to Jewish suffering to one that joins with them on behalf of the cause of human rights. The SJM, in short, along with the creation of the State of Israel (supported by Americans), marks another dimension of the Jewish experience. This book, then, is part history, part celebration of a bright page in Jewish and American Jewish life, marking a time when Jews came together with friends and allies to engage in an extraordinary rescue mission. It is also a testimonial to the human spirit and the thirst for freedom that remains unquenchable.

Notes

1. Henry L. Feingold, "Was There Communal Failure Among American Jews?" in *Bearing Witness: How America and Its Jews Responded to the Holocaust* (Syracuse: Syracuse University Press, 1995), pp. 205–17.

2. Howard M. Sachar, *A History of Jews in America* (New York: Knopf, 1992), 108; Daniel J. Elazar, *Community and Polity: The Organizational Dynamic of American Jewry*, rev. ed. (Philadelphia: Jewish Publication Society, 1995), 106.

3. Sidney Hook, *Out of Step: An Unquiet Life in the 20th Century* (New York: Harper and Row, 1987), 135; Elazar, *Community and Polity*, 103.

4. Peter Golden, *Quiet Diplomat: Max M. Fisher* (New York: Cornwall Books, 1992), 278.

5. Feingold, "Jewish Leadership During the Roosevelt Years," *Bearing Witness*, 226.

6. Ibid., 236.

7. Jay Winik, *On the Brink: The Dramatic, Behind-the-Scenes Saga of the Reagan Era and the Men and Women Who Won the Cold War* (New York: Simon and Schuster, 1996), 57; J. J. Goldberg, *Jewish Power: Inside the American Jewish Establishment* (Reading, Mass.: Addison-Wesley, 1996), 165.

8. Sachar, *History of the Jews*, 928.

9. William W. Orbach, *The American Movement to Aid Soviet Jews* (Amherst: University of Massachusetts Press, 1979), 4.

10. Sachar, *History of the Jews*, 906.

11. Elazar, *Community and Polity*, 111.

12. Sachar, *History of the Jews*, 924.

13. Golden, *Quiet Diplomat*, 75–76; Elazar, *Community and Polity*, 108.

14. Sachar, *History of the Jews,* 924.

15. For discussion of these issues, see Winston Pickett, "The Law of Diminishing Return," *Moment* (April 1997): 48–52, 88–97.

16. Nora Levin, "Home and Haven: Soviet Jewish Immigration to Philadelphia, 1972–1982," in *Philadelphia Jewish Life, 1940–1985,* by Murray Friedman (Philadelphia: Seth Press, 1986), 202, 220.

17. Sachar, *History of the Jews,* 927; Levin, "Home and Haven," 220; See, for example, *New York Times,* "Russian Submarine Surfaces in the Drug World," 7 March 1997.

18. Pickett, "Law of Diminishing Return," 97.

19. Ibid., 50.

20. Sachar, *History of the Jews,* 925.

21. *Jewish Forward,* 14 August 1994.

22. Alan M. Dershowitz, *Chutzpah,* (Boston: Little Brown, 1991), chap. 8.

I

Overview

Albert D. Chernin

Making Soviet Jews an Issue
A History

"S. M. Mikhoels, for many years the central personality in Jewish theatrical life in the Soviet Union, died in January, 1948." This is how the 1948–49 edition of the *American Jewish Yearbook* reported the death of Shlomo Mikhoels, the renowned director and actor of the Yiddish State Theater in Moscow.[1] According to an official Soviet announcement at the time, his life was cut short by a traffic accident in Minsk on 13 January 1948. The Soviet announcement cited his status as a significant figure in Jewish cultural life. That status had been acknowledged by Stalin seven years earlier in 1941, soon after the German invasion of the Soviet Union. Stalin appointed Mikhoels to cochair the newly created Jewish Anti-Fascist Committee of the Soviet Information Bureau with the latter's deputy chief, Solomon A. Lozovsky, a Jewish member of the Central Committee of the Soviet Communist Party and former chairman of the Trade Union International.[2]

Nikita Khrushchev recalled in his memoirs that the Jewish Anti-Fascist Committee was created by Stalin to undertake a public relations campaign "about the activities of our Soviet Army against the common enemy." The activities of the committee were aimed at "the Western press, principally the United States where there was a large, influential circle of Jews."[3] What followed was a reversal of Soviet policy. Contacts between Soviet Jews and Jews in the West were encouraged. On 24 August 1941, Soviet Jewish communists spoke on Moscow radio to world Jewry, addressing them in Yiddish as "brider yiden" (brother Jews). Even that simple salutation was a negation of Stalinist dogma.[4] It was one more instance where expediency, not ideology, dictated Soviet policy. To meet with Western Jews, Mikhoels traveled, as cochairman of the Jewish Anti-Fascist Committee, with its secretary, Itzik Fefer, the Soviet Yiddish poet, to the United States, Canada, Mexico, and Britain in 1943. On the eve of their departure, as Mikhoels and Fefer were concluding a courtesy meeting with Soviet President Kalinin, Stalin stepped into the room to wish them success. In the United States, they were greeted by record crowds, beginning with 46,000 in the now-demolished Polo Grounds in New York.[5]

After the war, the Jewish Anti-Fascist Committee continued to function. According to B. Z. Goldberg, a columnist for *Der Tag* (The Day), a New York Yiddish-language daily, its purpose was to continue to promote goodwill toward the Soviet Union. Goldberg, however, saw this body in a different light after meetings in Moscow with the leadership of the Jewish Anti-Fascist Committee during an extended visit to the Soviet Union in 1946: "Any local Jewish activity was irrelevant to the purpose for which the committee was organized," he asserted. "Nevertheless . . . so urgent [was] the need for a central Jewish body, that the greater part of the activity of the committee was, in actuality, concerned with local Jewish matters. It became the focal point of the entire spiritual life of Soviet Jews." Its Yiddish publication, *Einikeit*, "came to reflect the entire Jewish community,"[6] and its president, Mikhoels, was appointed by Stalin to chair the Soviet Commission on the Arts whose role was to designate winners of the Stalin Prize.

Nevertheless, the "Potemkin" village would soon come crashing down. The American Jewish community was unaware in 1948 that the death of Mikhoels signaled the launching of a campaign to eradicate the remnants of a once vibrant Jewish cultural life in the Soviet Union. At least that appears to have been the case if the Mikhoels obituary in the 1948–49 edition of the *Yearbook*, published more than a year after the death of Mikhoels, was any indication. That report gave no hint that Mikhoels had been murdered. Khrushchev, in his memoirs published in 1970, wrote: "They killed him like beasts. They killed him secretly. Then his murderers were rewarded and their victim was buried with honors. . . . It was announced that Mikhoels had fallen in front of a truck. Actually, he was thrown in front of a truck. . . . And who did it? Stalin did it or at least it was done on his instructions."[7] It was the beginning of what Soviet Jews called the "shvartze yoren" (the "black years"). Khrushchev claimed that members of "the Lozovsky committee" had drafted a paper addressed to Stalin. This alleged paper proposed that the Crimea be made a Jewish Soviet Republic within the Soviet Union after the deportation from the Crimea of Crimean Tatars. Khrushchev wrote, "Stalin saw behind this proposal the hand of American Zionists. . . . The committee members, he declared, were agents of American Zionists. They were laying the groundwork to set up a Jewish state in the Crimea in order to wrest the Crimea away from the Soviet Union and to establish an outpost of American imperialism on our shores. He was struck with maniacal vengeance" (260).

In contrast to the 1948–49 edition, volume 51 of the *Yearbook*, published in 1950, described in great detail the terror Stalin had unleashed against Soviet Jews in 1948. It reported that in November 1948, the Anti-Fascist Committee was suddenly dissolved and its Yiddish organ, *Einikeit*, discontinued. The Yiddish State Theater, a huge enterprise, was closed earlier that year; Shtern, the last Yiddish publishing house was shut down; all of the remaining journals were discontinued. The *Yearbook* reported that "leaders of the [Anti-Fascist] Committee and most of the well-known Yiddish writers were arrested and deported—Fefer, L. Goldberg, Markish, Nestor, S. Halkin, Bergelson, Broderzon, Kvitko." Further, "the campaign against Zionism and 'Jewish nationalism' was broadened to include attacks on all Jewish cultural and communal traditions, and all traditions of Jewishness were denounced as a form of both 'cosmopolitanism' and 'nationalism.' . . . The effect of the campaign was to identify all traditions of Jewishness with Jewish nationalism, Jewish nationalism with 'reactionary bourgeois Zionism,' Zionism with 'homeless cosmopolitanism,' and cosmopolitanism with 'service to imperialism and treason' against the Soviet Union."[8]

Years later, Soviet émigrés to the United States recalled in oral interviews that thousands, many of whom were totally assimilated, were purged and disappeared from academia, and spheres of culture and influence. One émigré remembered that "preparations for his bar mitzvah ended when the teacher disappeared." Another recalled a group of Jewish workers at the Stalin Automobile Factory who were put on trial as part of a Zionist plot.[9] Yet the knowledge in the United States of this campaign of terror against Soviet Jews did not trigger a collective response by the American Jewish establishment, or for that matter, even individual organizations, with the possible exception of the Jewish Labor Committee. The ineffectiveness of the American Jewish community in the face of the Nazi persecution in the 1930s and the Holocaust in the 1940s certainly was fresh in the minds of American Jewish leadership in the late 1940s. Nevertheless, those recollections did not impel them to act against Stalin's new campaign against Soviet Jews.

Of course, some may have been reluctant to believe these charges and may have seen them as another form of Red-baiting, which was growing in recklessness and intensity at that time in the United States. In that period, there still were those in the American Jewish community who romanticized Stalin's Soviet Union. The rose-colored view of the Soviet Union among some Jews may have been influenced in part by the Soviet Union's strong advocacy in the United Nations in 1947 of the establishment of a Jewish state in the British Mandate of Palestine. In May 1948, the Soviet Union was second only to the United States in swiftly recognizing the government of the new state of Israel. However implausible, Soviet support for a Jewish state was being asserted at Lake Success in New York on the very eve of Stalin's renewed campaign of terror against Soviet Jews. That advocacy included Andrey Gromyko's recollection in the

United Nations debate of the terrible suffering inflicted on millions of Jews by Nazi Germany.

By and large, however, the leadership of the American Jewish community did not have a romanticized perception of the Soviet Union. The articulate and forceful leadership of the Jewish Labor Committee in the 1940s and the highly respected executive director of the National Community Relations Advisory Council,[10] Isaiah M. Minkoff, had long recognized the despotic treatment of Jews by Stalin and the Soviet system, a view shared by many other Jewish leaders. Yet while they denounced the Soviet Union in 1949, they apparently did not press for a campaign. Most likely, the fear of the dangerous consequences for Soviet Jews of such a campaign was responsible for the restraint.

Ironically, there was a response by the editors of *Freiheit*, the Yiddish Communist daily, and leaders of the Jewish Section of the American Communist Party. In his memoir, *Being Red*, author Howard Fast recalled his meeting with Paul Novick and Chaim Suller, editors of *Freiheit*, on the eve of his departure for the Soviet-inspired World Peace Congress, which was to begin in Paris on 20 April 1949. Novick, a member of the National Committee of the Communist Party, claimed to be speaking "with full agreement of the National Committee, which had decided to issue a charge of anti-Semitic practices against the Communist Party of the Soviet Union. It charged "the entire leadership of the Communist Party was ridden with anti-Semitism." Fast, then a member of the Party, could not believe that such a charge could be true. Novick responded, "It is true. Can you imagine that we would make a charge like this if we didn't have proof? We have ample proof."[11]

Novick and Suller spelled out for Fast the actions taken against Jews that would be described later in the 1950 *Yearbook* (and the Khrushchev memoirs). They asked Fast to arrange to meet with the head of the Soviet delegation to the Peace Congress. In *Being Red*, Fast recalls being told: "You are to state that as a formal representative of the National Committee of our party, you make this charge against the Communist Party of the Soviet Union. . . . We accuse the leadership of the Soviet Union of grievous acts of anti-Semitism and of a non-Leninist position." They emphasized to Fast that a meeting at which charges of anti-Semitism would be leveled had to be held in secret: "If the press got hold of this, the consequences would be very bad" (207). Fast does not indicate for whom the consequences would be bad. For the Soviet Union? For the American Communist Party? For Soviet Jews?

As directed, Fast met in "absolute" secrecy in Paris in a basement room in Salle Pleyel with the head of the Soviet delegation, Alexander Fadeev, a Russian writer, and his translator. Fast made the charge he was instructed to bring. Fadeev replied, "There is no anti-Semitism in the Soviet Union" (217–18). Fast admitted that after the meeting he wondered whether Suller and Novick were wrong. Fast recalled, "Seven years later (1956) at the 20th Congress of the Communist Party of the Soviet Union, after Khrushchev's revelations of Stalin's monstrous deeds, Fadeev put a pistol in his mouth and blew his brains out" (219).

In 1953 at the time of the Doctors' Plot, Dr. Jacob Auslander, who had served in prison with Fast for being a member of the board in the 1930s of the Spanish Refugee Appeal, in a conversation with Fast characterized the Doctors' Plot "as a frameup of the worst kind." Fast then told Auslander about his meeting with Fadeev.

"Oh, my God, why have you not written of this?"

"Because the party asked me not to."

"Because they asked you not to? My God, Howard, what are you saying to me?"

Fast confronted Novick and Suller with Auslander's words. Novick answered, "What good would it do to accuse the Soviet Union of anti-Semitism before the whole world?" Fast replied, "Because if it's true, the world should know. It's important. Anti-Semitism is the meat of hate and murder, not of socialism." To which Novick replied, "But Russia is . . . the only socialist country. That's more important" (322 and 327–28).

On the night of 12 August 1952, twenty-three of the Yiddish poets, writers, journalists, and intellectuals who were among the leaders of the Jewish Anti-Fascist Committee arrested in 1948, including Fefer and Markish, were executed in the cellar of Lubyanka Prison. They were tried in July 1952 and charged with being agents of American imperialism who aimed to separate the Crimea from the Soviet Union and establish a Jewish national bourgeois Zionist republic to serve as an American military base against the Soviet Union. Despite brutal torture over a long period, they maintained their innocence to the very end.[12]

Five months later, on 13 January 1953, *Pravda* announced the arrest of nine leading doctors, six of whom were Jewish, as part of an international Jewish conspiracy, the American Jewish Joint Distribution Committee, to assassinate Soviet leadership, including Stalin. The official Soviet report charged that "the Joint . . . was established by American intelligence, ostensibly to aid Jews in foreign lands, but actually to serve as American agents and carry on widespread espionage, terrorist and inflammatory campaigns."[13] The doctors were accused of poisoning Andrey Zhadanov (supposedly Stalin's heir apparent) and Soviet military leaders and luminaries.

In the "Doctors' Plot," the Soviet regime perpetrated a fraud as treacherous as the publication by the czar's regime of the fraudulent *Protocols of the Elders of Zion*. Joseph Shapiro described the plot in the 1954 *American Jewish Yearbook* as "an unheard of outbreak of anti-Semitism. Together with the agents of [Lavrenti] Beria's [secret police] apparatus . . . Jews were to be made scapegoats for all the failures and crimes of the

Soviet regime. . . . [To this end] a worldwide 'Jewish conspiracy' was invented. . . . All this was accompanied by a barrage of propaganda . . . to show . . . Jews . . . [as] traitors, spies, imperialist agents, embezzlers and outright murderers . . . [It was] an immense cold pogrom."[14] Sovietologist Edward Crankshaw, who contributed commentary to Khrushchev's memoirs, suggested in his notes to the book that the plot against the doctors was designed to get rid of Stalin's closest colleagues: Beria, above all, but probably Molotov and Mikoyan too. Despite the torment Khrushchev says he felt during the episode of the Doctors' Plot, Crankshaw suggested that Khrushchev's role in this ghastly tale was suspect.[15]

Soviet émigrés to the United States later described their "overwhelming terror during the time of the Doctors' Plot." One recalled, "There began to be letters in the newspapers that Jewish doctors are poisoning people. We would hear people on the street saying . . . it's better not to go . . . to any Jewish doctors because it says in the papers they're murdering Russians." Many feared that Stalin would deport and possibly exterminate Jews. One émigré remembered, "The public prosecution of the doctors was thought to be the first step of a planned pogrom. We heard that it would be followed by public outrage and then Jews would be sent to Birobidzhan. The trains were supposed to be ready for transportation, and there were rumors of a plan to shoot people and throw them into clay pits. Such talk was very common. Everybody heard it."[16] Such deportations were not unprecedented under Stalin.

It was the 20–23 November 1952 trial in Prague of fourteen leading Czech communists that stimulated the first response from American Jewish organizations, even before the Doctors' Plot revelation. The anti-Semitic implications of those trials were self-evident. Eleven of those tried were Jewish, and their identity as Jews was obvious in the indictment. Dedicated Communists and bitter anti-Zionists, they were described by the prosecutor in his summation as "Trotskyite-Titoist Zionists" and "bourgeois nationalist traitors," recruited by Jewish agents to engage in sabotage and espionage. Confessing, the defendants attributed their crimes to their "bourgeois" and Jewish background.[17]

Every national member agency of NCRAC[18] and NCRAC itself issued a statement soon after the news of the Prague trials broke. On 21 December 1952, the Jewish Labor Committee held in New York City what the *Yearbook* described as "the first public meeting to protest Soviet anti-Semitism." More than fifteen hundred people attended. In a message to this meeting, President-elect Dwight David Eisenhower asserted, "This particular political act [the trial in Prague] was designed to unloose a campaign of rabid anti-Semitism through Soviet Russia and the satellite nations of Eastern Europe. The communists, like the Russian czars and the German Nazis, are using Jews as the scapegoats of their regime." Messages were received from other high government officials and trade union leaders, including Walter P. Reuther, president of the CIO.[19]

Distressed by the anti-Zionist atmosphere of the trials, NCRAC agencies agreed on the need to work closely with the Zionist organizations. The American Zionist Council responded to their suggestion to convene a meeting of thirty-four major national Jewish organizations. It was held 6 January 1952, only days before the Soviet "announcement" of the Doctors' Plot. At that meeting, Isaiah M. Minkoff, executive director of NCRAC, asserted that while Stalin had never adopted anti-Semitism as a racist theory, the Communists had long been engaged in the actual liquidation of organized Jewish life in the Soviet Union, and now (1953) had embarked upon the use of anti-Semitism as a political weapon. Minkoff urged "an intensive mobilization of world public opinion against Soviet anti-Semitism." He contended that a "soft" policy toward the Soviet Union on the part of world Jewry could not have "any salutary results." His call for such a campaign anticipated by ten years the campaign that would be launched by the American Jewish community. That meeting recommended a rally under the sponsorship of many organizations;[20] called for a nationwide and, if possible, a worldwide campaign for signatures to a mass petition to the United Nations; and requested a statement signed by one thousand representative citizens identified with important movements and organizations in American society.[21]

Two weeks later, on 20 January 1953, after the Doctors' Plot bombshell, Minkoff reiterated to the NCRAC executive committee the view he had expressed at the American Zionist Council meeting, and reported on the program that had been agreed upon. Myron Schwartz, executive director of the Saint Louis Jewish Community Relations Council, questioned the efficacy of the program Minkoff had urged. David Petegorsky, the executive director of the American Jewish Congress and an admirer of Nahum Goldmann,[22] questioned whether it was appropriate or desirable for the NCRAC executive committee to commit itself to a program without much more extensive discussion than was possible at that meeting. In the end, the executive committee approved in general the program.[23]

On 16 February 1953, about 3,500 people attended a protest rally in Manhattan Center. It was convened by virually all of the organizations that had met at the 6 January meeting of the American Zionist Council, with the exception of the American Jewish Committee.[24] In a resolution condemning the Soviet Union and its satellites for using anti-Semitism as a political instrument, the rally called upon those countries to permit the emigration of Jews to Israel.[25] The call for *aliyah* is of special interest in light of disputes years later in the American Jewish community over such a demand.

That protest rally was not an isolated manifestation. It was preceded and followed by a series of actions and statements by a wide variety of groups, non-Jewish as well as Jewish. The Soviet Mission to the United Nations was picketed a week after the announcement of the Doctors' Plot by 150 representatives of several Jewish and non-Jewish fraternal and labor groups. A week later, members of the Social Democratic Federation, the Socialist Party, and the Jewish Labor Bund picketed the offices of the Communist *Daily Worker* and *Morning Freiheit*.[26] Many national organizations such as the CIO, AFL, Americans for Democratic Action, National Council of Churches, Women's International League for Peace and Freedom, and Freedom House issued statements of protest. Among the statements was one sent on 12 February to President Eisenhower by fifty-one prominent church and civic leaders. A week later, another group of fifty-one church and civic leaders also appealed to President Eisenhower. However, the latter opposed any U.S. move to sponsor resettlement of Jewish refugees from Soviet areas. Their statement warned that such action would "undoubtedly alienate not only the Arab states adjacent to Israel, but, indeed, the whole Moslem world."[27]

On 16 February 1953, Senator James E. Murray (D-Mont.), joined by twenty-three of his Democratic and Republican colleagues, introduced a resolution that would express the Senate's profound sense of shock at the persecution of the Jews of the USSR. It was referred to the Senate Foreign Relations Committee. On 25 February 1953, committee chairman Senator Alexander Wiley (R-Wis.), favorably reported out a resolution that diluted the singular focus on Jewish persecution of the Murray resolution. The revised resolution condemned "the Soviet Government and its puppet states" for their campaigns against minority groups. It listed the Greek Orthodox congregations, Roman Catholic prelates, Protestant denominations, Moslem communities, ethnic groups in Poland, Ukraine, Baltic and Balkan States "and in many other areas under Soviet domination, and most recently the increasing persecution of the people of the Jewish faith." That resolution passed the Senate by a vote of 79 yeas, with 17 senators absent.[28] Ten years later, the Senate would again pass a watered-down resolution; the common denominator in each case was the attitude of the U.S. State Department. Between 22 January and 29 July 1953, eighteen resolutions were introduced in the House of Representatives. However, it was not until 29 July 1953, almost six months after the death of Stalin, that a resolution of Representative Jacob Javits (R-N.Y.), which condemned religious and political persecution behind the Iron Curtain, was favorably reported out of the House Foreign Affairs Committee. Even then, Congress adjourned that day before a vote was taken.[29]

From the start of the Prague trial on 20 November 1952, the American press devoted considerable space to reporting the anti-Jewish events behind the Iron Curtain. Editorials appeared in many of the nation's newspapers. Radio and television gave major emphasis to these developments in news broadcasts, commentaries, and news analyses. Probing articles appeared in most of the nation's leading periodicals and religious journals. The American Jewish Committee, ADL, American Zionist Council, and Jewish Labor Committee issued special publications.

What impact such a campaign may have had on the Kremlin is only a matter of conjecture, thanks to the death of Stalin on 5 March 1953. His death may have saved the Jews of the Soviet Union from being deported to Siberia or worse. On 4 April 1953, *Pravda* announced that the charges against the doctors were being dropped. This led a few weeks later to their release and exoneration. In statements that followed this announcement, the ADL, Jewish Labor Committee, and American Jewish Committee each warned that anti-Semitism in the Soviet Union was a continuing problem.[30]

Their warnings would be reflected in Soviet policy and practice in the weeks, months, and years that followed. None of the victims of Stalin's anti-Semitic campaign, except for the doctors, was rehabilitated. Even as Khrushchev exposed to the Twentieth Communist Party Congress on 26 February 1956, the terrible crimes committed by Stalin, he was silent on the crimes against the Jews. *Pravda* reprinted an article on his speech from the *Daily Worker* by the secretary-general of the American Communist Party, Eugene Dennis, but omitted his reference to "the destruction of lives of more than 20 Jewish cultural workers."[31]

The winds of change promised by Khrushchev did not blow for Jews. The Soviet media, in acts of undisguised anti-Semitism, continued their vicious campaign against "the international Zionist conspiracy" and "cosmopolitanism."[32] Contacts with Jewish communities abroad were suspect. There was virtually no interruption in the effort to strangle Jewish religious life. The closing of synagogues continued unabated. Prayer books, talesim, and phylacteries continued to be in scarce supply. Jewish cultural and communal expression continued to be effectively discouraged. Discrimination against Jews in employment, education, and housing was widespread. The opportunity to emigrate was almost nonexistent except for a handful of elderly men and women whose children lived abroad.

Paradoxically, the campaign to destroy Jewish identity had just the opposite effect. It kept alive that sense of being a Jew, but without substance and content. Soviet Jews were characterized, accurately, as cultural amnesiacs. For Khrushchev and the Soviet Union, as he once remarked to a foreign visitor, Jews stuck in the throat like a bone; they couldn't swallow them, nor could they spit them out.

Despite this continued repression and the warnings of several agencies, the vigorous response of American Jewish organizations to the call to action in January 1953 fizzled out soon after the exoneration of the doctors. As attested annually by reports in the *American Jewish Yearbook*, American Jewish leaders were well aware of what was taking place in the Soviet Union. Nevertheless, although there were sporadic protests throughout the balance of the 1950s, there was no sustained, coordinated campaign.

These intermittent protests were spearheaded primarily by an organization with close ties to the Jewish Labor Committee, the Congress for Jewish Culture, which represented Yiddish cultural institutions, writers, teachers, and artists. Periodically, it sent specific inquiries to Soviet government officials on the fate of several hundred Jewish intellectuals in the Soviet Union who had disappeared from public view. In September 1955 and again in April 1956, it sent detailed memoranda to the Soviet ambassador to the United States, Georgy N. Zaroubin. No replies were received. Thirty-six leading American intellectuals signed a protest statement issued by the Congress for Jewish Culture on 11 July 1956. The signatories included Dr. George N. Shuster, Upton Sinclair, Reinhold Niebuhr, Sidney Hook, Edgar Alan Mowrer, and Horace Kallen. They urged "freedom-loving individuals . . . to raise their voices in protest against these acts of brutality and discrimination against an entire people."

In a letter to the *New York Times,* seven prominent American writers (Saul Bellow, Leslie Fiedler, Irving Howe, Alfred Kazin, Philip Rahv, Lionel Trilling, and Robert Penn Warren) appealed to the Soviet government to permit Jews to emigrate, noting that Israel and other countries were ready to receive them. Eleanor Roosevelt expressed her concerns about Soviet government discrimination against Jews in a meeting with Khrushchev, who rejected the accusation. He also told her that in time the Soviet Union would permit Jews to emigrate.[33] Fifteen years would pass before the Soviet government would make even a gesture toward carrying out this promise.

In January 1958, the Congress for Jewish Culture marked the tenth anniversary of the murder of Mikhoels and the liquidation of Jewish intellectuals and Jewish culture in the Soviet Union with a meeting attended by more than one thousand people. At that meeting, Leon Crystal, a member of the staff of the *Forward,* the New York Yiddish daily, and a former president of the New York Yiddish Writers Union, urged the mobilization of public opinion on behalf of Soviet Jewry "not only by means of such gatherings as this one, but also by day-in and day-out efforts to enlighten progressive people in all civilized countries as to the anti-Semitic deeds of the present communist regimes." He contended, "Soviet leaders may pretend to be unconcerned about public opinion. In reality, they are sensitive to opinion in other countries. . . . If the truth about anti-Semitism in the communist countries becomes known in all civilized lands, it will blacken the reputation of communist regimes in the eyes of the progressive intelligentsia upon whom the communists are very anxious to make an impression."[34]

Nehemiah Levanon,[35] already a key figure in the 1950s in the Israel Prime Minister's Liaison Bureau [on Soviet Jewry], created by the government of Israel in 1953, recalled in a conversation with me that he had briefed Crystal in Paris prior to the journalist's visit to the Soviet Union shortly before he delivered this speech. Levanon said he had urged Crystal to call for the worldwide campaign. Crystal's call to action, however, did not lead then to an aroused and protesting Jewish community, let alone world public opinion. That would come later. Indeed, his speech articulated what would become the fundamental premises of the campaign the American Jewish community would launch in 1964.

Eleven months later, in December 1958, the American Jewish Committee received what it regarded as a reliable report that Soviet officials were considering a proposal to resettle Soviet Jews in Birobidzhan. According to the report, the plan was to be introduced as a resolution early in 1959 at the next congress of the USSR Communist Party. At that time, only about 35,000 Jews resided in this so-called autonomous Jewish region of the Russian republic. American Jewish Committee leadership feared that such a policy would lead to forced relocation of the Soviet Union's Jewish population.

The AJCommittee succeeded in arranging a meeting with Anastas Mikoyan, first deputy premier of the Soviet Union, during his visit to the United States in January 1959. It was the first meeting American Jewish leadership had held with any top Soviet official. In opening that nearly two-hour meeting, the AJCommittee delegation submitted a well-documented memorandum on the status of Soviet Jews. The delegation reported, "Mikoyan reacted indignantly; there was no intention to send the Jews anywhere. . . . He also denied categorically the charges of official discrimination against Jews. Not only was anti-Semitism nonexistent in the Soviet Union, he maintained, but Jews in fact were eager to give up their cultural distinctiveness." This standard line would be repeatedly asserted by Soviet leadership, especially Khrushchev. As for the Birobidzhan proposal, it did not come before the Communist Party Congress.[36]

Neither Mikoyan nor any other Soviet official subsequently responded to the American Jewish Committee memorandum. However, eight months later, on 7 August 1959, the *National Jewish Post and Opinion* reported that an official of the Soviet delegation to the United Nations had informed its correspondent that when Khrushchev arrived in the United States, "he would most probably welcome an opportunity to meet a representative body of American Jews." That report was given credibility by a similar report appearing that same week in the usually authoritative *London Jewish Chronicle*, based on comments a Russian embassy official in London made to a *Chronicle* representative. Khrushchev, then premier as well as secretary of the Communist Party, was scheduled to come to the United States on 15 September 1959, for a summit conference with President Eisenhower, and then remain for a tour of the United States. The U.N. Soviet official was quoted as saying, "As far as we are concerned, we would like once and for all to clean up the whole mess and the misleading information that Jews in the Western world have about persecution of Jews in the Soviet Union." Even absent a campaign, the issue of Soviet Jewry had become a nuisance, as one Israeli official observed.

These reports of Khrushchev's desire to meet took the national Jewish organizations by surprise. Almost immediately, Jules Cohen, national co-ordinator of NCRAC, was in touch with NCRAC's national member agencies to get their views on the value of such an unprecedented conference. To avoid jurisdictional conflicts, particularly with the Conference of Presidents of Major American Jewish Organizations, NCRAC national agencies[37] agreed that it would be best to address these issues in an ad hoc "no auspices" meeting. Such a meeting would include non-NCRAC agencies who were members of the Presidents' Conference, as well as the American Jewish Committee, which at that time belonged to neither body.[38]

From the start, Cohen kept Yehuda Hellman, executive director of the Presidents' Conference, fully apprised of the discussions among NCRAC national agencies, which were also members of the Presidents' Conference. Hellman told Cohen that he would attend, but that the Presidents' Conference "was not in the picture."[39] Nevertheless, the Presidents' Conference then convened a meeting under its auspices to discuss the Khrushchev issue. (Jurisdictional conflicts would plague American Jewish community advocacy for Soviet Jewry for years to come.) Many attending the meeting of the Presidents' Conference questioned its involvement in this matter. Philip Bernstein, executive director of the Council of Jewish Federations and Welfare Funds, expressed the view that the Presidents' Conference was set up to deal only with issues related to U.S.-Israel relations. Only a few months earlier, he recalled, it had been agreed unanimously that the issue of North African Jews was outside the scope of the Presidents' Conference. He also noted that only twenty-four hours before, Hellman had indicated that the Presidents' Conference would not seek jurisdiction.

Others supported Bernstein's position. Chairing the meeting in the absence of Philip Klutznik, then chairman of the Presidents' Conference, Label Katz, president of B'nai B'rith, asserted that he, too, had raised questions about the jurisdiction of the Presidents' Conference. On the other hand, representatives of several Zionist organizations urged the Presidents' Conference to assume jurisdiction. It was finally agreed that Katz, as chair of this particular meeting, should convene, as NCRAC agencies had previously recommended, an ad hoc meeting of all the agencies in the Presidents' Conference and other organizations that were not members.[40]

Jacob Pat, executive director of the Jewish Labor Committee, expressed his opposition to meeting with Khrushchev. What was to be gained, he asked, contending that Khrushchev would use the meeting as a forum for Soviet propaganda. In any case, if such a meeting were held, Pat urged that a carefully drafted memorandum be prepared that should spell out specific questions and demands, and that such a memorandum be published in advance of the meeting, or in the absence of a meeting with Khrushchev. Others shared Pat's concerns. Ben Koenigsberg, of the Union of Orthodox Jewish Congregations of America, agreed that Khrushchev would use the meeting as a propaganda vehicle to deny discrimination against Jews in the Soviet Union. However, the issues they raised were never joined in the discussion.[41]

Soon after the meeting, a Labor Zionist leader, Dr. Judd Teller, who was close to Nahum Goldmann, called Isaiah Minkoff, among others, to float a proposal, most likely from Goldmann, that the delegation to meet with Khruschev (although no decision had been made to hold such a meeting) should be Goldmann, as president of the World Jewish Congress; Jacob Blaustein, past president of the American Jewish Committee; and Philip Klutznik, past president of B'nai B'rith and chairman of the Conference of Presidents of Major American Jewish Organizations. When several national leaders and local federations learned of the proposal, they angrily rejected it as not truly representative. Their reaction led Teller to drop the proposal, presumably after consulting Goldmann.

In Stockholm, even before the national organizations had engaged in consultations in New York, Rabbi Joachim Prinz, then chairman of the International Commission of the American Jewish Congress, informed reporters covering a meeting of the World Jewish Congress that he had asked American Jewish organizations to request a meeting with Khrushchev. He also made that suggestion in a speech he delivered on Soviet Jewry a few days later to the Stockholm meeting. Most likely, Prinz made the proposal only after consulting with Goldmann, with whom he was close. Then, without consulting the agencies in New York, Klutznik, also in Stockholm for the World Jewish Congress meeting, and Prinz jointly wired Vice President Richard M. Nixon that they welcomed the news that Khrushchev was willing to meet with a Jewish delegation, and recalled Nixon's promise [during the Sinai crisis] that he would take a personal interest in such matters.[42] Back in New York on 25 August 1959, eighteen national organizations, meeting in the "no auspices" framework, agreed that they should seek a meeting with Khruschev and that they should be represented by a five-person delegation.[43] In the end, after all the discussions, meetings, phone calls, consultations (including with the State Department) and organizational jockeying over a two-week period, no meeting was held with Khrushchev.

The question remains whether Khrushchev was really interested in having such a meeting. It is hard to believe that the Soviet Mission in New York and the Soviet Embassy in London, which undoubtedly were most sensitive to concerns raised in those cities about the issue, put out "feelers" for such a meeting without having received a green light from the foreign ministry in Moscow.[44] In later years, American Jewish organizations would not seek meetings with top-level Soviet officials until the Gorbachev era. They concluded that their concerns and demands could more effectively be conveyed by U.S. government officials at the highest levels, reinforced by strong manifestations of concern about the issue in American public opinion. That was the heart of the strategy in pushing the U.S. government to press the Soviet Union on the issue of Soviet Jewry. And in September 1959, the issue was raised at a summit for the first time. At their Camp David meeting, President Eisenhower conveyed to Khrushchev the deep concern expressed to him by American Jews regarding the status of Soviet Jews. Khrushchev dismissed the matter by saying that Jews in the Soviet Union were treated as everyone else was. To Secretary of State Christian Herter's expression of concern about Soviet Jews, Foreign Minister Andrey Gromyko gave the standard response that would typify Soviet replies until the Gorbachev era: "It's an internal matter."[45]

Timed to coincide with the scheduled arrival of Khrushchev in the United States on 15 September 1959, the *New Leader* devoted its entire 4 September 1959, issue to a thoroughly documented, comprehensive exposure of the plight of Soviet Jewry. NCRAC urged its national and local member agencies to get this publication into the hands of prominent persons, Jewish and non-Jewish, especially those who were likely to be invited to receptions for Khrushchev "where occasions might arise for them to express to him their concern over the plight of Soviet Jewry." They also were urged to pass it on to clergymen as sermon material, and to TV, radio and newspaper journalists, and writers for editorial comment.[46]

When Khrushchev addressed the National Press Club in Washington during that trip, he was asked about Soviet anti-Semitism. He replied, "I think one fact can best illustrate the situation of Jews in our country, and it is the following: Among the people who participated in launching the Lunik, the Jews occupy a place of honor. On the whole, the national problem does not exist for us. We don't ask anyone for his religion. This is a matter of conscience that concerns no one but the individual himself. We consider each solely on his own merit."[47] Yet three days before Khrushchev arrived in the United States, Harrison E. Salisbury reported from Moscow in the *New York Times* that "anti-Semitic tendencies are still alive and powerful." He described how Jewish candidates for important jobs in Russia and Ukraine were disqualified on national grounds. On 29 September, he reported on the difficulties Jewish students experienced in entering certain schools, particularly calling attention to the small enrollments even in places with a substantial Jewish population.[48]

The Khrushchev visit to the United States produced no changes in the policies and practices of the Soviet Union. Discrimination against Jews in education, employment, and housing was as widespread as in czarist Russia. In a study in 1964 of Soviet educational practices, Nicholas De-Witt of Indiana University found "that Soviet authorities are employing a quota system to reduce the proportion of Jews enjoying opportunities of higher education."[49] The closure of synagogues continued. Between 1956 and 1963, Soviet officials closed 354 of the 450 remaining synagogues.[50] The Soviet media continued its vicious campaign against Zionism and Judaism. While there was no ban on baking matzoh, impediments to such baking prior to Passover began to appear in various Soviet cities that had the same effect as a ban. That was typical of Kremlin policies against Soviet Jews. Soviet officials would never do directly what they could achieve indirectly. In short, Jews still lived in fear, unable to fulfill themselves as Jews or to become secure members of Soviet society. Nor was the option to emigrate available to them; emigration was almost nonexistent.

To the horror of Westerners, Soviet Jews, as the traditional hated outsiders, were once again used as scapegoats from 1961 to 1964 in a government campaign against "economic crimes," which were endemic in the Soviet Union. The government sent its message by arresting and trying hundreds of Jews, and imposing death sentences on ninety-one of them. The Soviet media left little doubt as to the Jewish identity of those convicted of "economic crimes." This charge of scapegoating was well documented in a comprehensive white paper issued in Geneva in 1964 by the prestigious International Commission of Jurists: "They [Jews] have been made the target of a dangerous propaganda campaign, and Jewish participation in economic crimes has been highlighted if not actually magnified." It charged that the purpose of the campaign was to divert attention from "a veritable cancer in the vitals of ideology—capitalist corruption even within the party . . . and a spectacle of amazing fortunes made quickly."[51] Nobel laureate Bertrand Russell, a self-described friend of the Soviet Union, engaged in an exchange of correspondence with Khruschev in which he bitterly assailed these Soviet practices, as did other friends of the Soviet Union such as Jean-Paul Sartre and internationally respected champions of human rights such as Albert Schweitzer and Norman Thomas.

Until then, Jews in the West, though deeply troubled by the suffering of Soviet Jews, exercised great caution in publicly remonstrating against Soviet treatment of Jews. By mid-1963, growing concern about developments in the Soviet Union led Jews in the highest echelons of the U.S. government, top national Jewish leadership, the rabbinate, and grassroots to call for an end to the low priority and low profile the American Jewish community had given Soviet anti-Semitism.

Early in the summer of 1963, Meyer Feldman, special counsel to President John F. Kennedy, raised the issue of Soviet Jews with the president. Feldman was particularly concerned about the problem of Soviet Jews seeking to rejoin families abroad from whom they had been separated during World War II. Kennedy was favorable to the emigration of Jews from the Soviet Union, said Feldman. However, the president felt that there was little he could do about it at the time other than to send personal messages to Khrushchev or to use private diplomatic channels. Nevertheless, Kennedy raised the issue with Gromyko. Kennedy was well prepared; he had received, at his request, a memorandum on the problem drafted by Feldman and the State Department. While Kennedy felt Gromyko would inform Khrushchev, he told Feldman he had little hope that anything would be accomplished.[52]

Also in August, Lewis H. Weinstein, then chairman of NCRAC and a longtime friend of Kennedy from Boston, raised the issue of Soviet Jewry with the president. Kennedy told Weinstein he would ask Averell Harriman to raise the issue of Soviet Jews with Khrushchev, with whom he was engaged in discussions in Moscow on a nuclear test ban. Weinstein's discussion led him to draft an extensive memorandum on the issue for Attorney General Robert Kennedy, to whom he knew the president turned on certain Soviet issues. In that same month, Label Katz, president of B'nai B'rith, met with President Kennedy's adviser on Soviet affairs, Llewellyn Thompson, who in the late 1950s had served as U.S. ambassador to the Soviet Union. Thompson advised Katz that direct action by the United States on behalf of Soviet Jews would be "counterproductive."[53]

While all this was going on during that August, Weinstein, joined by Isaiah M. Minkoff, executive director of NCRAC, met with Rabbi Irving Miller, then chairman of the Presidents' Conference and also president of the Zionist Organization of America, and Yehuda Hellman, executive director of the Presidents' Conference, "to deal with the increasing mistreatment of Soviet Jews."[54] On 4 September Rabbi Abraham Heschel, a revered theologian, made an impassioned appeal for Soviet Jews at a Jewish Theological Seminary conference on the moral implications of the rabbinate. Haunted by "the failure . . . to do our utmost to save the Jews under Hitler," Rabbi Heschel warned, "Russian Jewry is the last remnant of a people destroyed in extermination camps, the last remnant of a spiritual glory that is no more. . . . Let the 20th century not enter the annals of Jewish history as the century of physical and spiritual destruction."[55] Spurred by Rabbi Heschel's outcry, representatives of major American Jewish organization met early in October in a session initiated by the Synagogue Council of America to explore proposals for the launching of a national campaign for Soviet Jewry. Among the proposals was a call for the convening of a national conference. A subcommittee that included the chairs and presidents of NCRAC, the Presidents' Conference, the Synagogue Council, and the American Jewish Committee was set up to examine these proposals.

Even before that meeting, according to a confidential memorandum by Philip Baum, then international affairs director of the American Jewish Congress, "Arthur J. Goldberg, then associate justice of the Supreme Court, together with Senators Jacob Javits of New York and Abraham Ribicoff of Connecticut, felt that perhaps the United States should officially broach the subject of discrimination against the Jews with the Soviet Union. The time had come, they believed, to end the silence in this matter, particularly among American Jews." They discussed the matter with Secretary of State Dean Rusk, who suggested that an international committee of leading Jews should seek a meeting with Soviet officials, rather than make it a unilateral American approach. They left the meeting with an impression that Rusk was "sympathetic, but cautious."[56]

A few days later, Goldberg and Ribicoff, as former members of the Kennedy Cabinet, were in the White House for ceremonial purposes, and used the occasion to raise the subject with President Kennedy. They were surprised by his comprehensive knowledge of the issue. During their meeting, Kennedy telephoned Thompson, who suggested that the matter be pursued with the Soviets by a delegation of American businessmen going to the Soviet Union on an exchange visit. Goldberg and Ribicoff disagreed, and suggested that as a prelude to a higher-level discussion with Khrushchev, they should meet with Soviet Ambassador Anatoly F. Dobrynin. In his call to Dobrynin to arrange the meeting, Thompson made clear that while he was not seeking the meeting directly on behalf of the president, there was no doubt of Kennedy's personal interest.[57]

On 29 October 1963, Goldberg and Ribicoff, joined by Javits, met with Dobrynin for four hours. They examined the entire range of grievances regarding Soviet policy and practice toward its Jewish population. Dobrynin challenged every point they raised: Jews were not singled out in the economic crime trials; no discrimination existed in employment and education. "They are treated like everyone else," he insisted. The Americans responded that Soviet anti-Semitism was a stumbling block on the road to improved East-West relations, a view, they noted, shared not only by Jews but by all men of goodwill. They asked whether the talks should be continued in Moscow with Khrushchev. Dobrynin replied that Khrushchev had already been apprised of the meeting and would receive a full report. If Khrushchev felt further conversations could be helpful, the answer would be communicated to Goldberg. Khrushchev never came back to them.[58]

At the urgent request of Goldberg, a special meeting of the Presidents' Conference was convened on 19 November. Goldberg and Javits gave a full report of their meeting with Dobrynin.[59] Goldberg felt that

Dobrynin's denials required a shift of the American Jewish community from quiet diplomacy to responsible protest. He cautioned that protest must never be imprudent, nor should protests to the U.S. government be linked to any direct relationship between the United States and the Soviet Union. Advocacy for Soviet Jews should be on humanitarian grounds. He endorsed proposals for the convening of a national mobilization conference. He also urged that Jewish organizations undertake a major educational program on this issue throughout the United States. Finally, Goldberg said that the three of them would continue to pursue a meeting with Khrushchev and explore other approaches by President Kennedy.[60]

At that same meeting, Lewis Weinstein, NCRAC chairman, was elected chairman of the Conference of Presidents of Major American Jewish Organizations. Immediately after the meeting, Weinstein called Kennedy, who expressed his readiness to meet with fifteen to twenty American Jewish leaders, designated by Weinstein, to discuss the issue of Soviet treatment of Jews. He suggested that Weinstein set up a specific date in early December for the meeting. Three days later, on 22 November, President John F. Kennedy was assassinated. A month before, in Cleveland, Dr. Herbert Caron and Dr. Louis Rosenblum, who were single-minded in their dedication to the cause of Soviet Jewry, organized the Cleveland Committee on Soviet Anti-Semitism. It was a group organized outside of the Jewish establishment. Their mission was to galvanize the American Jewish establishment, nationally and locally, to undertake a massive, ceaseless public campaign for Soviet Jews. It was the genesis of what would become the Union of Councils for Soviet Jewry.[61]

The emerging fundamental changes in the approach of American Jewish leadership were not unrelated to the role of Israelis representing the government of Israel. Binyamin Eliav, consul general of Israel in New York had been deeply involved in the issue of Soviet Jewry for a good part of the 1950s as a key member, with Nehemiah Levanon, of the little known Israeli agency, the Lishkat HaKeshar, the Prime Minister's Liaison Bureau (on Soviet Jews). It had been created in 1952 by Prime Minister Moshe Sharett to respond to the increasing repression of Soviet Jewry. Eliav succeeded Levanon in Israel's Moscow embassy after Levanon's expulsion. He adroitly drew upon this background and his role as consul-general to reach out to elite figures in government, national media, academia, the arts, and the Jewish establishment on the issue of Soviet Jews.

Working under Eliav's direction was a young Israeli, Meir Rosenne. In what was a new position at the consulate, Rosenne's role as consul was to focus solely on the issue of Soviet Jewry. While maintaining low profiles, there is little doubt that Eliav and Rosenne played key roles in influencing leadership and grassroots to put this issue on the agenda of the United States, and to encourage a campaign of responsible public protest. Before coming to New York, Rosenne, representing the Lishkat, organized in

Paris the first major international conference of intellectuals on Soviet Jewry. He was also in Paris when Eliav set up a research bureau on Soviet Jewry, the Bibliothèque juive. Soon after Rosenne's arrival in New York, he and Eliav were instrumental in the creation of the Jewish Minority Research, also a research bureau on Soviet Jewry, and the appointment of Moshe Decter as its director. Decter had edited the special *New Leader* issue on Soviet Jewry in 1959.

Drawing upon Rosenne's experience with the Paris conference of intellectuals, Decter organized a Conference on the Status of Soviet Jews, held on 21 October 1963, at the Carnegie International Center in New York, a week before the Dobrynin meeting with Goldberg, Javits, and Ribicoff. This assembly brought together prominent jurists, writers, civil rights activists, labor leaders and clergy, all strongly identified with campaigns for human rights. Out of these deliberations came an "Appeal of Conscience for the Jews of the Soviet Union." It appealed to Soviet authorities to take seven specific steps to remedy the inequities suffered by Soviet Jews. Its list of signatories included Supreme Court Justice William O. Douglas, Martin Luther King, Jr., Leonard Bernstein, the Reverend Theodore M. Hesburgh, Arthur Miller, Reinhold Niebuhr, Linus Pauling, Bishop James Pike, Walter Reuther, Norman Thomas, Whitney Young, and Roy Wilkins.

In the meantime, Rabbi Heschel became increasingly impatient with what he saw as the resistance of Jewish leadership to act on proposals for a national campaign for Soviet Jews. On 31 December 1963, Heschel wrote to Lewis Weinstein, chairman of the Presidents' Conference as well as NCRAC, that unless NCRAC or the Presidents' Conference took bold action, he would begin his own national movement. At the time, there was resistance among some within the Presidents' Conference to creating a separate vehicle for Soviet Jewry. Others feared what they saw as the dangerous consequences of a public campaign. One of the strongest opponents, Rose Halperin, chair of the American Section of the Jewish Agency, shared Nahum Goldmann's view that such a campaign would endanger Soviet Jews. However, Heschel's letter struck responsive chords in Weinstein and Isaiah Minkoff, who had called for a worldwide campaign for Soviet Jews in January 1953. The two were in agreement on convening as soon as possible a national mobilization conference. They envisioned such a conference as broadly representative of the total American Jewish community, involving all major national and local Jewish agencies.

To assure that goal, they gained the assent of Morris B. Abram, president of the American Jewish Committee, and John Slawson, its executive director. At that time, the AJCommittee was the only major community relations agency that was not a member of either NCRAC or the Presidents' Conference.[62] Their agreement reflected the action of the

American Jewish Committee board, which had just pledged "to arouse mankind to the plight of nearly three million Jews . . . who are threatened with the destruction of their cultural and religious identity."[63]

In mid-February 1964, Weinstein convened a meeting of the Presidents' Conference, with AJCommittee in attendance as observers. He invited Rabbi Heschel to address the meeting. The Presidents' Conference voted unanimously to convene a high-profile national assembly in Washington, out of which a new national body, the American Jewish Conference on Soviet Jewry, would be constituted. In light of the previous resistance, this unanimous action was a significant step. The American Jewish Committee agreed to participate as a member organization. It was planned as a two-day meeting on 5–6 April 1964, at the Willard Hotel in Washington, D.C., to be attended by every significant organization in the American Jewish community, key senators, congressional representatives and important non-Jewish national leaders in welfare, religion, labor, industry, and civil rights.[64]

Underlying this decision was a profound change in the premises that had guided the American Jewish community's response to Soviet Jewry. In the past, there was the ever-present fear among American Jewish leadership, as well as most Soviet Jews, that the ruthlessness of the Soviet regime could lead to reprisals against Soviet Jews.

Such fears were expressed to me by Chief Rabbi Yehuda Leib Levin in his study in the Grand Chorale Synagogue in Moscow in January 1967. "Even a fly can irritate an elephant, and the elephant will then smash it," he said. Thus, there had been a general tendency until the early 1960s to avoid public protests. Now, as a matter of strategy, there was a readiness to expose the anti-Semitic practices of the Soviet Union to the spotlight of public opinion, especially "progressive" opinion, in a sustained, concerted campaign, as urged in 1958 by the Yiddish writer Leon Crystal. A strong dissenting voice to such a public campaign was expressed by Agudath Yisroel, a right-wing Orthodox group, who shared the concerns and fears of Rabbi Levin. At its convention in November 1963, Agudath Yisroel passed a resolution deploring "the highly publicized aggressive tactics that various Jewish organizations have adopted . . . regarding the situation of the Jews in the Soviet Russia."[65]

The defensive responses of Soviet officials on the highest levels, particularly Khrushchev, to charges of anti-Semitism supported the perception of Soviet sensitivity to public exposure. The guarantee of equality for all minorities and the right to self-determination of nationality groups within a pluralistic Soviet Union were among the extravagant claims that could be exposed as the lies that they were. Protecting these myths was important to the Politburo. Its international Communist apparatus gave a high priority to propaganda to enhance the Soviet image in world public opinion as the progressive people's democracy. A case in point, as

Khruschev emphasized in his memoirs, was the creation and use of the Jewish Anti-Fascist Committee during World War II solely for public relations purposes, even when public relations collided with party dogma.

This change in strategic thinking was dramatically underscored shortly after the decision was taken at the Presidents' Conference meeting. Significantly, it was by the American Jewish Committee, which in earlier years had expressed strong reservations about public protests. On 24 February 1964, Morris Abram, president of the AJCommittee and a U.S. representative to the U.N. Commission on Human Rights, held a press conference to expose a book published in 1963 by the Ukrainian Academy of Science as crude, vicious anti-Semitism. The book, *Judaism Without Embellishment* by Trofim Kitchko, a Ukrainian professor, drew upon traditional anti-Semitic canards in its scurrilous attack on the Jewish religion. Abram's revelations stirred worldwide denunciations of the book. Even Gus Hall, secretary-general of the U.S. Communist Party, asserted, "There is no doubt in my mind about the anti-Semitic character of what I have seen. Such stereotyped, slanderous caricatures of the Jewish people must be unequivocally condemned."

Abram's charge drew a response on the eve of the opening of the historic American Jewish conference in Washington, D.C., on 4 April 1964, by the Ideological Commission of the Central Committee of the Soviet Communist Party. It declared in an official statement in *Pravda*: "The author of the book and the authors of the preface wrongly interpreted some questions concerning the emergence and development of this religion [Judaism]. . . . [A] number of mistaken propositions and illustrations could insult the feelings of believers and might even be interpreted in the spirit of anti-Semitism." *Pravda* then reiterated the standard Soviet denial: "There is no such thing as anti-Semitism in the USSR and cannot be."[66] Despite this qualified repudiation of this particular book, the anti-Semitism of the Kitchko book was hardly unique among official Soviet publications about Jews and Judaism. The exposure of the Kitchko book and the response supported the premises of the new Jewish strategy.

"The two days, April 5 and 6, 1964, at the Hotel Willard were exhilarating and produced highly satisfying results," Lewis Weinstein recalled. "The conference filled the hotel's large public room; every major American Jewish organization participated in a positive way [nearly five hundred Jewish leaders attended], and key members of Congress made strong statements of support. Forceful messages of support came from George Meany, president of the AFL-CIO; Dr. Martin Luther King Jr.; and leaders of many religious, social welfare, business and political groups. The press was heavily represented; among the reporters were several from *Pravda* and *Izvestia*."[67] Weinstein was disappointed that Israeli officials, including Israel's ambassador to the United States, Avraham Harman, declined to participate. His perception was somewhat puzzling in light of the behind-the-scenes role that Eliav and Rosenne had played in encouraging the new posture and the convening of this conference. Their refusal was not a reflection of any concern Israel had about the conference, although Weinstein thought that was the case. In those years, Israel chose to maintain a low public profile on the issue of Soviet Jewry precisely because of its deep involvement for more than ten years in reaching out to Soviet Jews through its embassy in Moscow. After the Six-Day War, when the Soviet Union ruptured diplomatic relations, Israel gradually moved toward a more public stance.

The high media visibility of the conference was important as a first step in launching the campaign. The twenty-four sponsoring organizations pledged to "extend [their] resources and [their] energies to the fullest to bring to the attention of the world the facts about the oppression of Soviet Jewry, through every means at [their] command, through every channel of communication available to [them], through every contact and association, in every place and in every season." Thus they established the American Jewish Conference on Soviet Jewry to single-mindedly press the issue of Soviet Jewry by coordinating and using the resources of the network of national and community agencies of the American Jewish community. Jewish leaders declared their purpose was "not to exacerbate 'Cold War' tensions." Their aim was "to mobilize public opinion into a worldwide moral force which will save the Jewish community from spiritual annihilation. The leadership of the Soviet Union," they asserted, "is not impervious to such world opinion." They expressed their belief "that the dissemination of the truth about discriminations and persecutions to which Soviet Jewry [was] being subjected [might] move the Soviet leadership to reappraise the political expediency of the present course of Soviet treatment of its Jewish citizens."

The nature and extent of these unique disabilities were spelled out systematically and in depth in five background papers carefully prepared for the conference by several of the sponsoring agencies. They set forth the themes of the campaign. They contrasted the "rights" proclaimed in Soviet law, constitution, and treaties with the reality of the USSR's repressive practices against Jews. They contrasted how the Soviet system denied to Soviet Jews those elements vital to sustaining Jewish identity with those elements available to other officially recognized religions and nationalities; the Soviet's declared policy of a pluralistic Soviet Union with the Soviet goal of seeking the total assimilation of Soviet Jews; the Soviet goal of the total assimilation of Soviet Jews with the discrimination Soviet Jews encountered in all aspects of their personal lives.[68] The conference adopted a comprehensive strategic "plan for action" that would guide the campaign for years to come. It charged the presidents of these organizations to meet "immediately upon the adjournment of the conference . . . [to] develop the means of continuing this conference on an ongoing basis, adequately staffed and financed to coordinate and implement the resolutions of this conference."[69]

The American Jewish community's campaign of public protest was not intended as a sporadic, flash-in-the-pan venture. The conference recognized that the occasional "spectacular project . . . may be necessary," but "the steady, ongoing job of interpretation . . . must lie at the core of our effort."[70] What the campaign required was the endurance of a marathon runner. In his meeting with Goldberg, Javits, and Ribicoff, Dobrynin expressed skepticism that the American Jewish community could sustain such a campaign over the long term. The "action plan" placed heavy stress on the crucial role of communities. "In the final analysis," it declared, "public opinion reflects the totality of judgments reached in communities throughout the nation. Long experience has taught that interpretation can most effectively be achieved on the level where people live and work together." The plan "deemed [the] effective [use of] all moral and lawful direct actions . . . on a selective basis, including the picketing of strategic buildings, offices and events," as acceptable tactics, as opposed to actions that would be undertaken in future years by such groups as the Jewish Defense League.[71]

In a statement addressed to Secretary of State Dean Rusk, the delegates called upon "the United States government [to] use its good offices to make known to the Soviet government the extent of our government's concern for the situation and status of three million Jews in the Soviet Union." It cited the "ample precedent in American history for appropriate actions to deal with the persecution and oppression of minority groups."[72] The statement stressed, "Our action is not to be considered in any sense as an exacerbation of political conflict between East and West. This is not a political issue."[73]

Thirty years later, making such requests to the secretary of state or even the president would be routine, certainly uncontroversial. However, prior to the conference, Dr. Nahum Goldmann, president of the World Jewish Congress and the World Zionist Organization, as well as the principal founder of the Conference of Presidents, expressed concern about such requests in letters to Lewis Weinstein. In a letter from Geneva on 20 February 1963, he stated his "grave doubts" about a proposed meeting of a conference delegation with the president: "Any formal intervention by the USA will probably be rejected by the State Department, and rightly so, and may be very harmful to the very sensitive Soviets. Just imagine if the Soviet Union would hold a conference on the civil rights situation of the Negroes and send a formal delegation to Krutchev [sic], asking him to intervene. What would be the reaction in America to such a procedure? And the Russians have the right to react in the same way."[74]

Weinstein replied, "If indeed there were Negroes in the Soviet Union, no one should be upset if a group of them, as Soviet citizens, spoke to General Secretary Khrushchev about the treatment of their black brothers and sisters in the United States. We should be talking to President Johnson as and for American Jews."[75] Weinstein's approach anticipated changes that would emerge in the 1970s, especially after the adoption of the Helsinki Final Act in 1975, and the posture toward international human rights violations by the Carter administration, given special meaning by the Reagan and Bush administrations in regard to Soviet Jewry.[76]

After the close of the conference, the presidents of the sponsoring organizations met with Secretary of State Rusk. They gave him the formal statement addressed to him and the conference resolutions. According to Weinstein, Rusk "enthusiastically agreed to express American concern to the Soviet authorities and to discuss all the issues with Soviet Ambassador Anatoly Dobrynin."[77] As the meeting was about to conclude, Meyer Feldman, now on President Johnson's staff, telephoned Weinstein that the president would meet with a small group within the next half-hour. The organizations quickly agreed on a delegation of the presidents of six organizations, and Hellman and Minkoff, directors of the Presidents' Conference and NCRAC. Weinstein recalled the president was well briefed as he made an "effective and welcome statement of his concurrence with our views and his intention of meeting with Ambassador Dobrynin and expressing his strong feelings to him and the Kremlin." Johnson met the very next day with Dobrynin in a meeting that Weinstein remembers was widely publicized.[78]

Two weeks after the conference, Yehuda Hellman, in a memo in which he identified himself as the secretary of the American Jewish Conference on Soviet Jewry, convened a meeting of the sponsoring organizations for 5 May 1964 to act on the recommendations of the conference. By the end of May, agreement had been reached on a plan presented by a committee, chaired by Rabbi Max Routtenberg of the Rabbinical Assembly of America, the Conservative rabbinate. The twenty-four organizations were divided into three groups of eight each. On the basis of a six-month rotation, each group was to serve as the steering committee of the American Jewish Conference on Soviet Jewry. The rotation sequence was determined by lot. The first steering committee elected George Maislen, president of the United Synagogue of America (the Conservative congregational body), as its chairman.[79]

This structure fell far short of the resolution calling for a conference "adequately staffed and financed." Certainly this was the judgment of embryonic Soviet Jewry grassroots groups (particularly in Cleveland and Oakland–San Francisco) and students, especially those in New York beginning to organize themselves into the Student Struggle for Soviet Jewry.

No budget was provided, and staff services were to be lent by member organizations. Initially working with Maislen and the steering committee as its professional coordinators were Hellman from the Presidents' Conference, Jerry Goodman of the American Jewish Committee, and Jerry Baker of the Anti-Defamation League of B'nai B'rith. The structure reflected the continued reluctance of some groups, particularly Zionist organizations pushed by Rose Halperin, even though such issues were presumably resolved at the Washington, D.C., convocation.

Nevertheless, the American Jewish Conference on Soviet Jewry (AJCSJ) was now in business. Over the summer of 1964, the AJCSJ, led by Maislen, attempted to get platform planks on Soviet anti-Semitism adopted by the national conventions of the Republican and Democratic parties. Testimony advocating such planks was presented by Senator Javits to the Republican Platform Committee and Senator Ribicoff to its Democratic counterpart. However, each of the platforms made only a parenthetical reference. Each party condemned discrimination by the Soviet Union against minorities in the Soviet Union, and added "such as Jews."

Maislen and the AJCSJ also tried to get support for a resolution in the Senate that Ribicoff had introduced in September 1963 condemning Soviet persecution of Jews. Even the effort to get hearings that summer of 1964 on the resolution in the Senate Foreign Relations Committee encountered resistance from Senator William Fulbright, its chairman. In light of Fulbright's evident anti-Israel and pro-Arab bias, his stance was not surprising. To get his resolution to the floor of the Senate for a vote, Ribicoff attached it as a rider to the foreign aid bill, and it was adopted on 23 September 1964, by a 60 to 1 vote, with Fulbright voting against it. As part of the foreign aid bill, it was sent to a House-Senate conference committee which, at the urging of Fulbright, changed the language to refer only to minorities in the Soviet Union without mentioning Jews. Nevertheless, Maislen and Ribicoff felt they had succeeded in getting the Senate to go on record on the issue of Soviet anti-Semitism.[80] Eight months later, on 14 May 1965, the Senate adopted by 68 to 0 a significantly stronger concurrent resolution. Although this resolution's initial finding referred to persecution "in varying degrees of intensity of elements of its [Soviet] Christian, Jewish and Moslem citizens," its focus was on the "abundant evidence that Jewish citizens have been singled out for extreme punishment" in various sectors of Soviet society.

This resolution represented a change in how this issue was approached by Congress, as well as by the State Department. As Theodore Comet, AJCSJ staff coordinator for that six-month rotation,[81] described it in a confidential memorandum, pressures on members of Congress from various sources inclined them to respond "with one omnibus bill in which the Jewish issue would be treated as all others and so swallowed up." Once the State Department withdrew its objections, it was expected that the resolution, as Ribicoff had originally introduced it, would sail through the Senate undiluted. However, Ribicoff alerted the AJCSJ that there was growing sentiment to absorb his bill into an omnibus resolution. His call activated a campaign of telegrams to members of the Senate Foreign Relations Committee by the national organizations and communities. Comet commented, "Our organizations came through beautifully." Thus the omnibus bill was stopped, except for its single reference to "Christian, Moslem and Jewish citizens."[82] Support for an omnibus bill underscored the challenge to deepen understanding of the singular nature of conditions confronting Soviet Jews, as distinguished from the Soviet Union's overall repressive antireligious and Russification campaigns.

Less than a month after the creation of the AJCSJ, more than a thousand people, mostly students, marched near the Soviet Mission to the United Nations in New York on May Day, 1 May 1964, a major holiday in the Soviet Union as well as elsewhere to celebrate the rights of the worker. Out of this action emerged the Student Struggle for Soviet Jewry, spearheaded by Jacob Birnbaum, who had emigrated to the United States from England a few months earlier, and Glenn Richter. On 18 October, the Student Struggle, operating out of Birnbaum's bedroom, held a rally attended by two thousand people on the Lower East Side of New York. The speakers included Senators Kenneth Keating and Javits, and Meyer Feldman, President Johnson's liaison to the Jewish community.

During that summer of 1964, Birnbaum met with the steering committee of the AJCSJ to seek financial assistance for the program of the Student Struggle. According to a report from George Maislen, then chairman of the steering committee, Birnbaum's request was rejected because of his refusal to accept the discipline of the American Jewish Conference on Soviet Jewry. Maislen noted that the Student Struggle was receiving financial help from sources outside the membership of the AJCSJ.[83] It is highly likely that Israeli Consul Rosenne, spiritual "godfather" of the Student Struggle, was instrumental in getting financial support for the group, as he did for the Jewish Minority Research, although Birnbaum strongly denies it.

The rejection of financial assistance was the beginning of what would be a long and at times stormy relationship between the Student Struggle and the AJCSJ and its successor organization, the National Conference on Soviet Jewry. The Student Struggle at no time had a large student following anywhere but New York. Even in New York, it comprised primarily religiously observant Jewish students. But those who were involved were dedicated and single-minded in their support for Soviet Jewry. Despite their occasional conflicts with the Jewish establishment, their activities generally were within the framework of the guidelines of the AJCSJ.[84]

Acting on the recommendations of the "Plan of Action" adopted at the national convocation in April 1964, NCRAC stimulated protest rallies over the summer and fall of 1964 in more than twenty-five major cities, including Boston, Cincinnati, Cleveland, Pittsburgh, and Washington, D.C. In Levittown, Long Island, more than 5,000 people jammed into a hall, with 3,000 people outside listening to the speeches on the outside loudspeakers. In New York on 28 October 1964, after marching from the United Nations to the barriers near the Soviet Mission, a capacity crowd filled Hunter College's auditorium, a block from the Mission, in the first protest rally convened by the American Jewish Conference on Soviet Jewry.

In Madison Square Garden on 3 June 1965, the American Jewish Conference on Soviet Jewry convened the largest protest rally ever held for Soviet Jewry. To the June 1965 Madison Square Garden rally, Johnson sent a message aimed directly at Soviet leadership: "In the spirit of peace and reason, we express our earnest hope that Soviet leadership will ameliorate the situation of its Jewish minority. Doing so would go a long way toward removing a moral and emotional barrier between us, and contribute to a relaxation of tensions." Dr. Philip Baum, then director of the International Commission of the American Jewish Congress, recalls that the day after this event, Nahum Goldmann denounced this mass demonstration of Jewish concern in a press conference at the American Jewish Congress. Goldmann sharply criticized the role Baum played as a key professional largely responsible for putting this rally together.

In a message to the October 1964 Hunter College rally (held a week before the election for president), President Johnson declared, "The position of the Jewish community in the Soviet Union is a matter of deep and continuing concern to me, to this administration, and to millions of thoughtful people throughout the United States. . . . In the Soviet Union today there is grave governmental, social and economic pressure against Jewish culture and religious identity. There is harassment of synagogues and interference with training in the great cultural heritage of Judaism. . . . All responsible officials in our government continue to search for practical methods of alleviating the position of Soviet Jews." He described the U.S. initiative in the United Nations in support of including an article on anti-Semitism in the draft convention on the elimination of all forms of racial discrimination, and its adoption over the "vigorous objections" of the Soviet delegate. Johnson urged, "Official actions . . . must be reinforced by the pressure of an aroused world public opinion."[85] This combination of continuing community protest rallies in various parts of the United States and strong statements from the highest levels of the U.S. government would become essential to the strategy for the next three decades. Each reinforced the other in influencing public opinion and in sending strong messages to Soviet authorities and words of encouragement to Soviet Jews.

Yet an uneasiness continued among some in the leadership about the protest campaign launched by the American Jewish Conference on Soviet Jewry. When George Maislen learned in the late summer of 1964 that four Conservative congregations in Philadelphia planned to take a busload of their congregants to Washington to picket the Soviet Embassy, he urged them not to take this action. Maislen informed them that the steering committee felt they should limit their rallies and protest meetings to Philadelphia. Philadelphia, however, told Maislen that a State Department official had suggested off the record that picketing was advisable. Similar encouragement came from an unnamed "agency" in New York, clearly Consul Rosenne. Nahum Goldmann, with whom Maislen consulted, concurred with the steering committee's opposition to such picketing and advised him that this was the point of view of many knowledgeable leaders throughout the world. In response to a request from the Philadelphia Jewish Community Relations Council,[86] which supported the congregations, NCRAC wrote to Maislen asking that the steering committee ruling be reviewed by the twenty-four member organizations of the AJCSJ.[87]

Maislen met with the board of the Philadelphia JCRC, but was unable to persuade it to call off the picketing. On 6 and 7 October 1964, the four Philadelphia congregations picketed the Soviet Embassy in Washington, D.C. It was the first time the embassy had been picketed on behalf of Soviet Jewry. This led to more than one thousand Philadelphians, including non-Jews from forty organizations, traveling on different, assigned days to Washington, under the auspices of the JCRC, to picket the Soviet Embassy over an eight-day period in March 1965.

Capping those activities, the newly created Greater Philadelphia Committee to Protest Soviet Anti-Semitism, staffed by the JCRC, held a mass rally at Independence Square on 28 March 1965, with Philip M. Klutznik as principal speaker.[88] This kind of activism would distinguish Philadelphia's role as a model of community activity for Soviet Jewry over the next thirty years, and was paralleled by other CRCs throughout the United States. Klutznik's speech to that rally laid out strategic themes that were aimed at sensitive Soviet nerves. In the years ahead, such themes would be repeated in thousands of speeches, pamphlets, and posters. As compared to other challenges to the Soviet Union, the demands expressed in those themes were modest and restrained. They were hardly counterrevolutionary, although in the eyes of the Kremlin, any challenge was counterrevolutionary.

Klutznik asserted, "We do not urge the Kremlin to change its commitments to itself and to the world. All we seek is that they keep them— that they give to the Jewish national who seeks them rights enjoyed by a

Russian Orthodox, a Baptist, or a Moslem in the Soviet Union." He pointed out that "the Declaration of Human Rights which honors the right of religious conscience upholds no less the right of emigration. . . . It is the very essence of elementary human rights that he who feels that he can no longer be what he wants to be in the nation of his birth or of his residence should be privileged to emigrate. Except in rare and extraordinary circumstances, the Soviet Union denies this right." Finally, he declared, "We are not here to shake our fists at the Soviet Union. . . . We are here to plead that she make real the promise of her law. We are here to plead that the Soviet Union do justice to herself by giving meaning to her international commitments and by letting those people go who cannot adjust to her new society."[89]

The Philadelphia experience underscored the potential of communities in the campaign. It is not clear whether this consideration led to rotating to NCRAC the staff role of the AJCSJ for the six-month period beginning 1 July 1964; in any case, the assignment was fortuitous for the newly launched campaign. As the national vehicle of CRCs, NCRAC brought a special relationship to the communities, and an understanding of how to apply basic community relations principles and tools to the campaign. Its executive director, Isaiah M. Minkoff, had been an advocate of a campaign for Soviet Jewry as early as 1953. Along with advocacy for Israel, the issue would become in the years ahead the highest priority of Jewish community relations.

Minkoff assigned Henry Siegman, then a member of the NCRAC staff, the responsibility of serving as coordinator of the AJCSJ. Even before taking the assignment, Siegman had proposed a major undertaking. Early in 1965, he recommended to the steering committee of the AJCSJ the Eternal Light Vigil project, which would take place in Washington, D.C. The steering committee approved, and set a June date for the vigil. However, less than two months before the scheduled date, the twenty-four member organizations of the AJCSJ decided to postpone it until 19 September over the objections of Siegman. He warned of the difficulties of enlisting mass support over the summer months. When Siegman acted on this new date in his new capacity as AJCSJ coordinator, he ran into repeated efforts, spearheaded by Rose Halperin, to postpone the vigil once again. It required the persuasiveness of Israel's ambassador to the United States, Avraham Harman, who flew up from Washington for a meeting of the AJCSJ, to maintain support for the project.[90]

More than 10,000 people, twice the number of the most optimistic projection, came from more than one hundred cities across the nation to Lafayette Park, across the street from the White House. Two chartered trains from New York were oversubscribed, as was a chartered plane from Cincinnati. Philadelphia, Baltimore, New Jersey, and Washington attended in unexpectedly great numbers. Large numbers of youth of all ages were present.[91] President Johnson, in a statement that was read to this huge gathering, declared, "History demonstrates that the treatment of minorities is a barometer . . . [of] the moral health of a society. Just as the conditions of American Jews are a living symbol of American achievement and promise, so the conditions of Jewish life (and that of other religious minorities) in the Soviet Union reveal fundamental contradictions between the stated principles and actual practices in the Soviet Union."

The demonstration closed with the kindling of the Eternal Light flame by a young boy and girl to symbolize future generations of Jews and the determination to carry on the struggle to assure Soviet Jews the freedom to practice and perpetuate their religion and culture. Following the lighting ceremony, the crowd joined in a march past the Soviet Embassy. A delegation comprising the new chairman of the AJCSJ, Rabbi Seymour Cohen of Chicago; Bayard Rustin; Father John Cronin; and Theodore Bikel was permitted by police to go to the door of the Soviet Embassy, where they intended to transmit boxes of petitions. They rang the bell. There was no response, and Bikel slipped a petition under the door. That scene was projected on the CBS and ABC network news that evening. The event was also covered by the Voice of America.[92]

Recalling that less than a year before, the AJCSJ steering committee opposed picketing the Soviet Embassy and then dragged its feet on this project, the Eternal Light Vigil was an important breakthrough as the first major protest rally for Soviet Jewry held in Washington under the auspices of the major national Jewish organizations. As a manifestation, it would become the measure and model of future demonstrations in Washington. Almost immediately after the vigil, Siegman left the staff of NCRAC to become executive director of the Synagogue Council of America. Minkoff turned to me,[93] who had been on the NCRAC staff since 1957, to take over the role of coordinator of the AJCSJ until 1 January 1966, when the six-month NCRAC rotation was scheduled to end. NCRAC's success in handling this assignment led the AJCSJ to ask the agency to take the rotation again for the six-month period from 1 January 1966, to 1 July. As that rotation period was coming to an end, Rabbi Israel Miller,[94] who succeeded Rabbi Seymour Cohen as chairman of the AJCSJ in March 1966, officially requested NCRAC to permit me to continue to serve as coordinator without any time limit, thus ending the six-month rotation pattern. While the responsibility was a heavy drain on the resources of NCRAC, I was allowed to do so. NCRAC[95] carried out this role until 1 August 1971, when the AJCSJ was reconstituted as the National Conference on Soviet Jewry.

When I left NCRAC in July 1968 to become executive director of the Philadelphia JCRC,[96] Abraham Bayer joined the NCRAC staff and served as AJCSJ coordinator on virtually a full-time basis. He continued in that role until 31 July 1971, when the AJCSJ became the NCSJ. Miller was succeeded as chair in November 1968 by Lewis Weinstein, who had just given up the position of president of the Council of Jewish Federations and Welfare Funds. Two years later, Rabbi Herschel Schacter, president of the Rabbinical Council of America, succeeded Weinstein and served as chairman until 10 June 1971, when Richard Maass, chair of the foreign affairs committee of the American Jewish Committee and later its president, became the last chairman of the AJCSJ, and on 30 August 1971, the first chairman of the National Conference on Soviet Jewry.

While many in the grassroots responded to the cause of Soviet Jews, many more American Jews. even leaders and professionals, were uninformed and thus insensitive to the plight of Soviet Jews. Many equated the assimilation of Soviet Jews with assimilationist tendencies in the American Jewish community, blind to the Soviet government's deliberate policy of forced assimilation. Many failed to grasp the uniqueness of the Soviet repression of Jews. They saw it as an expression of Soviet hostility toward all religions. For some, the pain index of anti-Semitism was whether they were "killing Jews," so they were unable to feel the severity of Jewish pain resulting from the complex and subtle repressive policies and practices of the Soviet regime. Even among those concerned about Soviet Jews there were some who viewed it from the perspective of the Holocaust, seeing it as a new genocidal war, this time against Soviet Jews. In light of the issue's low public profile in the preceding years, it was not surprising that there was such widespread misunderstanding.

Thus, a major educational effort among the rank and file, as well as leadership, was regarded as vital by the ACSJ. The success of a massive, sustained campaign depended upon an informed Jewish community, whose commitment grew out of understanding the true nature of Soviet repression in all its Orwellian forms. Its success required its advocates to tell the truth without distortion or stretching the truth. The reality of Soviet Jews was bad enough; it did not require embellishment. To that end, the AJCSJ published in 1966 a comprehensive 53-page manual, prepared with the assistance of CRC and federation directors. It had sections on the nature of the issue, organizing the community for action, using the mass media, reaching the total community, involving youth in the campaign, and providing a number of program aids.[97] It set up a national Soviet Jewry speakers bureau. That same year, it published and distributed in the thousands a "Q and A" brochure on Soviet Jewry. It arranged for five copies of a dramatic 14-panel graphic exhibit on Soviet Jewry to be displayed throughout the United States. It conducted regional conferences and seminars for Jewish leadership on religion and nationality in the USSR, utilizing leading authorities on the Soviet Union.

Further, it reprinted in the tens of thousands articles on Soviet Jews, and produced and distributed tapes made by prominent figures (one by Martin Luther King, Jr.) for radio and other purposes. One simple approach exceeded expectations: when I drafted the "Matzoh of Hope" in the spring of 1967. It was a 60-second litany on the repression of Soviet Jews that was to be recited at Passover seders. That first year, the AJCSJ printed 125,000 copies and exhausted the supply; in addition, the "Matzoh of Hope" was reprinted in national Jewish periodicals, daily newspapers (in their Passover articles), Anglo-Jewish weeklies, synagogue bulletins, and federation mailings, reaching more than a million people. Radio stations around the country broadcast as radio spots tapes of actor Edward G. Robinson reading the selection. On the eve of Passover in 1969, the ACSJ ran it as a half-page ad in the *New York Times*. The ad announced that the ACSJ petition campaign, marking the twentieth anniversary of the Universal Declaration of Human Rights, had resulted in 300,000 signators. The petitions were presented to the United Nations.

The ACSJ actively drew upon the resources of its member organizations to carry out a wide variety of projects. Stimulated by the ACSJ, the National Jewish Welfare Board[98] published in 1966 a handbook for summer camps providing interpretive and programmatic material on Soviet Jewry, which was extensively utilized that summer and future summers. Similarly, the JWB dedicated National Jewish Music Month in 1967 to the historic contribution of Russian Jewry to Jewish music," and then published a manual on the subject.

The project "Operation Pekuach Nefesh" was another example of education joined to public advocacy. It was undertaken in 1967 by the Jewish Education Committee of New York in consultation with the AJCSJ. It was an intensive program to educate Jewish children attending Jewish schools in the New York area to the plight of Soviet Jewry. The program culminated in a series of three full-page ads in the *New York Times* addressed to Soviet Premier Alexey Kosygin. The ads were signed and paid for by one-dollar contributions from the children.

In April 1966, three hundred college students gathered at the Isaiah Wall, opposite the United Nations, for an all-night study vigil. This was followed a week later, during Passover, by a march of nearly fifteen thousand young people to the United Nations.[99] To dramatize Soviet obstacles to teaching the Jewish religion and culture, the United Synagogue Youth, affiliated with a constituent of the AJCSJ, conducted in May 1969 an all-night "teach-in" on the first night of Shavuot, traditionally a time of study, at Dag Hammarskjold Plaza opposite the United Nations. Rabbi Abraham Joshua Heschel led it off. Like the Passover March, it was reported in the New York media.[100]

Such public exposure of the issue was key to the success of the campaign. Thus, demonstrations had to catch the interest of the mass media to reach the general public, and, especially, catch the attention of Washington and Moscow officialdom. Getting such media coverage was not easy in that period of widespread demonstrations on civil rights and Vietnam. Numbers alone, unless they were huge, were not enough. Although not intended, the demands of the media tended to encourage outrageous acts such as those undertaken by the Jewish Defense League after 1969. The media would denounce such acts in their editorials, while giving them full coverage in their news columns. Irresponsible actions of groups like the JDL gave additional visibility to the issue, but did not win support for Soviet Jews among opinion molders and those responsible for American foreign policy. On the contrary, it shifted the focus from Soviet Jews to JDL behavior.

The challenge was to find creative and multifaceted means to tell in a responsible way what was essentially the same story with different wrinkles. Otherwise, the Soviet Jewry campaign ran the risk of boring the media, public, and even participants in the effort. By and large, the responsible advocacy movement met the challenge in a variety of innovative approaches. For example, two nights after more than 20,000 Moscow Jews gathered on the night of Simchat Torah 1967 in front of the Grand Chorale Synagogue and in Leningrad, 3,000 persons, mostly young people, came together, under the auspices of the New York Coordinating Committee, to sing and dance as well as protest for Soviet Jews within shouting distance of the Soviet Mission to the United Nations. Then those who were able to do so squeezed into the jammed Park East Synagogue, directly across the street from the Soviet Mission, for speeches by prominent public figures denouncing Soviet discrimination against Jews.

That first Simchat Torah demonstration in 1967 would grow the following year into similar demonstrations of solidarity with Soviet Jewish youth held the same day coast to coast in more than thirty major cities. Eight thousand gathered to "dance in the streets" of Los Angeles, with TV coverage from NBC and CBS; in Washington, 4,000 people, led by actor–folk singer Theodore Bikel, rallied in front of the Washington Monument; in San Francisco, a crowd of 4,000, led by folk singer Rabbi Shlomo Carlbach, sang, danced, and marched for Soviet Jews. In Philadelphia, the annual Simchat Torah manifestation grew from 3,500 in 1968 to more than 10,000 young Jews from area colleges and high schools. In New York, the major demonstrations were undertaken by the Coordinating Committee on Soviet Jewry of the then embryonic New York Jewish Community Relations Council. Neither group had staff or budget. What the committee had was the dedication of its chairman, Rabbi Jacob Goldberg, representing the Board of Rabbis, and the staff services of myself, as the coordinator of the AJCSJ.

In a large tent erected in the shadow of the United Nations on Dag Hammarskjold Plaza, the New York Coordinating Committee on Soviet

Jewry conducted during Passover 1967 a different kind of 24-hour vigil. Nearly ten thousand people attended, and influential religious and political leaders spoke in the hour assigned to each of the twenty-four national member organizations of the AJCSJ. Variations on this Passover event were held in seventeen other cities in every section of the United States, and the rallies stimulated broad coverage via television, radio, and the press.[101]

The Jewish holidays provided an effective way to apply their particular themes to Soviet Jews, such as the exodus of Passover or the forced assimilation of Chanukah. The holiday calendar also provided the means of sustaining programming for Soviet Jews on a year-round basis. The timing of Chanukah enabled the AJCSJ to link it to the annual observance on 11 December of the anniversary of the Universal Declaration of Human Rights, adopted by the United Nations in 1948. While it lacked treaty status, the Universal Declaration set forth agreed-upon international principles of basic human rights, and the Soviet Union was a signatory.[102] With this as the focus, the AJCSJ coordinated on 11 December 1966, a national demonstration held simultaneously in thirty-seven cities, with 50,000 people participating.

Martin Luther King, Jr. addressed twelve of these rallies by telephone hookup from Atlanta, Georgia. King warned "of the possibility of the complete spiritual and cultural destruction of a once flourishing Jewish community . . . deprived by the Soviet government of elementary needs to sustain even a modest level of existence and growth. . . . If [the Soviet] government expects respect for itself in the international community of nations, the sincere and genuine concern felt by so many people around the world for this problem should impel the Soviet government not only to effect a solution, but to do it with all deliberate speed."[103] These appeals triggered editorials on Soviet Jewry in several major newspapers. Similar programs were held in subsequent years in a number of cities during Chanukah and the anniversary of the Universal Declaration of Human Rights.

In hammering away at the Soviet Union's human-rights obligations to Soviet Jews, the campaign gave priority to gaining the support of those figures prominently identified with peace movements and civil rights. Support of Soviet Jews by such individuals as King was believed to be disturbing to the Soviet regime. Soviet reactions tended to support that judgment. King was not alone among human rights activists in supporting Soviet Jewry. On 18 March 1966, the Ad Hoc Commission on the Rights of Soviet Jews held a full day of public hearings, put together by Moshe Decter, director of Jewish Minorities Research. The commission comprised people like King; Dr. John C. Bennett, president of the Union Theological Seminary; Father George Ford, veteran Catholic champion of civil liberties; Emil Mazey of the United Automobile Workers; Telford

Taylor, a prosecutor in the Nuremberg trials; Norman Thomas, a leader of the Socialist Party; and as its chair, Bayard Rustin, who in 1963 ran the historic march on Washington for civil rights. Their testimony was given broad circulation in a special issue of *Congress Bi-Weekly*, a publication of the American Jewish Congress.[104]

In May 1967, King; Rustin; Roy Wilkins, the executive director of the NAACP; A. Philip Randolph, the patriarch of the civil rights struggle and the leading African American trade union leader; and Whitney Young, executive director of the National Urban League, were joined by ninety local African American leaders in an appeal to the Soviet Union for Soviet Jews. In December 1967, the *New York Times* and other major newspapers published an open letter to Premier Kosygin from Roger Baldwin, the founding director of the American Civil Liberties Union; Randolph; and Norman Thomas. They called upon Kosygin to act on the promise he made one year earlier on 3 December 1966, to permit emigration to reunite families. These efforts were spawned by the AJCSJ.

The human rights theme was dramatically expressed by the AJCSJ in Philadelphia in April 1966 at its first biennial. Sitting in historic Congress Hall at the desks where the founding fathers voted to add the Bill of Rights to the Constitution, the presidents of the twenty-four national member organizations of the AJCSJ adopted and signed the Declaration of Rights for Soviet Jewry. Its six demands called upon the government of the Soviet Union (1) to restore Jews to "a position of equality with . . . other nationalities"; (2) to "remov[e] all discriminatory measures designed to restrict [the] freedom" of Jews "to practice, enhance and perpetuate their culture and religion"; (3) "to make available the institutions, schools, text books and materials necessary" to transmit to their children their Jewish culture and religion; (4) to permit Jews "to freely develop communal life and to associate and work with Jewish communities and groups" inside and outside the Soviet Union; (5) "to use all means . . . to eradicate anti-Semitism"; and (6) "to permit Soviet Jewish families, separated as a result of the Nazi Holocaust, to be reunited with relatives abroad."[105] That fall, on the eve of High Holy Days, replicas of the declaration were posted in hundreds of synagogues and other Jewish communal institutions around the United States in ceremonies that involved prominent local figures such as Mayor John Lindsay in New York.

To assure that the strong support of Congress for Soviet Jewry came across to its primary targets in Washington and Moscow, the AJCSJ, an organization without a budget and dependent on NCRAC's tight budget, expended substantial sums for ads, primarily in the *New York Times* and the *Washington Post*, to publish statements of Congress.

On 4 December 1966, the Sunday before the anniversary of the Universal Declaration, the AJCSJ ran a statement signed by ninety U.S. senators as a full-page ad. The statement grew out of a declaration of sixty-seven senators issued earlier that year in April on the eve of the biennial of the AJCSJ. That statement was run as a news report in a number of major newspapers including on page one of the *New York Times*. In May 1967, newspapers throughout the country carried news stories about a plea for Soviet Jewry from 315 members of the House. The treatment the press gave these statements was a clear sign that an issue that in the past had been invisible was increasingly being recognized by the media. As part of its ongoing effort to reinforce that recognition, the AJCSJ published a statement by 357 members of the House as a full-page ad in the *New York Times* later that year, 10 December 1967, once again using the anniversary of the Universal Declaration on Human Rights to link the issue of Soviet Jewry to Soviet obligations under the declaration. That statement was run soon after the Soviet Union, as a delayed reaction to the Six-Day War, ended the small trickle of emigration that it had permitted starting in January 1967, a month after the Kosygin statement on "the doors are open" for family reunion. Lining up support in Congress for these various statements was a result of the valuable cooperation given the AJCSJ by I. E. Kenen, then executive director of AIPAC, the American Israel Public Affairs Committee,[106] a member organization of the AJCSJ, and the office of Senator Ribicoff.

Indeed, the multifaceted campaign altered not only media perceptions but the awareness and posture toward Soviet Jewry of the American Jewish community, American public opinion, and those who shaped American foreign policy, beginning with the president. As Abba Eban, then Israel's foreign minister, said to a small, closed meeting of the Presidents' Conference (which I attended) in 1966, "The campaign has made Soviet Jews a worldwide issue." No longer were they or their plight invisible, and that was of great significance in trying to affect Soviet practices.

For the AJCSJ, a top priority of the Soviet Jewry issue was to put it on the agenda of U.S.-Soviet relations. From April 1964 to July 1971, numerous meetings were held by the AJCSJ with key Johnson and Nixon administration officials responsible for U.S.-Soviet relations. They included Presidents Johnson and Nixon; Vice President Hubert H. Humphrey; Secretaries of State Dean Rusk and William P. Rogers; Nicholas Katzenbach, under-secretary of state; Elliot Richardson, under-secretary of state under Nixon; McGeorge Bundy, national security adviser; Walt Rostow, special assistant to the president; Meyer Feldman, special assistant to the president; Foy D. Kohler, former ambassador to the Soviet Union and deputy under-secretary of state for political affairs; Walter Stoessel, deputy assistant secretary of state for Eastern European affairs; Llewelyn Thompson, former ambassador to the Soviet Union; Arthur Goldberg, ambassador to the United Nations; Charles W. Yost, ambassador to the

United Nations (under Nixon); Morris Abram, U.S. delegate to the U.N. Human Rights Commission; and Rita Hauser, U.S. delegate to the commission under Nixon.

The meetings such as those held by Rabbi Miller and myself with Stoessel were almost on a monthly basis. Normally in such meetings, the State Department provides the briefings, but in the meetings with Stoessel, the pattern was reversed. Miller and I usually provided Stoessel with new information and assessments of developments in the Soviet Union in regard to Soviet Jews. In a meeting with McGeorge Bundy, he admitted that U.S. intelligence on conditions of Soviet Jewry was not as good as it should be. At that time, there was no one in the American embassy in Moscow whose portfolio included Soviet Jews. This would change in future years.

From the start, the AJCSJ found these officials sympathetic to the plight of Soviet Jewry. Yet there seemed to be some reticence in vigorously pressing the case officially through diplomatic channels. They seemed to acquiesce in the Soviet contention that the issue was an internal matter, not the business of the U.S. government. On the other hand, privately and publicly, they encouraged the AJCSJ to continue its campaign to expose Soviet repression of its Jewish citizens. However, AJCSJ leadership, while agreeing on the importance of its campaign of public exposure, was convinced that such a campaign had to be paralleled by American diplomatic pressure to bring about a change in Soviet policy. Little by little, the White House and the State Department began to move in that direction. In one of the meetings with Walt Rostow, he said American diplomats had been advised to use every informal opportunity available to raise the issue of Soviet Jews with high Soviet officials. Rusk told Miller and me that he had raised the issue with Ambassador Dobrynin. He said he had told Dobrynin that, unlike many other issues, the problem of Soviet Jews could be easily resolved, and in return, the Soviet Union would gain substantially in public esteem in the West. He stressed to Dobrynin that the Soviet Union could gain so much at a relatively low cost.

When the campaign was launched, the issue of Soviet Jewry was not on the agenda of U.S.-Soviet relations. As Rostow, then a Johnson adviser, indicated, it was put on the agenda, however unofficially, and year by year it grew in importance. In 1970, Secretary of State Rogers raised with Soviet Foreign Minister Gromyko the issue of Soviet citizens seeking to join their relatives abroad. For the first time, an American secretary of state handed Gromyko "an official representation list of Soviet citizens, including many Jews, who have been refused permission to join close relatives in the United States." Rabbi Schacter, then chairman of the AJCSJ, was informed of this action in a letter from Martin J. Hillenbrand, assistant secretary of state for European affairs. In that letter, Hillenbrand said, "United States government officials, at various levels, intend to convey both officially and privately to Soviet Authorities the adverse reaction on American public opinion of the unfair treatment of Jews and other minorities in the USSR." He also stated that the United States would continue to raise these issues in international fora, carefully choosing the forum, "so that our efforts cannot be dismissed as merely 'cold war propaganda.'"[107]

What had evolved was a fundamental change in the State Department's interpretation of this issue. By October 1967, Walter Stoessel, who was then acting assistant secretary of state for European affairs, described Soviet Jews to an AJCSJ leadership conference in Washington "as the most disadvantaged minority" in the Soviet Union. Such a view would be reflected in official State Department publications. On 4 June 1971, the official information bulletin of the State Department on the "mistreatment of Jews in the Soviet Union" represented a striking change from the official information bulletin of the State Department in 1964. The 1964 document described the problems of Soviet Jews within the context of Soviet antireligious campaigns, essentially as problems suffered by all religious groups in the Soviet Union. In contrast, the bulletin in June 1970 asserted, "Judaism fares better than non-recognized religious sects such as Jehovah's Witnesses, but worse than other officially recognized religious groups." It spelled out the discriminatory denials suffered by Judaism. Similarly, it pointed out, "Unlike most other nationality groups . . . their distinctive language, activities and community institutions have been severely restricted." The publication also described the virulent Soviet propaganda attacks on "Zionism as a weapon of subversion" and the vulnerability of Jews "to official attacks on grounds of divided loyalty." It noted, "They are also suspect for having ties to Western Jewry." This represented an accurate account of the miserable status of Jews in the Soviet Union. There can be little doubt the campaign was responsible for this awareness and understanding in the American government.

In addition to the White House and State Department, the AJCSJ also put pressure on the Voice of America to have scheduled programs at fixed times beamed to the Soviet Union and aimed at Soviet Jews. In the latter part of 1966, it sent a memorandum spelling out its recommendations to John Chancellor, then director of the Voice of America. Rabbi Miller, chairman of the AJCSJ, and the writer followed it up in early 1967 with several meetings with Chancellor and key staff of the U.S. Information Agency (USIA). These discussions were continued in 1968 by telephone and correspondence with John Daly, who succeeded Chancellor as VOA director. While expressing concern about the plight of Soviet Jewry, the VOA resisted scheduling regular programs for Soviet Jews. As Daly wrote in a letter to Rabbi Miller, "The directive under which the Voice operates establishes that it shall be used on behalf of the people of the

United States and shall not be used to serve primarily the interests of any specific group."[108] Nevertheless, the AJCSJ persisted in its efforts to achieve its goals with the VOA.

In the end, the efforts of the AJCSJ did result in the VOA broadcasting news accounts of actions that demonstrated American concern about the problems of Soviet Jewry. The VOA news coverage included a statement of twenty-seven U.S. senators; the open letter to Kosygin from Norman Thomas, Roger Baldwin, and A. Philip Randolph; the statement of 344 members of the House of Representatives; a VOA tape of a Washington, D.C., Simchat Torah solidarity demonstration; and the full text of an "Open Letter to the Jews of Moscow," published in the *New York Times*, from the American Association for Jewish Education. Every few weeks, a portion of a regularly scheduled Sunday morning feature on religion in America was devoted exclusively to questions of interest to Jewish listeners.[109]

That the campaign was touching raw nerves in the Kremlin was becoming increasingly evident. In the Soviet Union, *Komsomolskaya Pravda*, one of the Soviet Union's major newspapers, in a 3,000-word article in its 4 October 1967 issue (hardly coincidental that it was on the eve of Rosh Hashanah), bitterly attacked protest activities in the United States. It accused American Jewish organizations as being part of "an international Zionist conspiracy," singling out the American Jewish Conference on Soviet Jewry, B'nai B'rith, and the American Jewish Committee for special criticism.[110] In a long article in its 29 May 1968, issue, *Literaturnaya Gazeta*, a weekly of the Union of Soviet Writers, denounced Rabbi Israel Miller and the AJCSJ.[111]

These articles were meant to have a chilling effect on Soviet Jews. They were intended as a warning to Soviet Jews to avoid any signs of affinity with Jews outside the Soviet Union, and to young Soviet Jews to avoid distinctively Jewish means of expression. They were published in an atmosphere of vicious, almost daily attacks by the Soviet media on Israel and Zionism in the aftermath of the Six-Day War; they were, in fact, vitriolic anti-Semitism whose parallels could be found in Nazi propaganda and the last years of Stalin. They were described in the *White Paper on Soviet Jewry*, issued in April 1968 by the AJCSJ. "Altogether, the campaign revived the theme of the anti-Semitic classic, *The Protocols of the Elders of Zion*, and conjured up the favorite canard of anti-Semites—the notion of a sinister "international Jewish conspiracy" to control the world.[112]

The Soviet propaganda machinery made futile, if not foolish, public relations attempts aimed at the West, particularly the United States. These included an issue of *Soviet Life*, an English-language Soviet propaganda publication, which described the "happy" lives of Jews in the Soviet Union, and letters to the editor of the *New York Times* from "happy" Jews such as General Dragunsky, denouncing the "libelous attacks" on the Soviet Union. Such efforts failed to convince even the editors of *Freiheit*, the New York Yiddish communist daily, or its fellow traveler *Jewish Currents*.

What Soviet propagandists must have conceived as a "public relations coup" was their sending to the United States in June 1968 the 73-year-old Chief Rabbi Yehuda Leib Levin of Moscow and Leningrad Cantor David Stiskin to foster goodwill and a "sympathetic understanding" of Jewish life in the Soviet Union. Presumably, the Soviets believed that these two would have the same impact on the American Jewish community that Shlomo Mikhoels and Itzik Fefer had when they came to the United States as leaders of the Jewish Anti-Fascist Committee in 1943. Although Rabbi Levin had received previous invitations to come to the United States from such groups as the Synagogue Council of America and the Rabbinical Council of America, the Soviets arranged for them to come under the notoriously anti-Zionist American Council for Judaism and the Friends of Jerusalem (Neturei Karta). These two groups were seen as sympathetic to the goal of the PLO, namely, the destruction of the state of Israel.

While in the United States, Rabbi Levin and Cantor Stiskin, "guided" by such groups, turned down repeated requests to meet with the Synagogue Council, the Presidents' Conference, and NCRAC.[113] Some feared that Rabbi Levin's denials of anti-Semitism in the Soviet Union and the false information he gave, such as a radically inflated number of synagogues and rabbis in the Soviet Union, would undermine the efforts of the AJCSJ campaign. These fears proved to be unjustified. The visit had no impact on either the Jewish community or the general public.

More significant in the Soviet response to the campaign than Rabbi Levin's coming to America was an exceptional response by the Kremlin eighteen months earlier. To a written question submitted in advance at a Paris press conference in December 1966 on the reunion of Jewish families separated by the war, Premier Alexey Kosygin responded, "In regard to the reunion of families, if any families wish to come together or wish to leave the Soviet Union, for them the road is open and no problem exists here." The AJCSJ saw this statement as a significant indication of the campaign's impact on the Soviet regime and viewed it with cautious hope. His statement was followed in January 1967 by the beginning of a modest emigration pattern to Israel of about 100 to 200 people a month. While these numbers were minimal, some in the American Embassy in Moscow thought they might prove to be an important crack in the closed gates of the Soviet Union. However, four months after the Six-Day War of June 1967, emigration was halted. In January 1969, emigration of Soviet Jews bound for Israel started up again. The initial numbers of 200 to 300 were small, but they gave encouragement to the AJCSJ that a ceaseless advocacy campaign, backed by diplomatic pressure, could change Soviet policy.

Most important, the campaign touched Soviet Jews. No longer did they feel alone and forgotten. Little by little, the response in the West emboldened the embryonic Jewish movement in the Soviet Union, originally nurtured by Israeli emissaries, to speak out and act in behalf of their cause. Even in the 1960s they had begun to organize *ulpanim* (classes in Hebrew), hold picnics in the country to celebrate Jewish holidays and Yom Ha'atzmaut (Israel Independence Day), conduct study groups on Jewish history, pass from hand to hand typewritten carbon copies of their Russian translations of books about Israel such as *The Exodus* and *The Source,* and publish Jewish *samizdat* (underground publications).

Before the well-known bravery and inspiration of the Sharanskys and the Slepaks in the 1970s came the courage and dedication of men and women, little known in the West, like Dr. Pechersky and Natan Tzurilnikov, both from Leningrad, who in the early 1960s had been imprisoned for their involvement in Jewish education. On their release, they still continued their work for the Jewish people. They and an increasing number like them had begun to emerge, even before the outpouring of support by the Soviet Jews for Israel during the Six-Day War. In the end, they would make the difference in the campaign for Soviet Jews, but they had to pay a painful price for their bold and determined advocacy.

To reach out to these Jews who were not permitted to have ties to the organized Jewish community abroad, travel to the Soviet Union by groups from the American Jewish community began to grow little by little in the 1960s. As president of the Rabbinical Council of America, Rabbi Israel Miller led a nine-man delegation to the Soviet Union in the summer of 1965. They were followed by other groups, including the national leadership of Hadassah and the Central Conference of American Rabbis, the association of the Reform rabbinate. While serving as coordinator of the AJCSJ, I led a group of six CRC directors and their spouses to the Soviet Union in January 1967. The American Jewish Congress, which had a major travel program, included a Soviet itinerary among its tour options. As a deliberate policy, AJCSJ recommended to its member organizations, and particularly CRCs, that they encourage concerned and informed American Jews to travel to the Soviet Union. On a more systematic basis, the travel of certain individuals whose meetings with Soviet Jews could be of value was made possible by various groups and individuals.[114] The end result was the nurturing of profound relationships and friendships between Soviet Jews and American Jews, as well as those from Western Europe.

What has been characterized as "the Jewish movement" in the Soviet Union was in fact a Zionist movement; they saw redemption of the Jews as the "return" to Israel. Starting in the late 1960s, these Soviet Jews demanded their right to emigrate "to their national Jewish homeland" under international law, particularly the Universal Declaration on Human Rights. In later years, they would characterize their demands as repatriation. In these courageous acts, whose frequency made the exceptional seem routine, they would release to the media petitions, letters, and declarations addressed to the government of the Soviet Union, to the United Nations, to the president, and the Congress of the United States. These demands were expressed by the thousands of Soviet Jews seeking exit visas to Israel. The growing demands for exit visas were probably the single greatest pressure on the Soviet Union to open the gates of emigration.

To smash the emerging Jewish movement and stem the rush to emigrate, the Soviet Union used an iron fist. This led the campaign in the United States to go beyond exposing Soviet treatment of Jews as a group to exposing Soviet persecution of individual Jews who expressed themselves as Jews and petitioned for the right to emigrate. One of the first cases was that of Boris Kochubiyevsky: He was raised as an orphan without any Jewish education or awareness except for his experience as a Jew in the Soviet Union, and was expelled from his factory trade union because of his defense of Israel at a factory meeting during the Six-Day War. He protested Soviet silence about the Nazi massacre of Jews at a memorial meeting at Babi Yar, where his parents were killed; resigned under pressure from his job in May 1968; and applied that summer with his wife, a Ukrainian, for exit visas to Israel. The request was first refused; later, the family was told on 28 November to pick up their passports. On that day, their apartment was searched in their absence, and letters were seized, including protest letters to authorities. Kochubiyevsky was arrested one week later for anti-Soviet slander, and was sentenced to three years of forced labor on 16 May 1969. In response to the call of the AJCSJ, vigils protesting his imprisonment were held throughout the country. The *New York Times* published a letter to the editor from Lewis Weinstein, chairman of the AJCSJ, and the AJCSJ urged that similar letters be sent to local newspapers. The case of Kochubiyevsky was described in the *Times*, the *Washington Post,* and other major newspapers throughout the nation.[115]

No longer would the campaign allow the Soviet Union to engage in such outrages without the world taking notice. The AJCSJ and others involved in the campaign would treat each Soviet Jew victimized by the Soviet Union as a specific responsibility. Thus, for example, in November 1969, an AJCSJ delegation gave the U.S. ambassador to the United Nations, Charles Yost, a letter addressed to the U.N. General Assembly from Elizaveta Kapshitzer of Moscow in behalf of her son. He was denied an exit visa to Israel and prevented from earning a living after being expelled from the Soviet Writers' Union. Rita Hauser, U.S. delegate to the Human Rights Commission, attempted to read the letter to the General Assembly's human rights committee, but, according to the *New York Post*, she was interrupted three times by the Soviet and Ukrainian delegates and was unable to finish the letter. However, their interruptions helped Hauser make her points about the particular case, as well as indict the Soviet Union on its overall treatment of Soviet Jews. The interruption succeeded in bringing the letter to the media's attention.[116]

On 15 June 1970, nine Soviet Jews and two other Soviet citizens were arrested at Leningrad's Smolny Airport for allegedly planning "to seize a scheduled aircraft." At the same time, eight Leningrad Jews were arrested in other locations. In Leningrad, Victor Boguslavsky protested the arrests in a letter to the Soviet procurator-general. It promptly led to Boguslavsky's own arrest. Using the pretext of the alleged hijacking, nineteen other Jews were rounded up on charges of anti-Soviet agitation.

In Moscow, Riga, and Kharkov, as well as in Leningrad, the homes of many Jewish activists were searched. Authorities uncovered such "anti-Soviet material" as books of Hebrew poetry and recordings of Hebrew songs. These attacks on the Jewish movement took place in a climate permeated by an intensification of the virulent anti-Israel and anti-Zionist campaign in the Soviet media. "The Soviet press seemed to compete with itself in the increasing hysteria of its language," reports indicated.[117] Still, Soviet Jews would not be silenced by these arrests and the intimidation of the Soviet media.Within weeks of the Leningrad arrests, the *New York Times* reported that three different groups of Soviet Jews sent documents, signed by more than eighty persons, to the Supreme Soviet, which had just convened. They demanded that they be permitted to immigrate to Israel. The documents were made available to Western correspondents.[118]

In the United States, after receiving reports of new arrests in Riga, a delegation of the AJCSJ met with key State Department officials on 13 July 1970. The Jewish Community Council of Washington, D.C., followed up with a press conference on "these ominous developments." Such press conferences in the nation's capitol were covered by the *Washington Post,* and had considerable impact. Demonstrations were held in other communities, including Philadelphia, Boston, Los Angeles, and San Francisco. In New York, the Student Struggle demonstrated behind the barriers near the Soviet Mission to the United Nations. In September, Stanley Lowell, a confidant of New York City Mayor John Lindsay and former mayor Robert Wagner, was appointed by Rabbi Schacter, chair of the AJCSJ, to head a newly formed National Lawyers Committee for Soviet Jewry. This committee planned to monitor Soviet implementation of due process in its trials of Soviet Jews, to speak out when it saw violations of Soviet and/or international law, and to volunteer legal services.

Expecting the Leningrad trials to be held soon, the AJCSJ encouraged an ongoing barrage of manifestations of concern. Between 18 October and early November 1970, there were at minimum 125 rallies, marches, and vigils in at least 90 cities. Newspapers in every section of the United States carried editorials.[119]

After the Leningrad arrests were announced in the Soviet press, the incarceration of Soviet Jews prior to trial became shrouded in silence. Ominously, a Moscow dispatch on 3 December 1970, cited the official announcement of the sentencing to death a year before of an accused hijacker. Then, six months to the day after the arrests at the Leningrad Airport, on 15 December 1970, the trial began in the Leningrad City Court. Soviet authorities imposed a news blackout on the proceedings, a move that triggered worldwide discussions of the trial and the conditions confronted by Soviet Jews. A week later, on Christmas Eve, as the Western world had closed down to observe the holiday, the Soviet government shocked the world in the announcement of sentences given the eleven defendants. Two were condemned to death and the other nine to prison terms ranging from four to fifteen years.[120]

Outraged protests erupted throughout the world. In Philadelphia, for example, a rally was held in the heart of the city on Christmas Day. Around the country, special Sabbath services were held in crowded synagogues and in some churches. In some cities, including Washington, church bells were rung at prearranged times. A delegation of the National Council of Churches met with Ambassador Dobrynin. Twenty-four senators sent a joint letter of concern to President Nixon; similarly, forty congressmen joined in a letter to the president. The Senate and the House of Representatives each adopted resolutions calling on the Soviet Union to commute the two death sentences and "to provide fair and equitable justice for its Jewish citizens."[121] On three days' notice, 500 Jewish leaders from 66 cities in 33 states, representing the entire range of Jewish organizational life, came to Washington on 30 December 1970, for an Emergency Conference jointly convened by the AJCSJ and the Presidents' Conference. Delegations fanned out to meet with ambassadors or chargés d'affaire of thirteen embassies. Poland, Czechoslovakia, Hungary, and Congo declined requests to meet. A lawyers' delegation met with U.S. Deputy Attorney General Richard Kleindienst.

A press conference was held by Rabbi Heschel, Isaac Bashevis Singer, Bayard Rustin, Professor Hans J. Morgenthau, and playwright Arthur Miller. Later, Miller announced the creation of the Ad Hoc Committee of Concern for Soviet Jewish Prisoners. Its original members included Leonard Bernstein, historian Henry Steele Commager, Robert Penn Warren, Nobel laureate George Wald, Dwight MacDonald, Alfred Kazin, Telford Taylor, Lionel Trilling, and Notre Dame President Theodore M. Hesburgh. A delegation from the conference met with Secretary of State Rogers. The delegation included Rabbi Schacter, chairman of the AJCSJ; Dr. William A. Wexler, chairman of the Presidents' Conference; and Max Fisher, president of the Council of Jewish Federations and Welfare Funds. During the discussion, Rogers telephoned President Nixon to arrange an immediate, unscheduled meeting with the president. In the 40-minute White House meeting, the president impressed the delegation with his knowledge of the situation and of what the U.S. government was doing and planned to do.[122]

Widely covered by the media, the conference adjourned late in the evening of 30 December. In the early hours of Thursday, 31 December, one week after the sentences had been decreed, it was announced in Moscow that the death sentences had been commuted and some of the other sentences reduced. "When dictator regimes commute death sentences, it suggests that world opinion is not the ineffectual phantom that skeptics have taken it to be. . . . I confess that I thought the Soviets too rigid to bend with the wind of world opinion in the Leningrad sentences. . . . [It] suggest[s] a new emerging force whose potency bears no relation to its lack of hard power," Max Lerner wrote on 4 January 1971, in his column in the *New York Post*.

This concept of the power of public opinion is what had driven the AJCSJ from its very creation in April 1964, and it was this overriding strategic judgment that was the basis of the unprecedented decision of Jewish leadership of Western Europe, North and South America, Australia, and Israel to convene a world conference to mobilize a global response to the ominous developments in the Soviet Union. Such a conference was urged in a resolution adopted by a gathering of Jewish leaders from seventeen European countries, held in Paris in April 1970. The AJCSJ in June, and the British Board of Deputies and the Israel Public Council for Soviet Jews in July each endorsed the urgent need for a world conference.[123] There is little doubt that the proposal originated with the Israel Liaison Bureau. It was agreed that such a conference would be convened by national groups such as AJCSJ and international bodies such as the World Jewish Congress, the World Zionist Organization, and B'nai B'rith International.

With a view toward holding such a conference in London before the end of the year, an international secretariat was designated that summer composed of Abraham Marks, director of the British Board of Deputies; Pierre Kaufman, director of the Representative Council of the Jews of France (CRIF); Joe Fuchs, representing the Israel Public Council on Soviet Jewry; and myself, who was asked by the AJCSJ to take a leave from my role as director of the Philadelphia JCRC to represent the American Jewish community on the secretariat. Later, the dates and site were changed to the Palais des Congrès in Brussels, from 23 to 25 February 1971. Representatives of the sponsors of the proposed world conference met in London on 5 August 1970, and proclaimed 20 September 1970—the week of the opening of the United Nations General Assembly—as World Day for Soviet Jewry. On that day, major demonstrations were held in London, Paris, Sydney, Melbourne, Buenos Aires, Montreal, Toronto, and major cities in the United States, including New York at Dag Hammarskjold Plaza.

Four days before this demonstration, the *New York Times* reported that two documents were distributed to Western correspondents in Moscow from Soviet Jews, no doubt in anticipation of the 20 September observance. One was a letter signed by eighty-three Jews, giving their addresses and occupations. They called on "brother Jews" to unite in their cause. Another, signed by seventy-seven Jews, was addressed to the delegates of the U.N. General Assembly. The first letter asserted, "We are the only people in the Soviet Union who are ordered openly, in plain terms, to dissolve, to disappear among other peoples."

The secretariat of the scheduled world conference, which had been augmented by David Susskind of Brussels, Yehuda Hellman of the Conference of Presidents, and Abraham Karlikow of the American Jewish Committee office in Paris, met for the first time in Brussels on Thanksgiving Day, 1970. At that time, no one anticipated the magnitude of the impact that this first world conference of Jewish communities for Soviet Jewry would have. Nor did they anticipate the draconian sentences that the Soviets would hand down in the coming month and the worldwide outrage inspired by these excesses. A few members of the secretariat warned that the Brussels conference would be poorly attended, receive little visibility in the media, and fail to have any impact.

How wrong they were! That convocation of Jewish communities, held in Brussels from 23 to 25 February 1971, proved to be historic. From thirty-eight countries on five continents came more than fifteen hundred delegates, including scores of prominent public officials, civil rights activists, scholars, poets, writers, financiers, union leaders, and philosophers. More than three hundred delegates came on chartered flights from the United States. To the astonishment of the secretariat, the Soviet media on the eve of the conference launched a propaganda attack that captured the attention of the world media. Nearly three hundred journalists from every part of the world covered the Brussels event. Even the brief disruption of the conference by Rabbi Meir Kahane of the Jewish Defense League could not weaken the unity of purpose and resolve of that assembly.

From the World Conference came the demand for Soviet authorities "to recognize the right of Jews who so desire to return to their historic homeland in Israel." This demand went beyond the American campaign's demand that had focused on family reunion. It mirrored the demands of the Jewish movement in the Soviet Union. As stated to the conference by a Soviet Jew who had just emigrated after five years in a Siberian labor camp, "All I demand is the right to live among my own, in my own culture, as a Jew. I am not anti-Soviet, but I want to express myself as a Jew. This is basic to me, and this is why I wanted to go to the Jewish homeland."

This was the raison d'être of the movement in the Soviet Union. It was essentially a Zionist movement, although it had other dimensions. When the resolution, including this demand, was first presented to the presidium of the World Conference, Lewis Weinstein, a representative of the NJCRAC, found himself alone in urging it be modified to call for not only aliyah (emigration to Israel), but for the right to emigrate anywhere. The Israelis contended that the Soviet Union could ideologically live more easily with a nationality group seeking to return to their national homeland than with a flood of emigration to the West. While the call for aliyah was overwhelmingly adopted by the Brussels conference, it would become in the mid-1970s a source of severe tension among some within the American Jewish community establishment and Israel. Many Soviet Jews, leaving with Israeli visas, sought American visas when they arrived in Vienna en route to Israel.

At the close of the conference, five representatives including Weinstein were chosen to present the declaration to the Human Rights Commission of the United Nations, then beginning to meet in Geneva. Dr. Yoram Dinstein, who had served from 1967 to 1969 as Israel's (Soviet Jewry) consul in New York and was an authority on international human rights legal principles, served as consultant to the delegation.[124] In Geneva, they met with the Venezuelan chairman of the Human Rights Commission, Dr. Ribon Merenfeld of Caracas. They also met with Soviet representative Nikolai Tarrasov, who vehemently rejected the charges against the Soviet Union, and with Rita Hauser, U.S. representative to the U.N. commission. Ambassador Hauser presented a powerful indictment of the Soviet Union's treatment of Jews. She quoted *Pravda* that any Soviet Jew who wished to migrate was automatically "an enemy of the Soviet people." Tarrasov angrily responded that her quotation was deceptive as well as slanderous. He then read the quote as stating that any Jew who wished to emigrate to Israel was a Zionist, and thus automatically an enemy of the Soviet Union. In his denial was affirmation of the charges against his country.[125]

The impact of the World Conference was seen almost immediately after its adjournment. Indications emerged of some loosening of emigration policies. As many as 1,000 Soviet Jews emigrated in March. In April, it went up to 1,300. By the end of 1971, the total for the year had reached more than 13,000, in contrast to about 4,200 in 1970. In 1972, emigration surged to 31,681.

The Soviet crackdown on Soviet Jews in 1970 moved the leadership of the organizations composing the American Jewish Conference on Soviet Jewry and the Council of Jewish Federations and Welfare Funds at its General Assembly in Kansas City to agree in November 1970 to raise from local Jewish federations a Soviet Jewry emergency fund of $100,000 for the AJCSJ. Until then, the AJCSJ had been barred from such fund-raising. Except for seeking assessments from member organizations project by project, the AJCSJ relied on NJCRAC's budget for all of its operating expenses. By 1970, that included virtually a full-time NJCRAC professional with a full-time secretary; substantial staff backup, ranging from the NJCRAC director of public information to the mailroom staff; and hidden but very tangible costs such as telephone, mail, rent, and travel. Each year, this put an increasing strain on NJCRAC's small budget. The $100,000 fund was not to be used to reimburse NJCRAC in any way for these expenditures; its purpose was to provide funding for specific programs and material.[126]

From the very beginning, the constraints on the AJCSJ were attacked by some community groups that eventually formed the Union of Councils for Soviet Jewry. In April 1964, the Cleveland group urged that this newly created AJCSJ be "funded and staffed to coordinate and implement this protest." At the biennial in Philadelphia in April 1966, they called for a new body with a $500,000 budget. Similar demands were made before and during the April 1968 biennial in New York, although they were expressed in a more irresponsible fashion by students from Columbia University, which reflected the temper of the times.[127] Even without a budget, the AJCSJ had been much more effective than its critics would concede. It had radically changed the American Jewish community's response to the plight of Soviet Jews, the priority the U.S. government gave to this issue, how the Kremlin approached this issue, and the isolation of Soviet Jews from the rest of the world Jewish community.

In the course of its history from 1964, the American Jewish Conference on Soviet Jewry was buffeted by many crosscurrents. Among its constituents were those who still looked to Nahum Goldmann for leadership on the Soviet Jewry issue, although as time went on, his influence waned. There were others who were troubled, and with good reason, by the concept of creating a single-issue organization for every critical threat to Jewish security. However, they recognized that to bring the conference within the Presidents' Conference or under the rubric of NJCRAC would be perceived as reducing the priority given to the issue.

Some who were strongly identified with the Presidents' Conference were concerned about the close identification of the AJCSJ with NJCRAC. The "grassroots" critics, who in reality represented only a handful of people on the community level (albeit profoundly dedicated true believers), were distressed by what they regarded as excessively cautious responses to information coming directly from sources in the Soviet Union. They attacked the AJCSJ for being too deferential to the Israel Liaison Bureau, although some, including the Cleveland group, had been nurtured by the bureau's representatives and had been funded as a result of its intercession on their behalf.[128] In the end, their frustration was no different than the frustration of the leadership in confronting this behemoth that was the Soviet Union.

The ever-expanding demands of this issue on NJCRAC led its officers to declare that resources had been taxed to the point of prejudicing the proper discharge of the longtime coordinating responsibility for the whole gamut of community relations. They asserted that if coordination of the national activities for Soviet Jewry were transferred to any new national organization, NJCRAC was prepared to continue, and even to augment, its coordination of the work of the communities through its member agencies. NJCRAC concerns were reinforced by growing pressures, particularly after the Brussels conference, for the restructuring and independent funding of the AJCSJ. It led to appointment of a joint committee by Rabbi Schacter, chairman of the AJCSJ, and Dr. Wexler, chairman of the Presidents' Conference, to develop recommendations for reorganizing the AJCSJ. The committee was chaired by Stanley H. Lowell. Without a dissenting vote, its recommendations for reconstituting the American Jewish Conference on Soviet Jewry with its own staff, independent funding, and annual budget were adopted by member organizations on 4 June 1971.

Financial support was pledged by Jewish federations. The recommendations provided for the reorganized body to have special relationships with the Presidents' Conference in regard to officials of the federal government and international organizations, and with NJCRAC in regard to working with the communities. The new arrangement also reconstituted the New York Conference on Soviet Jewry, which was then staffed by David Geller, on loan from the American Jewish Committee, as an independent local agency with its own full-time staff and budget.[129] Richard Maass, chairman of the foreign affairs department of the American Jewish Committee, who succeeded Rabbi Schacter as chairman of the AJCSJ on 4 June, became the first chairman of the reconstituted body when these recommendations went into effect on 30 August 1971. Jerry Goodman, who had been a member of the foreign affairs department of the AJCommittee, became the first executive director of what soon was to be renamed the National Conference on Soviet Jewry. Malcolm Hoenlein, then a member of the staff of the Philadelphia JCRC, became the first director of the Greater New York Conference on Soviet Jewry.

Driven by the impact of the World Conference on Soviet Jewry and the reconstituted National Conference on Soviet Jewry, a new chapter was now to be written in American advocacy for Soviet Jews.

Notes

1. Jerzy G. Gliksman, *American Jewish Yearbook* [hereafter *AJY*] 50 (1948–49): 400.

2. Molotov's Jewish wife, Madame Zhemchuzhina, was also a member of the committee. Khrushchev thought that the committee was created at the suggestion of Molotov, although, he added, "It may have been Stalin's own idea."

3. Nikita Sergeevich Khrushchev, *Khrushchev Remembers*, with an introd., commentary, and notes by Edward Crankshaw, trans. and ed. Strobe Talbott (Boston: Little, Brown, 1970), 259.

4. In 1913 in his *Marxism and the National-Colonial Question* Stalin wrote, "Jews are not a people"; that is, they must become a part of the all-Russian melting pot and relinquish all ties binding them to other sections of the Jewish people. Stalin rejected a concept of a Jewish people.

5. Isaiah M. Minkoff, who was then the executive director of the General Jewish Council, recalled to me that he deliberately avoided any meeting with Mikhoels when he was in the United States, although they had been close personal friends in earlier years. Minkoff was concerned that his long history of opposing Soviet Communism might embarass and even harm Mikhoels, who had played an instrumental role in helping Minkoff escape from the Soviet Union in the early 1920s. Ben Zion Goldberg, *The Jewish Problem in the Soviet Union: Analysis and Solution*, with a foreword by Daniel Mayer (New York: Crown, 1961), 45 and 47.

6. Goldberg, *Jewish Problem*, 61, 63, 64.

7. Khrushchev, *Khrushchev Remembers*, 261–62.

8. Joseph Gordon, *AJY* 51 (1950) 336–40.

9. Sylvia Rothchild, *A Special Legacy: An Oral History of Soviet Jewish Emigrés in the United States* (New York: Simon and Schuster, 1965). The book was a collection of interviews conducted by Ms. Rothchild under the auspices of the American Jewish Committee.

10. In 1969 the name was changed to the National Jewish Community Relations Advisory Council. It was created in 1944 by the General Assembly of the Council of Jewish Federations to serve as the national coordinating and planning body of the field of Jewish community relations. Its orginal membership included the American Jewish Committee, the American Jewish Congress, the B'nai B'rith-/Anti-Defamation League, the Jewish Labor Committtee, and fourteen local Jewish commmunity relations councils. NCRAC would play a major role in future years in the campaign for Soviet Jews.

11. Howard Fast, *Being Red (A Memoir)* (New York: Houghton Mifflin, 1990), 206.

12. Goldberg, *Jewish Problem*, 102–3.

13. Report to annual conference of Jewish Labor Committee, April 1953, 15–17.

14. Joseph Gordon, *AJY* 55 (1954): 263–64. The Doctors' Plot dovetailed with the arrests and trials that were held in late 1952 in Prague of Rudolph Slansky, vice premier and former secretary-general of the Czech Communist Party, and other Party leaders in Rumania, Hungary, and East Germany, who for many years had been disciplined, obedient servants of the Moscow apparatus. They were charged and executed for "cosmopolitanism" and "Zionist" conspiracies.

15. Crankshaw commentary, in Khrushchev, *Khrushchev Remembers*, 282–83.

16. Rothchild, *A Special* Legacy, 96, 47, and 97.

17. Lucy Dawidowicz, *AJY* 55 (1954): 148–49.

18. American Jewish Committee, American Jewish Congress, B'nai B'rith/ADL, Jewish Labor Committee, Jewish War Veterans, and the Union of American Hebrew Congregations. Many local CRCs sent statements of concern to the new president, Dwight D. Eisenhower, and to Henry Cabot Lodge, the new U.S. ambassador to the United Nations.

19. Dawidowicz, *AJY* 55 (1954): 146.

20. The American Jewish Committee abstained on the motion to convene a mass protest meeting, possibly at Madison Square Garden. In the protests against Nazi Germany before World War II the American Jewish Committee also opposed mass protest meetings in Madison Square Garden.

21. Minutes of NCRAC executive committee meeting, 20 January 1943, 6–7.

22. Dawidowicz, *AJY* 55 (1954): 149.

23. Minutes of NCRAC Executive Committee meeting, 20 January 1943, 8.

24. The American Jewish Committee declined to cosponsor it on the grounds that the original plans called for a nonsectarian meeting.

25. Dawidowicz, *AJY* 55 (1954): 109.

26. Ibid.

27. Ibid, 148–49.

28. Ibid, 150–51.

29. Ibid, 150–51.

30. Ibid, 156.

31. Goldberg, *Jewish Problem*, 106.

32. The idea of a worldwide conspiracy against Russia has deep roots in Russian history and was repeatedly reflected in scurrilous attacks on Jews throughout the history of the czars and the Soviet Union. It still manifests itself today in the post-Soviet era.

33. "A Decade of Destruction, Jewish Culture in the USSR, 1948–1958," report of the Congress for Jewish Culture, New York, January 1958.

34. Ibid, 20.

35. At the behest of the Liaison Bureau in 1953, Levanon, who at the time was agricultural manager of Kibbutz Kfar Blum, served in the Israeli embassy in Moscow as agricultural attaché. In that capacity he reached out to Soviet Jews, and was expelled from the Soviet Union for that activity in 1955.

36. Naomi W. Cohen, *Not Free to Desist: American Jewish Committee, 1906–1966* (Philadelphia: Jewish Publication Society, 1972), 504–5.

37. American Jewish Congress, Jewish Labor Committee, Jewish War Veterans, Union of American Hebrew Congretions, Union of Orthodox Jewish Congreagations of America, and the United Synagogue of America. The American Jewish Committee and the B'nai B'rith/ADL withdrew from the NCRAC in 1952 in the conflict over the MacIver Report. They would rejoin NCRAC in 1965 and 1966.

38. Jules Cohen, NCRAC memorandum, 10 August 1959, NCRAC archives, American Jewish Historical Society, Boston.

39. Ibid, Jules Cohen notes, 12, 13, 14, 17 and 18 August 1959.

40. Ibid, Jules Cohen, NCRAC memorandum, 19 August 1959.

41. Ibid.

42. Ibid.

43. Isaiah M. Minkoff, NCRAC memorandum (as in note 38), 26 August 1959.

44. In 1984, almost a year before Gorbachev came to power in March 1985, NJCRAC received similar "feelers" through a credible interlocutor about the

desire for a meeting by a "very high" Soviet official with a "representative" American Jewish organization. As in the case of Khrushchev, nothing ultimately came of it.

45. Gunther Lawrence, *Three Million More?* (Garden City, N.Y.: Doubleday, 1970), 8.

46. Samuel Spiegler, NCRAC Memorandum (as in note 38), 4 September 1959.

47. Goldberg, *Jewish Problem*, 233.

48. Shapiro, *American Jewish Yearbook Bulletin* [hereafter *AJYB*] 61 (1960): 262.

49. Nicholas DeWitt, "The Status of Jews in Soviet Education" (New York: American Jewish Congress, 1964).

50. Zvi Gitelman, "The Jews: Problems of Communism," USIA, September–October 1967, 92.

51. *Journal of the International Commission of Jurists* 5, no. 1 (1964): 45–46.

52. Lawrence, *Three Million More?* 170–71.

53. Ibid, 172.

54. Lewis H. Weinstein "Soviet Jewry and the American Jewish Community," *American Jewish History* 77, no. 4 (June 1988): 600.

55. Abraham Joshua Heschel, *The Insecurity of Freedom: Essays on Human Existence* (New York: Farrar, Straus and Giroux, 1966), 273.

56. Lawrence, *Three Million More?* 169–75.

57. Ibid.

58. Ibid.

59. The Baum memorandum was based on the Goldberg-Javits report to the Presidents' Conference.

60. Lawrence, *Three Million More?*, 160.

61. William W. Orbach, *The American Movement to Aid Soviet Jews* (Amherst: University of Massachusetts Press, 1979), 20.

62. Weinstein, "Soviet Jewry," 601–4.

63. Naomi Cohen, *Not Free to Desist,* 508.

64. Weinstein, "Soviet Jewry," 603.

65. *AJYB* 65 (1964): 77.

66. Lawrence, *Three Million More?* 161–62.

67. Weinstein, "Soviet Jewry," 664.

68. Five background papers on Judaism, Jewish culture, economic crimes, discrimination in science and higher education, and on reunion of families. AJCSJ archives, American Jewish Historical Society, Brandeis University, Boston.

69. American Jewish Conference on Soviet Jewry Declaration of Purposes, 6 April 1963, AJCSJ archives.

70. Proposals for local followup, AJCSJ archives.

71. Ibid.

72. In 1840, the United States protested the arrest and torture of Jews in Damascus on "blood libel" charges. In 1860, it took steps to cancel a discriminatory clause against Jewish emigration in a treaty with Switzerland. In 1912, it nullified a mutual travel and commercial treaty with czarist Russia because of discrimination against American Jews traveling in Russia.

73. Statement to Secretary of State Dean Rusk, 7 April 1963, AJCSJ.

74. Nahum Goldmann letter, 20 February 1963, in Weinstein, "Soviet Jewry," 616.

75. Weinstein, "Soviet Jewry," 604.

76. Max Kampelman, who served as U.S. ambassador to the Helsinki Review Process under Presidents Carter and Reagan, recalls that in the Madrid review

meetings in the early 1980s, the Soviets insisted that the United States was violating Helsinki by criticizing the Soviet Union for its human rights behavior. They claimed that Helsinki made such interference unacceptable. Kampelman asked, If we had reached an agreement on disarmament, would it be internal interference to charge a failure to comply with the agreement's provisions? It would make such negotiations a farce. The same concern applies here. In signing Helsinki in 1975, the Soviet Union assumed certain obligations. Thus, inquiring about Soviet compliance was not improper interference in its internal affairs. There were those who argued in the 1960s that that same principle grew out of the adoption of the Universal Declaration of Human Rights in 1948. Indeed, that was the original posture of the American Jewish Conference on Soviet Jewry.

In a case somewhat similar to the hypothetical one that Goldmann put to Weinstein, Kampelman recalled that the Soviets made a tactical move that he welcomed. They criticized the human rights records of the United States. He welcomed the criticism, "declaring that it legitimized the review at the meetings of a state's compliance with the human rights obligations of the Helsinki Final Act."

77. Weinstein, "Soviet Jewry," 615.

78. Ibid., 604–5. In his book, Gunther Lawrence (*Three Million More?*) recalls the events and sequence somewhat differently: "A delegation finally obtained an invitation to the White House where they talked with McGeorge Bundy (the president's national security adviser). . . . Weinstein explained that silence could no longer be tolerated . . . and outlined steps the government could consider. . . . During the meeting, the president entered the room . . . and reviewed his own human rights record. . . . He promised to discuss the matter with . . . Rusk the following morning. . . . The following day, the delegation met with Rusk and formally requested the State Department to convey the views of the conference to the Soviet government."

79. Report of George Maislen to AJCSJ, 19 October 1964, AJCSJ archives [hereafter Maislen report].

80. Ibid.

81. Ted Comet, executive director of the American Zionist Youth Foundation, served as coordinator of the AJCSJ from 1 January 1965 to 1 July 1965. Label Katz, president of B'nai B'rith, became chairman of the new steering committee, also serving for the same six-month period.

82. Comet memorandum, 17 May 1965, AJCSJ archives.

83. Maislen report.

84. As executive director of the Philadelphia JCRC from 1968 to 1975, I found the relationship with students involved in the Soviet Jewry campaign on several campuses, particularly Penn and Temple, constructive and helpful. The JCRC provided them with staff assistance, as well as occasional financial help.

85. NCRAC memo of selected statements on Soviet Jewry, 26 March 1965, AJCSJ archives.

86. Even before the creation of the American Jewish Conference on Soviet Jewry, the Philadelphia JCRC had already undertaken a series of activities for Soviet Jewry, beginning its campaign as early as December 1962 with a citywide conference on the plight of Soviet Jewry. This leadership of the Philadelphia JCRC on behalf of Soviet Jewry anticipated the exemplary role it would play in the campaign well into the 1990s.

87. Maislen report.

88. Summary Reports on Soviet Jewry project by Jules Cohen, 2 March and 15 April 1965, Philadelphia JCRC archives.

89. Address by Philip M. Klutznik, 28 March 1965, Philadelphia JCRC archives.

90. Siegman report on Eternal Light Vigil, 4 October 1965, AJCSJ archives.

91. Ibid.

92. Ibid.

93. In addition to serving as AJCSJ coordinator, I was also NCRAC director of community consultation, the group responsible for NCRAC's annual plenary session and staffed of the committee charged with Israel advocacy. It was easier for me to undertake this role as a result of the repeal that summer of the racist national-origin quota system of American immigration law (for which I received a pen from President Lyndon Johnson for my leadership role in achieving this long-sought goal). The change in the law would have ramifications for the immigration of Soviet Jews to the United States.

94. Rabbi Miller was president of the Rabbinical Council of America, a national association of Orthodox rabbis.

95. In 1969, the National Community Relations Advisory Council inserted "Jewish" into its name, changing it to the National Jewish Community Relations Advisory Council.

96. I returned to NJCRAC in July 1975 as its executive vice chairman, succeeding Minkoff, who retired after thirty-one years in that position.

97. *Manual on Guidelines for Action*, 1966, AJCSJ archives.

98. Renamed years later as the Association of Jewish Community Centers.

99. Chernin summary of AJCSJ activity, 2 April 1968.

100. AJCSJ Report to COJO, 9 July 1969, AJCSJ archives.

101. Chernin summary (as in note 99).

102. Eleanor Roosevelt played a crucial role in getting the Universal Declaration adopted and in getting the Soviet Union to support it. In the 1950s, she raised the issue of Soviet Jewry on various occasions with high Soviet officials, including Khrushchev.

103. Text of King address, 11 December 1966, AJCSJ archives.

104. AJCSJ memorandum of 9 December 1966.

105. Text of Declaration on Rights for Soviet Jewry, April 1966.

106. In those years, AIPAC, under Kenen, was a small, tightly run, low-profile operation (in many respects similar to NCRAC), but it was highly respected and trusted in the corridors of power in Washington. AIPAC maintained a close working relationship with NCRAC and the CRCs.

107. Hillenbrand letter to Schacter, 6 November 1970, AJCSJ archives.

108. Daly letter to Miller, 30 January 1968, AJCSJ archives.

109. When I was in the Soviet Union with my family in October 1969, an old Jew in a synagogue in Kiev, learning that I was from Philadelphia, exclaimed in Yiddish, "Philadelphia! Golda was in Philadelphia yesterday, and thousands of children sang and danced on the streets to greet her." He had heard that on a broadcast beamed to the Soviet Union. Of personal interest to the writer was that he had described a program arranged by the Philadelphia JCRC to welcome Prime Minister Golda Meir.

110. Chernin memorandum, 31 October 1967, NJCRAC archives.

111. Jerry Goodman, *American Jewish Yearbook* 70 (1969): 114.

112. White Paper on Soviet Jewry, AJCSJ archives, 4.

113. Rabbi Israel Miller, chairman of the AJCSJ, had personally extended an invitation to Rabbi Levin in the Great Chorale Synagogue of Moscow in the summer of 1965. He did so at that time as the president of the RCA, the Orthodox rabbinate. The invitation was formalized in a letter to Ambassador Dobrynin in September 1965. Early in 1968, Rabbi Jacob Rudin, president of the Synagogue Council, extended a similar invitation.

114. Similarly, trips to the Soviet Union were arranged for two members of

my staff on the Philadelphia JCRC, Malcolm Hoenlein and Rabbi Maurice Corson. This was replicated throughout the United States, as well as in Western Europe. Hoenlein is today the executive director of the Conference of Presidents of Major American Jewish Organizations. Corson is currently president of the Wexner Foundation. The writer made five such trips between 1966 and 1991.

115. Abraham Bayer memorandum, 25 June 1969, AJCSJ archives.

116. Bayer memorandum, 5 December 1969.

117. Richard Cohen, ed., *Let My People Go* (New York: Popular Library, 1971), 76–78.

118. *New York Times*, 15 July 1970.

119. Bayer memoranda, 17 July and 8 September 1970. Richard Maass report, 30 December 1970, AJCSJ archives.

120. Cohen, *Let My People Go*, 79–81.

121. Maass report, 30 December 1970.

122. *Report on Emergency Conference on Soviet Jewry*, 15 January 1971, AJCSJ archives.

123. A. J. Karlikow, AJCommittee memorandum, 15 April 1970, AJCSJ archives.

124. Dinstein is now the chancellor of Tel Aviv University.

125. Weinstein, "Soviet Jewry," 608–9.

126. The process in the AJCSJ for moving toward securing a programmatic budget began six months before in the spring of 1970 when it started to redefine its charter in order to become a 501(C) 3 agency under IRS regulations, which would have enabled it to become a direct recipient of tax-deductible contributions. Abraham Bayer, AJCSJ coordinator, had drafted a fund-raising letter as early as May 1970. The letter was to be sent to major federations. All of this was aimed at expanding the work of the AJCSJ.

127. William W. Orbach, *The American Movement to Aid Soviet Jews* (Amherst: University of Massachusetts Press, 1979), 25, 30, 40–41.

128. Nehemiah Levanon prevailed upon Edward Ginsburg, a major donor to federations in those years, to persuade the Cleveland federation to give $10,000 to the Cleveland group, which was the first of a series of grants.

129. Stanley Lowell memorandum, 9 June 1971, AJCSJ archives.

Israel's Role in the Campaign

The "good old days" for Jews under Soviet communism lasted only a short period in the early years after the revolution. Only then did the new regime tolerate, if not encourage, Yiddish culture and education. The very existence of the Jewish section of the Communist Party, Yevsektsiya, was short-lived. Similarly, experiments such as the Jewish settlements in the Crimea and the much-publicized project of the Jewish autonomous region in Birobidjan suffered the same fate. Jews as a nationality apparently did not fit into the Stalinist mold of a multinational Russian-dominated Soviet empire. Jews who saw themselves as a nationality were not to be trusted. All elements of Jewish national identity were expected to assimilate and disappear as quickly as possible. Jewish religious activities were confined to local synagogues. No nationwide Jewish organization or association was permitted. Even the slightest contact with Jews in the West was not allowed. Jews in the Soviet Union were effectively walled in. As far as Israel and world Jewry were concerned, Jews in the Soviet Union had become almost a lost tribe.

It was only during World War II that some hope for Soviet Jews was aroused. In its critical days, the Soviet Union felt compelled to create the Jewish Anti-Fascist Committee. A number of prominent Jewish writers, many of them well known in the West, were drawn into it. They were expected to mobilize public support for the Soviet war effort, particularly among the Jews in the United States. Those of us in Eretz Yisroel, the land of Israel, were excited, and even entertained the hope that ties with "the lost tribe" would be renewed. We raised funds for ambulances that were driven to Iran, and handed over to Soviet army units. However, when the war ended, the Iron Curtain was dropped. The era of the cold war settled in, and our hopes melted away.

In 1948, a new flicker of hope appeared. The Soviet Union voted for the establishment of a Jewish state in part of Palestine. In Moscow, a large crowd of Jews followed Golda Meir, Israel's first ambassador to the

Soviet Union, as she walked to the synagogue. Sadly, however, the last years of Stalin's reign became the black years for Jews in the Soviet Union. The last vestiges of Jewish cultural life were eliminated; many synagogues were closed; and those remaining were put under the watchful eye of the Committee for Cults and Religion. In 1952, Yiddish writers were secretly shot. A vicious, thinly disguised campaign of anti-Semitism was launched against so-called international, cosmopolitan, unpatriotic citizens who were allegedly not to be trusted. A number of Jewish physicians were arrested, accused of a plot to poison Soviet leaders. An atmosphere of pogroms was brewing. In that atmosphere in 1952, a small group of Israelis who had come from the Soviet Union on aliyah (emigration to Israel) in the late 1920s and early 1930s, met in a private home near Tel Aviv. The gathering was convened by Isser Harel, head of the Mossad, and Shaul Avigor, Israel's "gray eminence," who on the eve of the emergence of the State of Israel, led the spectacular effort to smuggle masses of Jewish survivors of World War II into British-held Palestine.

I was the only one among those present who had never lived under the Soviet regime. But I had a good Russian cultural background, even though I came from Estonia (before it had been occupied in 1939). Harel spoke about the ominous campaign against Jews in the Soviet Union and laid out the dilemma: Should or should not the Israeli Embassy in Moscow become involved in a clandestine effort to establish contacts with Jews in the Soviet Union? Most of the participants were skeptical about the possibility of achieving anything useful from an embassy isolated in Moscow and under close surveillance by the KGB. Some warned that such activities might only harm Soviet Jews, already subjected to a cruel and heartless regime. Though we were not outspokenly optimistic, some of us thought it was Israel's duty to give it a try.

At that time, I was farm manager in my kibbutz, Kfar Blum. A few weeks after this meeting, Harel came to inform me that a decision to undertake such an effort had been made at the highest level. Three Russian-speaking Israeli families were to join the embassy staff on a special mission. I was asked to lead the mission, and, as I learned, a small special department was formed, led by Harel and Avigor. This department came to be known in later years as the Liaison Bureau; the code name was "Nativ." (Only now have I been allowed to disclose the code name in print.) The Liaison Bureau was to work through the Israeli embassies behind the Iron Curtain in Moscow, Bucharest, Budapest, Prague, and Warsaw. Its task was to maintain contact with Jews in those countries; help them in every possible way; provide them with information; smuggle in Jewish cultural and religious material; explore the possibilities for aliyah; and, in some cases, help Jews escape across borders. Bear in mind what it meant for this small, struggling state to undertake this daring step in 1952, only four years after the Jewish state emerged from a bloody war.

I worked for two years in Moscow with my small team. We toured the country as much as possible. We learned a great deal about the fate of Jews, not only those in Moscow and the other great cities, but also those in remote parts of the Soviet empire. We managed to establish a number of lasting contacts with Jews in Moscow, Leningrad, Kiev, Odessa, and a few smaller places. In our first steps, we provided new information on Israel and world Jewry, including literature, prayer books, religious accessories, and Israeli souvenirs.

All this could be done only on a very limited scale. In the first year of our mission, we were elated after almost every meaningful encounter with a Soviet Jew. However, we were careful not to draw hasty conclusions. We could not be sure that what we heard represented the mood and feelings of a larger number of Jews. The very fact that a Jew dared to communicate with us made him exceptional, rather than typical. Only later, during our second year, did we feel that our experience was sufficient to try to put together our impressions and experiences.

During the first year following Stalin's death in March 1953, the atmosphere eased a little. Gradual changes initiated by the new leadership could be detected, but fear still prevailed among Jews. Many political prisoners were released from the camps and returned to their families and friends. Then suddenly, out of the blue, posters announcing concerts of Yiddish songs could be seen in the streets of Moscow. We never missed any of those concerts. We were well rewarded, if not by the artistic standards of those concerts, then by the wonderful new experience of sitting in the midst of an excited, almost jubilant crowd of Jews who filled the small halls. On one occasion, we attended a concert of a Latvian folk singer who also sang Yiddish songs. The hall was packed mainly by Jews. Upon hearing her sing a translation of a Negro spiritual, a shocked silence fell upon the hall: she had sung "Let My People Go." Thunderous applause erupted, and we were left speechless.

Though robbed by the regime of all elements of Jewishness, Jews in the Soviet Union were not a lost tribe after all. The emergence of Israel, the Jewish state, apparently had a great impact upon them. This was a central point I stressed in my reports to Avigor and Harel. Second, I urged that we widen and deepen our mission. My third and crucial point was that the time had come to launch a campaign in the West. And indeed, in the summer of 1955, a number of our Jewish contacts pointed out that the post-Stalinist leadership was striving to improve its image in the eyes of the West. Therefore, we felt that it was time to alert the West to the plight of the Jews in the Soviet Union, and to encourage pressure on Soviet leadership to change Soviet treatment of the Jewish minority.

In the fall of that year, I was expelled from the Soviet Union, along with several other members of my team. Avigor and Harel met with me in Europe on my way home, and we had a thorough discussion of the situation following our expulsion. As I expected, I was told that the mission in the Soviet Union would go on, and our replacements would be sent as soon as possible. Then, to my surprise, I was informed that a decision had been made to launch a campaign in the West, "the campaign you spoke about in your reports from Moscow. You will be in charge until we find the right man to replace you. Then you will be able to return to your home in Kfar Blum." So I was to form a department for this task within the Liaison Bureau in Tel Aviv, and to recruit capable and dedicated representatives who were to work out of the larger Israeli embassies in the West. In the United States, that person would work out of the consulate general in New York. I was to submit to Avigor and Harel my ideas and concepts regarding the content and principles of the campaign, as well as my plans for immediate action. I was more or less assured that in less than a year, my replacement, Dr. Binyamin Eliav, would be ready to take over.

From the very beginning of my return to Israel, and more so on my first visit to Europe, I was shocked and discouraged. Most Israelis and European Jews poured cold water on my appeals. Their reaction had a sobering effect upon me. Two years in the Soviet Union had opened my eyes and heart to Soviet Jews, but had left me unprepared for the response of Jews in the free world. The fate of Jews in the Soviet Union was not occupying their minds and troubling their hearts. At best, their immediate response was, "It's so sad, but what can one do?" Occasionally, some Israelis whom I approached responded warmly, but many others regarded our efforts as tilting at windmills. As a start, we managed to recruit only a small number of Israelis in the press and public life. Abe Harman, who was heading the information department of the Jewish Agency, was one of them.[1] He asked me to prepare a position paper for Israeli embassies in the West.

In the reports I sent home, I suggested that we would be better able to carry out our task only when we had our "own man" stationed in each important embassy. We hoped that our people would enjoy the assistance and cooperation of ambassadors and the embassy staff in reaching the Jewish communities in the West. I reported that it would require systematic, patient, and persistent work with Jewish organizations, their leaders, and the rank and file to awaken the Jewish community to the kind of effort this cause demanded. A lot of work had to be done, I felt, and so I reported. What encouraged me were my first encounters with non-Jewish politicians, journalists, and intellectuals in London and Paris. They listened attentively. My story and my request for help apparently made sense to them, and some of them agreed to help us right after my first visit. They responded with sympathy and understanding to our view that starting such a campaign would probably enrage the mighty Kremlin.

I realized that while my Russian experience and background knowledge would suffice for my first steps, our future work would require our small office in Tel Aviv to systematically produce timely and up-to-date information, position papers, statistical data, history, and other background materials. The Tel Aviv office would have to work in close cooperation with our team in Moscow to get the up-to-date information and data from Soviet newspapers and other relevant literature. Such material would be needed by even the best people we could recruit for positions in our embassies. At the beginning at least, we anticipated that they were likely to have had little personal experience and knowledge, and probably no relevant background. So the kind of support the Tel Aviv office had to provide would be essential to their work. Avigor was extremely helpful. First, he found several good people at Hebrew University in Jerusalem. Within a few years, a small institute would be working in Jerusalem, with knowledgeable and devoted historians building the academic base for our work. The institute was called Yeda ("knowledge" in Hebrew).

Upon my return from my first visit to Europe, I outlined to Avigor and Harel the content, targets, tactics, and style of our campaign. We discussed the outline thoroughly, and I felt again their strong backing. We were about to confront the mightiest propaganda apparatus of the time. We also faced a West actively involved in the so-called cold war with the Soviet Union. From the very beginning, it was clear to me that our campaign should in no way become another theme on the cold war agenda. We had to find the right way to present our case so that it could gain maximum sympathy and support in the widest circles of public opinion in the West. We had to build a case that would convince moderates and even some who sympathized with the Soviet Union. Only then would our efforts draw the attention of Moscow and—we hoped—gain respect among Western governments.

A visit to Britain by Bulganin and Khrushchev, the heads of the Soviet Union, presented us with our first opportunity. I was sent a month in advance to London to prepare for their visit. With the help of the embassy, I met with Labor and Conservative party leaders. My experience in working for a couple of years in England as a much younger man led me to what I felt was the right approach. The British were about to host Soviet leaders for the first time, and they would do so respectfully, even though they were not in love with the Soviet regime. So I decided to ask them to raise questions, rather than to criticize the Soviets: Why are Jews treated differently than other nationalities? Why aren't there Jewish schools? Why aren't there Jewish theaters? What happened to the Jewish culture of these millions of Jews in the Soviet Union? Why aren't Jews who want to emigrate to the Jewish state allowed to do so? An indication of the effectiveness of our effort was reflected in the experience of Bulganin and Khrushchev in Leeds, a big city in Yorkshire. There they met with the Yorkshire trade union leaders, who asked them a few embarrassing questions, upsetting the temperamental Khrushchev. He suddenly turned around, "Why doesn't anybody ask me about the Jewish question in the

Soviet Union?" Then I realized that our first performance was at least a partial success.

Binyamin Eliav seemed to me the right person to take over my job. An eloquent speaker and brilliant and highly cultured publicist, he spoke English, French, German, Russian and Spanish, in addition to Hebrew. Most important, we were in full agreement on the targets, tactics, and style of our campaign. This proved to be crucial in assuring the continuity of the campaign, as in those years we twice had to replace each other. The differences in our personalities and backgrounds served our work well. Eliav concentrated his efforts on the intellectuals in Europe, particularly such influential thinkers as Bertrand Russell in England, and Jean-Paul Sartre in France. My efforts were directed at mobilizing Jewish leaders and organizations, and seeking support among parliamentarians and politicians. Brick by brick, we laid the foundation for a worldwide network. We realized it was important not to operate solely from our embassies and consulates. The next steps were to produce in each community indigenous activists, and to organize conferences and symposia.

In London, we were successful in getting the highly regarded English-Jewish writer Emanuel Litvinoff to join our efforts in a professional capacity as director of a Jewish library on current affairs. It published *Jews in Eastern Europe*, a highly respected and trusted periodical that Litvinoff edited and drafted. The library helped our cause immensely. Its strength lay in its high quality and credibility; not once over the years did the Soviets catch a false statement or incorrect data in it. A similar Jewish library was set up in Paris, run by a local director with the assistance of an Israeli contributor. The materials issued in London were sent to Holland, Scandinavia, and America. Those published in Paris were sent to Belgium, Switzerland, and Italy.

In the United States, the Jewish Minority Research did a wonderful job. Moshe Decter, its director, wrote, edited, and published brochures and special authoritative publications, and organized conferences of prominent public figures, artists, intellectuals, and journalists. Like Litvinoff, he was careful in sticking to thoroughly verified material, facts, and figures. Decter was invulnerable to any attempt by the Soviets to discredit him and the Jewish Minority Research. In Latin America, materials from London and New York were translated and published by local Jewish activists who cooperated with our *shlichim* (emissaries). When Eliav was appointed consul general in New York, I was called back from my kibbutz to replace him in Tel Aviv. I found a well-functioning office with capable, energetic and devoted people working for us in London, Paris, and New York. (In New York, we had Uri Raanan, an Israeli student.)

During the second half of the 1950s, there were important developments in the Soviet Union. In 1957, the Liaison Bureau, Nativ, organized a large Israeli delegation to participate in the world youth festival the

Soviets were hosting in Moscow. The Israeli delegation assembled a choir and several soloists, and held a concert that was broadly publicized in the Soviet Union. Our team in the embassy in Moscow worked hard to spread the information among Jews about the expected arrival of the Israeli delegation, even details about the route it was to travel by train from the Rumanian border to Moscow. The Israelis on the train were surprised and elated during several en route stopovers. They were greeted by groups of Jews who gathered on the platforms. In Moscow, jubilant, admiring Jews from all over the Soviet Union crowded the halls where the Israelis performed. Hundreds of Jews, some from the most remote corners of the Soviet Union, managed to meet Israelis in person, exchange words with them, and pocket some Israeli souvenirs. The reports of the delegation upon its return sounded an urgent message: Get on with the job. It definitely inspired us and strengthened our determination. We intensified and widened our efforts in Europe and in America.

The Jewish communities and their organizations in the West gradually became more cooperative. However, we still did not enjoy the support or encouragement of the World Zionist Organization and the World Jewish Congress. Nahum Goldmann, the president of both, considered crude public pressure confrontational. According to him, it would anger the mighty Kremlin and boomerang. Goldmann hoped eventually to persuade the Soviets to renew, at least partly, Jewish cultural activities in the Soviet Union. To demand much more would only hurt the Jews, he thought. We had several discussions with Goldmann. Ever polite and understanding, always using intelligent and sharp arguments, Goldmann stubbornly stuck to his concept. When we mentioned our intention to seek the support of Western intellectuals, Goldmann surprised us. He was prepared to sponsor and preside over a conference of intellectuals in Paris, and cooperate with us with regard to the content and spirit of the conference. The ever-cautious but highly skilled politician chose to cooperate with us, "the hotheads," apparently to minimize the possible damage that could result from a conference that was "too aggressive."

We were pleased to cooperate because we realized how important it was for the first international conference on Soviet Jewry to be impressive and distinguished. In those days, Goldmann was the right person to get the right people to participate. The challenge to us was to see to it that Goldmann's overmoderate speech would be followed by speakers who would give what we believed was the right tone and direction. Both Goldmann and we did a good job. It was quite an impressive conference. Goldmann's speech was brilliant, but bland. It had very little fight. So, too, was Professor Martin Buber's speech. But the veteran ex-Communist Berger Barzilai, and a number of prominent personalities from England, France, Scandinavia, and other countries kept the conference on the right track.

Shaul Friedlander, Goldmann's young assistant, and Meir Rosenne,[2] our man in Paris in those days, did an excellent job organizing the event. Emanuel Litvinoff, who brought his English and Scandinavian friends to the conference, demonstrated then what an asset he was to our work. Our team was happy, and I think Goldmann was happy, too. He showed the Soviets that he was "the moderate and reasonable Jew." In the ensuing years, however, Goldmann's approach did not work. He never received an invitation to Moscow.

In 1965, Ambassador Harman and Consul General Eliav came to the conclusion that Nativ had to have its own man at the embassy in Washington. I was asked to take up the post of minister counselor in Israel's Embassy in Washington. In addition to serving as an expert on Soviet policy, my main task was to keep the State Department, Congress, and influential news media informed on the fate of the Jews in the Soviet Union, and to seek sympathetic and active support from them for our cause. I soon learned that the plight of Soviet Jewry had drawn little attention in Washington. American Jewish organizations had involved the two Jewish senators, Abraham Ribicoff and Jacob Javits, to a certain extent, but that was about all.

I realized I had to do a lot of basic groundwork among officials of the State Department, on the Hill, and with the top journalists of the American press. I also tried to enlighten some of the better-known Sovietologists, who appeared to know very little about Jews in the Soviet Union. To a certain extent, I ignored the protocol. I regularly met with senior officials of the Soviet section of the State Department, as well as with desk men and those in the back rooms. I kept them informed, and gradually won their support for our view that public and political pressure by the West could produce positive results in Moscow. I believed that the State Department and the White House could be pulled into our cause in the framework of their bilateral relations with Moscow. The Liaison Bureau in Tel Aviv urged me also to do something to persuade the Rumanians to rectify difficulties that had occurred in Jewish emigration from Rumania. Congressman Emanuel Celler, chairman of the House Judiciary Committee, spoke to the Rumanian ambassador to the United States. He proved to be very effective.

In the fall of 1965, American Jewish organizations took an important and impressive step in the right direction. It was not an easy one: the American Jewish Conference on Soviet Jewry, the umbrella body for Soviet Jewry advocacy, planned a mass demonstration in Washington. I was excited and convinced that such an event, if successful, would make a great contribution to our efforts. But Meir Rosenne, now our man in the New York consulate, called to inform me that some national Jewish leaders were seeking a reconsideration of holding such a mass demonstration, questioning its wisdom. He asked me to come to New York for a meeting on this issue of the American Jewish Conference on Soviet Jewry. I was very new at that time. I had just arrived in Washington, and only a few Jewish leaders knew me personally. I asked Ambassador Harman to join me. It was Rose Halperin of the World Zionist Organization who made the Goldmann-like argument against the demonstration. It would be counterproductive, and would anger Moscow too much. Harman, a brilliant speaker and highly respected by American Jewish leadership, was persuasive.

The mass demonstration, the so-called Eternal Light Vigil, took place in Lafayette Park, across the street from the White House. A crowd of about ten thousand Jews, who arrived by trains and buses from New York and other Jewish communities on the East Coast, and by planes from cities from all parts of the United States, filled the park. Senators Ribicoff and Javits were the key speakers. The success of the demonstration surpassed all expectations. I could feel the immediate impact in my subsequent meetings with officials in the State Department, with journalists, and with people on the Hill. The vigil in Washington encouraged those Jewish leaders who were working hard to persuade Jewish organizations to build an effective organizational framework to carry on a persistent and expanding campaign. I reported to the heads of the organizations on the impact the vigil had on the State Department and Congress, and urged them to maintain systematic and ongoing contacts in Washington. Meir kept the organizations informed of the latest developments in the Soviet Union and the West. Slowly but surely, the ball started rolling.

During the late 1960s, Rosenne and I were confronted with an increasingly unpleasant problem. Parallel with the growing activities of the large national Jewish organizations and the rest of the Jewish establishment, so-called grassroots groups sprouted up in a number of Jewish communities in the United States. Active, impatient, and temperamental, the various grassroots groups criticized the establishment as inactive and ineffective. They urged us, as Israel's representatives, not to rely on the Jewish establishment, but rather to cooperate with and help their grassroots supporters. Initially, we thought that both elements were important. Only the establishment could draw masses of Jews into the campaign. Only the establishment was considered as representative of the American Jewish community by the administration and Congress. On the other hand, we hoped that these grassroots groups would push the establishment to make greater efforts to expand its activities. On occasion, those "grassroot radicals" acted as a whip to awaken some sleeping elements in the establishment.

As an indication of our relations with the Union of Councils, the umbrella of these grassroots groups, I prevailed upon Edward Ginsburg, a major contributor to the United Jewish Appeal, to help me persuade the Cleveland federation to give $10,000 in the 1960s to one of the original local groups that organized the Union of Councils. I flew to Cleveland; I saw their people; I liked the way they worked, and told Sidney Vincent, one of the heads of the federation, "They are doing a good job." Jacob Birnbaum brought me up from Washington to help him raise money for the Student Struggle for Soviet Jewry.

We tried to maintain a balanced approach toward these grassroots groups, but it soon proved futile. They charged that we were siding with the establishment, and they became more and more critical, sometimes almost hostile. As the years passed, these groups, while at times positive, were sometimes damaging to the cause. When we were pushed by them to make a decision about a rumor, we had no choice but to check it out first, which would anger them. Impatient and eager to be first, they often publicized unverified and inaccurate information. That sometimes led some of our people to denounce what they saw as irresponsible actions. On several occasions, the grassroots groups projected as heroes those whom we regarded as shady characters among the activists in the Soviet Union.

An example: In 1969, I received a cable from Tel Aviv that an activist in Riga had immolated himself by fire to protest Soviet emigration policies. I cabled back immediately, and said that I would not tell the Jewish organizations to publish this because of my serious doubts about its veracity. From reliable sources in Washington I had learned that the young man was in fact protesting against the Soviet invasion of Czechoslovakia. "Where did you get your stuff?" I asked. It turned out that three *olim* (émigrés to Israel) from Riga insisted that this was the story. I had to fly to Tel Aviv and argue with key staff at the Liaison Bureau. When I spoke to one of the *olim*, he said, "Look, what the hell difference does it make if we can use it to dramatize the issue?" I felt strongly that to publish a rumor as fact before it was checked out would be a terrible mistake. It would seriously undermine the credibility of the campaign. We realized from the very outset of the campaign that we could expose Soviet behavior and propaganda only by scrupulously adhering to the truth, and not by using their methods.

Toward the end of the 1960s, most of the Jewish communities in the free world had gradually become actively involved in the campaign, both nationally and locally. The Jewish establishment everywhere formed bodies to run the campaign. Our bureau in Tel Aviv fed them information, data, figures, and supplied brochures and publications in several languages. Shortly after returning to Israel in 1969, I was appointed by Prime Minister Golda Meir to head the Liaison Bureau. Zvi Nezer was running the department of the bureau that dealt with the campaign in the West, but I personally kept our contacts with the campaign in the United States.

In 1971, the American Jewish Conference on Soviet Jewry not only changed its name, but became an agency with its own substantially increased budget and staff that enabled it to function more effectively. A very important development in my eyes was the spectacular performance of the Greater New York Conference on Soviet Jewry, which, under Malcolm Hoenlein, its first director, became increasingly active. As years passed, the annual mass demonstration on Solidarity Day became tremendously valuable for the campaign in the United States. Strengthened and inspired by the campaign in the West, the open struggle for aliyah by Jews in the Soviet Union, starting in 1968, was reflected in a subtle renewal of emigration by Soviet authorities.

How did we manage to keep our cause in the limelight over so many years, including the focus on cases that sometimes stretched out over years? The answer is that we had the support of Jews all over the place. We had good *shlichim* (emissaries), but most important was the action that took place in the Soviet Union on the part of the activists. They made it possible to keep the campaign going year after year, gaining more and more strength. Two developments jolted not only us, but the entire worldwide movement: a letter of appeal from eighteen Jewish families from Georgia to Golda Meir that she read over Israeli radio, and the drama of the Leningrad trials and other trials that followed. These developments had tremendous impact. A worldwide conference became imperative because that same year, 1970, the Russians once again suddenly stopped virtually all emigration.

The idea for such a conference was not new. While I was still in Washington in 1969, I felt the time had come to call a world conference of Jewish organizations of every shade of political opinion and social calling, religious and secular—a conference of Jews that would actively support the cause of redemption of Soviet Jewry. The response of a few Jewish organizations in the United States was positive, but the international Jewish organizations—the World Zionist Organization, the World Jewish Congress, and B'nai B'rith International—opposed the idea. They suspected that the conference might bring about the creation of a new permanent organization. I also suspect that it was Nahum Goldmann who persuaded Prime Minister Levi Eshkol not to rush ahead with such a problematic initiative. Upon my return to Israel, when the conditions had underscored the need for such a conference, Golda Meir not only supported the idea, but used every opportunity to persuade Jewish leaders. The sudden drop in the number of exit permits that the Soviets issued, and the arrests and trials that were supposed to follow them, made us set the beginning of 1971 as the date for holding the world conference in Brussels.

We worked very hard on preparations for the conference. In Tel Aviv and in most of the Jewish communities in the world, we were in a hurry. Zvi Nezer ran the technical preparations out of Tel Aviv. I was in touch with Jewish leaders in every community in the West to try to set the program and the agenda of the historic Brussels gathering. Jews from all walks of life, from all shades of political coloring, gathered at the conference. It was a wonderful demonstration of Jewish solidarity and unity. The conference took an important step: it elected a presidium that would continue to function after the adjournment of the Brussels conference.

I'm not ashamed to say we managed to maneuver the international Jewish organizations into going along with what became a new coordinating body to deal with the campaign on a worldwide basis. Global coordination wasn't simple because each country has its own distinctive conditions. We felt it was important that this body meet twice a year. American Jews were well represented; they had the skills and know-how. They were represented by the National Conference on Soviet Jewry, the National Jewish Community Relations Advisory Council (NJCRAC) and the Conference of Presidents of Major American Jewish Organizations. Other Jewish communities were represented by their counterpart organizations. For years we worked together. We met, assessed what was happening in the Soviet Union and the West, and set annual programmatic goals for worldwide activities.

After substantially increasing the number of exit permits, the Soviets issued in 1972 their infamous decree that demanded every emigrant to repay the expenses for his or her education, amounts of money that very few could afford. We recommended to Prime Minister Meir that she reject this infamous tax, and refuse to raise money to help Jews pay the tax. We urged all Jewish communities to launch major campaigns of protest. The movement in the West, as well as the activists in the Soviet Union, was unanimous in supporting this decision. The outrage expressed in the United States, and the stormy protest all over the world, resulted in the Jackson-Vanik amendment. Special tribute must be made to the late Senator Henry Jackson and his dedicated assistants, Richard Pearl and Dorothy Fosdick, for their determination and devotion to the cause of Soviet Jewry.

For me personally, one of the saddest periods in the struggle for Soviet Jews was the conflict over *noshrim*, the Soviet Jews who left the Soviet Union with Israeli visas, and then "dropped out" in Vienna to go to some other destination, usually the United States. The differences over this issue sharply divided American Jews, and Israelis as well. Feelings were especially bitter among the *olim*, Russian Jews who came to Israel. I remember an *oleh* writing in a newspaper that a scientist who had been active in the Jewish movement in the Soviet Union was "an anti-Zionist." Why? Because he thought that those who "drop out" should be allowed to do so without interference. The scientist responded to the writer by calling him "a fascist." In separate meetings with each of them, I said, "Look, you are now in the free world. It's not the Soviet Union anymore. If somebody has a different opinion than you, even on such an emotional issue as *neshira*, he doesn't become your enemy. Sasha hasn't changed because of what he wrote in the newspaper; you haven't changed." But it was a bitter and very sad period.

I understood to a certain extent the emotions that moved many American Jews to call for freedom of choice. While I did not vocally agree, I recognized why so many American Jews, as children and grandchildren of immigrants, particularly from Russia, could not accept our arguments. We were convinced that making it easy not to go to Israel, while leaving the Soviet Union on an Israeli visa, legitimized that step. Here we had Jews living in a country that saw the United States as the ultimate paradise, regardless of what Soviet propaganda said about America. They also were bombarded by press and television that ceaselessly painted Israel as a poor, terrible country whose very existence was endangered. An ignorant man who believes his choice is between going to a paradise or to a country where his son will be shot in the Israeli army does not really have a free choice. We could not reach the Jewish masses. With all our efforts, including those of American Jews, we reached very few Jews out of the millions of Soviet Jews. The mass of Jews were very different from the refuseniks and activists with whom Jews from the West met.

What troubled me was that some very militant fighters for the freedom of Soviet Jews spoke about physical danger of Jews in the Soviet Union. I knew there was no physical danger. But I knew that there was a danger to Jewish identity in the Soviet Union. The danger was survival of Jews as Jews. While there have been problems with absorption in Israel, every Jew who came to Israel from the Soviet Union remained a Jew. His children remained Jews. We have not been so sure that this would happen with every Jew who came to the United States, Canada, or Australia. In dealing with the issue of the *noshrim*, I realize that none of us was a hundred percent right; it was a very difficult issue.

Nevertheless, despite these differences, we all can take enormous pride in the success of this great campaign that lasted so many years. It was the result of a concerted effort of a wonderful triangle: Jewish activists in the Soviet Union, Israel, and the Jews of the Diaspora. What it has meant to us in Israel is 721,472 Jews from the Soviet Union coming to our country, a half-million in recent years. It is unbelievable that a small country like Israel could absorb such numbers in just a few years. It will gradually change Israel, one hopes, in the right way. Already it has changed the economy of the country: 500,000 consumers in just the last couple of years; tens of thousands of doctors, engineers, scientists, excellent mathematicians, good musicians and good teachers, especially high school teachers in mathematics, physics, and chemistry. And their education didn't cost us a penny. More that 60,000 are coming annually from what was once the Soviet Union. By the end of the century, we hope to have among our citizens close to a million Jews from the former Soviet Union.

All of this we did together. To realize the dimensions of this achievement, remember where we were in 1952, when we created Nativ; the 1960s, when we launched the campaign in the West; and the many years of the struggle that followed with many bitter disappointments. As Soviet Jews persisted, even in the face of many discouraging setbacks, so, too, did Israelis, American Jews, and tens of thousands of Jews all over the world. The result has been this historic exodus.

Notes

1. Avraham Harman later joined the Israeli Foreign Ministry, and in the 1960s, during the Kennedy and Johnson administrations, would serve as Israel's ambassador to the United States.
2. Meir Rosenne would serve in the 1980s as Israel's ambassador to France and the United States.

Soviet Jews
Creating a Cause and a Movement

The movement for emigration of Soviet Jewry has been remarkably successful, perhaps second only to Zionism, as a twentieth-century Jewish political movement. From 1968 through 1994, 1,215,558 Jews left the USSR and its successor states. More than 750,000 (62 percent) have gone to Israel, thus constituting the largest aliyah (emigration) from any single country. There is a special irony in this: the USSR, which allowed no Zionist organizations or activity, no *shlichim* (Israeli representatives to Jewish communities abroad), no fund-raising for Israel, no tourism to Israel and very little from it, and which did not have diplomatic relations with Israel from 1967 until the late 1980s, has "exported" more Jews to Israel than any other country. Moreover, those who did attempt to agitate for emigration or to emigrate themselves were often harassed, imprisoned, and denied the right to emigrate, a right that had been subscribed to by the Soviet Union in at least three international agreements.

How can we explain this extraordinary achievement in the light of these unfavorable circumstances? First, we must acknowledge that nearly 30 percent of the emigrants (312,888) left between 1992 and 1994, after the Soviet Union had collapsed, and that an astonishing 72.5 percent (776,867) of the total left between 1989, when radical changes had occurred in the system, and 1994. Thus, it was the collapse of the Soviet system that both spurred Jewish emigration and made it easy to leave the country. The second factor, without which the great exodus during the collapse of the USSR would have been far less likely, is, of course, the aliyah movement within the Soviet Union and the direct and indirect aid rendered to it from a parallel movement outside it, mainly in North America, Western Europe, Australia, and Israel.

The main question to be addressed is how and why such a movement arose in a country that actively discouraged and repressed all spontaneous political and even cultural or social activity. After all, when a group of eager *Komsomoltsy* (Communist youth activists) in Tashkent, capital of Uzbekistan, tried to do in 1965 what they saw as their civic duty by cleaning up municipal parks and trying to maintain order within them, they were arrested on suspicion of "working for a foreign organization." Why else would a group band together without having been ordered to do so by the authorities?

The emergence of the Soviet Jewish movement, in the main a movement for free emigration to Israel, can be explained as the outcome of a process that combined the courage of a very small number of Soviet Jews; the desperation of a larger number; the willingness to take a gamble of an even larger number; changes in the mentality of Diaspora Jewry; the existence of a Jewish state; and a subtle, but profound, change in the nature of the international system and its influence on domestic politics, including Soviet politics.

The initiators of the Jewish movement came from various parts of the USSR. Eighteen Georgian Jewish families may have been the first to call publicly for free emigration when they wrote a letter to the United Nations Human Rights Commission on 6 August 1969, demanding that they be allowed to emigrate to Israel.[1] Around the same time, individual Jews in Latvia, Lithuania, Russia, and the Ukraine were petitioning Soviet leaders to be allowed to leave.[2]

Remarkably, there is no evidence that they knew each other, let alone coordinated their activities. However, despite the efforts of the Communist regime, Zionism had never been completely stamped out in the USSR. It had been the strongest single political tendency among Jews in 1917–18, but was vigorously attacked in the two decades following, its activists often being arrested and exiled.[3] Nevertheless, some Zionist activity was carried on, especially after World War II when many Jews became disillusioned with their prospects not only in the USSR, but anywhere they would be a minority. Encouraged by Israeli diplomats and others, these Zionists formed small groups, sometimes penetrated by the police, to learn more about Zionism and Israel. Some even tried to leave the Soviet Union, legally and illegally, and get to Israel.[4]

As Benjamin Pinkus points out, between 1964 and 1967, Jewish cultural activity, much of it with a Zionist tinge, increased considerably.[5] A Jewish *samizdat* (underground publications) developed, and the materials were transported from one city to another. Jewish amateur dramatic groups formed and served as foci of Jewish activity and as symbolic statements of adherence to Jewish culture. Younger Jews began to visit synagogues on certain holidays, not necessarily to pray, but to meet each other and to sing and dance, with Jewish and Israeli music. The synagogue was the only permitted Jewish institution in the USSR and became the natural meeting place for nationally minded Jews. Finally, in a few places, Jews began to gather at the sites of mass murders by the

Nazis, almost none of which were designated by the authorities as places of Jewish martyrdom, and some of which were totally neglected.

In the late 1960s, following the Six-Day War in the Middle East, agitation for Jewish rights, including the right to leave the country, spread among small numbers of Jews. As with all social movements, there were concentric circles of activism. It is difficult to say how many people were in the leadership core of the movement. Pinkus has calculated that 5,454 people signed petitions for emigration between 1969 and 1978, most of them between 1968 and 1973. He classifies nearly 300 people as "leaders" in the 1969–83 period, including 87 who were put on trial.[6] The petition signers may be considered the second circle around the core, people who were publicly active in the Zionist movement. In this group one might include also those who demonstrated at Soviet offices, wrote open letters, or even met in groups that they assumed were penetrated by the KGB, thus demonstrating their willingness to have the authorities know of their association with the cause. Obviously, the line between activists and leaders is not a clear one. Backing up both groups, and sometimes moving into the ranks of the public activists, were the third circle, people who risked their positions, social and political standing, and economic security by applying to leave even when their prospects were very poor (late 1960s, 1980–89). They were strongly motivated to leave and courageous enough to take high risks in order to do so.

A fourth circle consisted of the people who rode the waves of emigration, those who took advantage of what seemed to be a liberalization of policy, and left in "good" years, such as 1978 and 1979. Some of those were people who had applied when their chances were slim and were being "cleaned out," but others had applied only when they thought their chances were better. Finally, there was the panic migration of 1989–92 when more than three-quarters of a million people, including a growing proportion of non-Jews attached to Jewish family members, fled what they saw as a collapsing economy, state, and social order. They feared that this collapse would result in scapegoating Jews and that, in any case, their economic and educational futures were seriously endangered.

Since about 1992, the migration is being driven less by panic than by cooler assessments of prospects in the post-Soviet republics, and by the existence of critical masses of previous immigrants in Israel and the United States who serve as magnets for their relatives and friends still in the former Soviet Union. Three long-term factors explain the emergence of Jewish consciousness in a public and demonstrative way in the USSR. The first was the psychological dissonance of being forced to become Russian culturally (because Jewish culture was not available), while being forced to remain Jewish legally and socially. This dual enforcement was accomplished politically through the nearly immutable identification on the internal passport, and socially because most others regarded Jews as such, no matter how an individual Jew might have thought of himself.

Thus, Jews were deprived both of their own culture and of the ability to become someone else, even though they might have adopted whole-heartedly someone else's culture—in most cases, Russian. Unlike in the United States, where one could be simultaneously American—a political and cultural concept, rather than an ethnic one—and Jewish, in the So-viet Union, one could not be simultaneously Russian and Jewish as both of these were defined by the state as ethnic categories and hence were mu-tually exclusive. That is, while everyone in the USSR was "Soviet" by cit-izenship, they were also classified additionally in one of the more than a hundred ethnic groups, called "nationalities" in Soviet parlance. Jews were thus Soviet and Jewish, but never Russian (or Ukrainian, Lithua-nian, Georgian, Uzbek, and so forth) and Jewish.

The second long-term force shaping the consciousness of Jews in the Soviet Union was the influence of the million or so *Zapadniki* (people from the West) who entered the USSR in 1939–40. They became Soviet citizens as a result of the annexation of the Baltic states, eastern Poland, and Bessarabia and Bukovina (from Romania). Because they had lived in-tensely Jewish lives, for the most part, and were involved in the full range of Jewish religious, political, and cultural life, their mere presence in the USSR reconnected Soviet Jews to the Jewish world and its culture. It is not by chance that many of the first teachers and activists of the reemer-gent national movement in the 1960s were *Zapadniki* or were inspired by their teachings.

The last long-term influence on Soviet Jews was, of course, anti-Semitism on both the state and societal levels. Anti-Semitism on the grassroots level and, following 1948, clearly and militantly anti-Semitic government policies, shattered illusions about "friendship of the peo-ples" and "internationalism" that many Jews had entertained in the two decades following the revolution. The Soviet state and society were send-ing a clear message to Jews that they were regarded as second-class citi-zens at best, and that, in the words of the nineteenth-century Russian Jewish Zionist Leon Pinsker, Jews were "everywhere in evidence, but no-where at home," at least not in the USSR.

In the shorter range, what made the first activists turn to a Zionist agenda was, again, three factors. The one with the widest impact was the 1967 Arab-Israeli war, which demonstrated that the USSR, "their" coun-try, was fully prepared to collaborate in the annihilation of the Jewish state and its inhabitants, and this only twenty-two years after the Shoah. Even a highly acculturated and patriotic Soviet Jew, the writer Ilya Ehren-burg, commented in a private conversation, "If, following in Hitler's footsteps, the Arabs had started massacring all the Jews in Israel, the in-fection would have spread. We would have had here a wave of anti-Semitism. Now, for once, the Jews have shown that they can also kick you hard in the teeth."[7] Physicist and prominent refusenik Mark Azbel noted, "The . . . war was the most exciting experience of a lifetime to thousands and thousands of Soviet Jews. None of us thought of anything but the war during that agonizing week. . . . Overnight, we recognized how close was the fate of Israel to our hearts."[8]

Second, even Jews who were not especially concerned with Israel but were involved in cultural life were impelled by the 1966 trial of writers Andrei Sinyavsky and Yuli Daniel to wonder about the prospects for reform in the USSR. The trial signaled that there would be no relaxation of state control of ideas and expression. A very high proportion of Jews were members of the creative intelligentsia, and some began to despair of their prospects. Moreover, the invasion of Czechoslovakia in 1968, designed to reverse Czech political and economic reforms—ironically, many of them the same as those adopted by Mikhail Gorbachev twenty years later—and prevent the ideas from spilling over to the Soviet Union, reinforced the idea that Brezhnev's USSR would not permit meaningful political and economic reform. These two events drove some Jewish reformers, who previously had hoped that the system would be relaxed and reformed, to give up on the USSR and instead of attempting to change it, to adopt a more modest agenda of leaving it.

Finally, the Leningrad hijacking trial of 1970, widely covered in both the Soviet and international media, demonstrated that there were some highly committed aliyah activists, and that the world was paying attention to them and could provide them with some measure of protection. Three related trials of Soviet Jews in 1971 in Russia, Latvia, and Moldavia kept the issues of Soviet Jewry and the desire for migration in the headlines. One Soviet Jew noted that it was the trial, rather than the 1967 war, that impelled her to seek to leave. "Look here, we said at home, here are Jews who don't simply talk about Israel, don't just dream, but they do something, and are not afraid of the danger and the punishment."[9]

The aliyah movement overlapped to some extent with the democratic or dissident movement, especially in its early days. People such as Mikhail Zand, Vadim Meniker, Vitaly Svechinsky, and Yuli Telesin were active in both. Zionists learned tactics from democrats and there was a considerable amount of mutual support. Boris Tsukerman, a Zionist activist, had taught himself the details of Soviet law and provided legal advice to physicist Andrey Sakharov, perhaps the most prominent democrat. In turn, Sakharov supported the right of Jews to emigrate to Israel. Anatoly Sharansky later served as a link between both democrats and Zionists and representatives of the Western media, which may explain why the Soviets meted out particularly harsh punishment to him.

There were tensions between the "pure" Zionists, who argued that involvement in trying to reform the Soviet system would divert energies from the Zionist struggle and would subvert the claim of simply wanting to leave the USSR, and others who felt a moral obligation to assist the democrats. Israeli authorities strongly opposed any involvement with the democrats and urged that only one goal, aliyah, be pursued. There were also differences about tactics. Some maintained that the aliyah movement should act strictly within the letter of Soviet law, while others said this was unrealistic. Some sought highly publicized confrontations with the authorities, while others felt it was best to avoid them. A few activists publicly renounced their Soviet citizenship and declared that they were citizens of Israel, while others maintained that they had nothing against the USSR. A few even said that if they would be allowed to emigrate, they would join the Communist Party of Israel.

Despite these differences, there seems to have been a consistent consensus on one point. The movement began as one for aliyah, and although in the 1980s the overwhelming majority of emigrants did not go to Israel, it always remained an Israel-oriented movement. Those who went to the United States did not set up a separate or even allied movement, nor did they make emigration to the United States or elsewhere a public goal. Rather, the decision where to immigrate was treated as a private one, with the public agenda being to establish the right to leave the country.

Strikingly, this was a movement that never had an organization. The aliyah movement had no formal structure; no appointed or elected leadership; no headquarters, address, or phone number. And yet it succeeded. Why did the movement never become an organization? First, an organization was inherently difficult to create under Soviet conditions, and would have been more vulnerable than a movement to discovery and repression. Had an organization been set up, the authorities would have no doubt succeeded in arresting its leadership, leaving the mass following without direction and inspiration. Instead, the fluid nature of informal leadership meant that the repression of any leader would not have widespread effects as there was nothing to prevent another person from assuming a leadership role, no formalities to be gone through before this would be done.

It is likely that the Soviets' initial decision in 1971 to allow a few thousand to emigrate was based on the assumption that if the leadership of the movement were allowed to leave, the movement would die a natural death. The Soviet authorities clearly did not understand either the nature of the movement or of chain migration, the latter ensuring that once a group was allowed to leave, they would inevitably attract others to do the same. Another reason for the lack of organization was that Soviet Jews had had no communal structure since shortly after the 1917 Revolution, and not even state-sponsored organizations and institutions since the dissolution of the Jewish Anti-Fascist Committee in 1948. Soviet Jewry was a community of memory and of fate, but it had no formal means of communicating (newspapers, magazines, books, radio, and television programs).

But Jews had shared experiences and could exchange "glances of recognition." Shared memories and fates cut across class, educational, geographic, and cultural lines, and created invisible, informal communities. By the 1960s, within these nonorganized communities, a much more visible, but still informal, subcommunity of aliyah activists and then refuseniks had emerged, and it became the focus of both Soviet and foreign attention. The informality of the movement may have had its costs, but it had advantages. The authorities thought that by incarcerating, exiling, or expelling its leaders, they could kill it off. But because leadership was largely moral and certainly informal, as soon as one group or generation was removed from the scene, another arose to take its place.

Another advantage of the movement was that it was spread all over the Soviet Union. Other national movements (for example, the Ukrainian and Baltic) were limited to one republic, and thus could be more easily isolated and attacked. Moreover, many leaders of the Jewish movement were located in those cities—Moscow and Leningrad, primarily—which had the largest concentrations of foreigners, and especially the foreign media. That may be a large part of the reason that the Muscovites and Leningraders became the spokesmen, and hence the recognized "leaders," of the movement. Jews took advantage of occasional regional variations and policy, and moved to places from which emigration appeared to be easier, or conducted their emigration-oriented activities in those places until they had to move them elsewhere. For example, in the early 1970s, it seemed that republic and local authorities in Latvia and Lithuania were more lenient about granting exit visas than their counterparts in the Ukraine and Russia. Therefore, some determined activists moved to the Baltic republics to improve their prospects for emigration.

It should be stressed that there were important differences between the Jewish activism and other movements. First, the former did not demand changes in the Soviet system or in the shape of the USSR. The democratic movement demanded the former, and other nationality movements (Ukrainian and Baltic) demanded a fundamental reordering of federal arrangements and the state structure, even to the point of seceding from the USSR. Jews simply demanded to leave it—and leave it alone. This was less threatening to the authorities. Second, an implicit collusion among Jews, Israel, and the Soviet authorities allowed the movement to define itself as one for the reunification of families, a simple humanitarian aim, or for repatriation to the national homeland, a stickier demand that, certainly from the Soviet official and even unofficial view, implied clearly that the Jews were disloyal to the USSR. Both these rationales, however, applied to very few groups in the USSR: Greeks and Spaniards, who were few in number, and Germans, who were more numerous than the Jews. Only the "reunification of families" argument, and not the one about "repatriation to the homeland," applied to Armenians, the third major "privileged" group (in addition to Jews and Germans) allowed to emigrate. But these rationales applied to almost no other groups. Thus, the danger of spillover of Jewish demands could be contained.

Why did mass emigration of Soviet Jews, not seriously envisioned until the late 1960s, become an issue on the international agenda? After all, this issue is what enabled foreign pressures to be exerted successfully on the USSR. James Rosenau has pointed out that today, there are more actors in world politics than ever before, many of them not states but nongovernmental organizations (NGOs), multinational corporations, international organizations, ethnic and religious groups, and so on.[10] They have been legitimized and have proved effective at times. What used to be dismissed as "interference in the internal affairs" of a country has come to be seen as proper concern for violations of human rights. American president Jimmy Carter did a great deal to put human rights on the international agenda, and the 1975 Helsinki agreements provided the internationally agreed-upon principles enabling foreign individuals and organizations to become involved in what had previously been considered the domestic affairs of another state.

Moreover, education and mass media have involved ordinary people more in world affairs, none more so than Western Jews who have unusually high levels of education, and are generally affluent and urban. These demographic characteristics are generally associated with greater involvement in world affairs. In addition, Jews historically have paid more attention to world affairs than many other peoples, if only because they have had coethnics and coreligionists in so many parts of the globe. In addition, modern technology facilitated the penetration of the Iron Curtain. Over many years, tourists brought in literature, cassettes, textbooks, and other materials that lessened the intellectual, spiritual, and social isolation of activist Jews who had been removed from their professional posts and had been made into political and social pariahs because of their agitation for emigration. Telephone calls from abroad boosted the morale of refuseniks and may well have provided some measure of protection from official persecution. Soviet Jews could be made aware of events outside the USSR, and their supporters could be kept up-to-date on what was happening inside it.

There is little doubt that Soviet Jews benefited from the feeling by many Jews in the West that they had not done enough to save more European Jews in the 1930s. Decades later, they had become more affluent, better educated, and less hesitant to assert their positions. They took advantage of their greater financial and political power in the 1970s and 1980s to ensure that massive persecution of Jews would not be repeated. The African-American civil rights movement, the consensual nature of the Soviet Jewry issue, the origins of so many Western and Israeli Jews in the old Russian Empire, and traditions of cross-boundary solidarity—all played a role in mobilizing world Jewry on behalf of Soviet Jews and their emigration.

Similarly, Western governments responded to calls for action because some felt guilt for the Shoah and their immigration policies of the time, which had effectively condemned hundreds of thousands to death. At the same time, the existence of Israel relieved them of the burden of having to take in would-be immigrants. This situation permitted them the luxury of demanding free emigration from the USSR without committing themselves to free immigration to their own shores. Finally, in the United States, the Soviet Jewry campaign could be endorsed by conservatives, who welcomed the chance to tilt against the "evil empire," and by liberals, who saw it as a human rights issue. Just about all American Jewish organizations advocated on the issue, so elected officials felt they could only gain by supporting it.

By 1989, just when the largest emigration period by far began, the movement had become unnecessary. The Soviet Union had opened its gates, and most of those who wished to leave could do so. This freedom remains true of all the successor states of the USSR. Moreover, after 1989, Jewish emigrants were being moved not so much by ideology or a desire to better themselves economically or vocationally, but by sheer panic at what they saw as the disintegration of the Soviet economic and political systems, and of the very society itself. After 1991, when the system did, indeed, collapse, emigration became further routinized. The current emigration is propelled largely by the traditional forces spurring migration: the search for better economic and educational opportunities, and the wish to join relatives and friends who have already emigrated. The movement had achieved its aim and by so doing, no longer needed to exist. As it had never become institutionalized, there were no organizational interests to defend even after the organizations had outlived their purpose. (Would that could be said of other organizations.) The one million émigrés are living testimony to one of the great accomplishments of Soviet and world Jewry, including the State of Israel, in this century.

Notes

1. The text of the letter in Russian, with a Hebrew translation, is reproduced in "Anu hai mishpekhot yehudiyot migruziyah," pamphlet published by the Prime Minister's Office (Israel), Jerusalem, December 1969.

2. Their petitions are conveniently reprinted in Moshe Decter, ed., "Redemption: Jewish Freedom Letters from Russia" (New York: American Jewish Conference on Soviet Jewry, May 1970). The letter of the eighteen Georgian Jews is translated on pages 32–35.

3. See Zvi Gitelman, *Jewish Nationality and Soviet Politics: The Jewish Sections of the CPSU, 1917–1930* (Princeton: Princeton University Press, 1972), chap. 5; L. Tsentsiper, *Eser shnot redifot* (Tel Aviv, 1930); Don Pines, *Hehalutz*

bekur hamahpecha (Tel Aviv: Davar, 1938); Katsir, *Kovetz lekorot hatnuah hat-sionit berusiya*, 2 vols. (Tel Aviv: Masada, 1964, 1972); Benjamin West, *Struggles of a Generation* (Tel Aviv: Massadah, 1959); Guido Goldmann, *Zionism Under Soviet Rule* (New York: Herzl, 1960).

4. See Yaacov Ro'i, *The Struggle for Soviet Jewish Emigration, 1948–1967* (Cambridge: Cambridge University Press, 1991); and Binyamin Pinkus, *Tehiya u'tekuma leumit* (Beersheva: Ben Gurion University Press, 1993). Pinkus's book covers the period from 1947 to 1987.

5. Benjamin Pinkus, *The Jews of the Soviet Union: The History of a National Minority* (Cambridge: Cambridge University Press, 1988), 312–14.

6. Ibid., 316.

7. Alexander Werth, *Russia: Hopes and Fears* (New York: Simon and Schuster, 1969), 218–19, quoted in William Korey, *The Soviet Cage: Anti-Semitism in Russia* (New York: Viking, 1973), 125.

8. Mark Azbel, *Refusenik* (Boston: Houghton Mifflin, 1981), 214–15.

9. Interview with Dov Goldstein, *Maariv*, 18 March 1977.

10. James N. Rosenau, *Turbulence in World Politics: A Theory of Change and Continuity* (Princeton: Princeton University Press, 1990).

II

Impact of Strategic Pressures

Jackson-Vanik
A *"Policy of Principle"*

A major study of worldwide emigration policies, sponsored by the prestigious Twentieth Century Fund and published in 1987 by Yale University Press, lauded the Jackson-Vanik amendment as "the single most effective step" taken by the United States to cope with "the new serfdom" of restrictions upon emigration. It was a rare compliment. Foreign policy establishment figures in the United States held the amendment in contempt, and former secretary of state Henry A. Kissinger, in his volume *Diplomacy*, harshly denounced it.

But the study's comment accorded with the perspective of Jews from the former Soviet Union for whom the amendment constituted a potent—if potential—liberating lever. A similar attitude was held by American Jews for whom the amendment served as a powerful weapon in their historic struggle on behalf of their brethren held in virtual bondage with respect to emigration. Far more significant than the view of Jews was the perception of the modern world's greatest humanist, Nobel Laureate Andrey D. Sakharov. He had extended the amendment a unique and unprecedented endorsement as a "policy of principle" that could have extraordinary ramifications.

Yet the enactment of the Jackson-Vanik Amendment was by no means quick and easy. It required a two-year legislative struggle involving intense battles with a determined Nixon administration, bolstered by powerful corporate interests. At the center of the struggle stood Henry M. Jackson, a senior U.S. senator who espoused a vigorous civil liberties perspective joined to a pronounced anti-Soviet posture. When Senator Jackson formally introduced his amendment on the Senate floor on 15 March 1973, he specifically referred to Article 13/2 of the Universal Declaration of Human Rights, which holds that "everyone has the right to leave any country, including his own, and to return to his country," as the principal source of inspiration for the proposed legislation. The crucial importance ascribed to this right was evident from the three-year study by the United Nations Subcommission on Prevention of Discrimination and Protection of Minorities. It found that the right is "a constituent element of personal liberty" and a precondition for the exercise of other human rights. Indeed, the principle this right upholds has been the cornerstone of international law since the Magna Carta.

The relevance of the Declaration of Human Rights to the Jackson-Vanik amendment was critical. Sakharov was to underscore it in an "open letter" to the U.S. Congress. In it, he spoke of the appropriateness of the declaration for legislative action in that it would attach a "minimal condition" for the consummation of détente agreements involving trade. The U.S. Congress, after all, reflected "the traditional love of freedom of the American people." Senator Jackson went beyond this general point to a specific attribute of American tradition, the country's basic character as a "nation of immigrants," which justified the introduction of the amendment. It is precisely because of this character, he insisted, that freedom of emigration is "an American issue." Jackson reminded his colleagues in a major speech on the floor of the Senate that "I would not be in this chamber today if Norway, the country of my parents' birth, had practiced the sort of emigration policy that the Soviet Union has today."

Jackson's initiative was sparked by an extraordinary decision of the Soviet government: the enactment, on 3 August 1972, of a decree requiring would-be emigrants who had acquired a higher education to pay a "diploma tax." On 14 August, the decree was reaffirmed by an "order" of the USSR Council of Ministers, directing appropriate Soviet agencies to establish a scale of fees. These were so exorbitantly high that payment by those holding advanced degrees was virtually impossible. Soviet Jewish activists, at a 15 August press conference, warned that the effect of the decree would be the creation of "a new category of human beings—the slaves of the 20th century." The diploma tax was but the latest of a massive series of devices created by the Kremlin to stop the drain of talent. Even as the barrier to emigration was lifted in March 1971, and the flow of 13,000 Jews to Israel was increased to 32,000 in 1972, the highly educated and technically trained were compelled to run an obstacle course of prolonged torment.

The Kremlin had not reckoned with the revulsion the tax would generate in the United States. Especially shocked were the scientific and academic communities. Twenty-one Nobel laureates issued a public statement in the fall of 1972 expressing "dismay" at the "massive violation of human rights" by the imposition of "exorbitant head taxes." At an emergency meeting of the leadership of national Jewish organizations, called for 26 September in Washington, D.C., by the National Conference on Soviet Jewry, it was decided to move from a largely public-relations campaign to a predominantly political one focusing on a particular piece of legislation. Senator Jackson, who had asked to be invited to the gathering, outlined to the 120 participants a legislative proposal tying trade benefits to removal of curbs on emigration.

In part, the Jackson proposal was a response to negotiations for a comprehensive trade agreement that had been carried on between American and Soviet officials since the beginning of August. The provisions of the agreement, as finally signed by the two powers in October, were that the United States was to receive from the USSR $722 million of the enormous lend-lease debt owed it since World War II; in return, the administration pledged to seek congressional authorization for extending to the Soviet Union most-favored-nation (MFN) tariff treatment.

By early October 1972, Senators Jackson and Abraham Ribicoff had gathered thirty-two sponsors for their proposal, which they offered as an amendment to an East-West trade bill. Senator Jacob Javits, who had been reluctant to support the initial Jackson-Ribicoff draft because he thought it "unnecessarily irritating" to the Nixon administration, joined when it was somewhat modified, bringing with him thirty more senators. Shortly thereafter, when the number of sponsors had grown to seventy-six, or more than three-quarters of the Senate, Jackson formally introduced his amendment.

The amendment would refuse a "nonmarket economy country" MFN (most favored nation) status, as well as credits, credit guarantees, and investment guarantees, if that country denied its citizens the right to emigrate, or imposed more than a nominal tax on emigration. At the time, observers viewed the Senate action as a show of strength and a warning to the Russians, rather than a serious legislative move. Their reasoning was based on the fact that time was too short for the East-West trade bill to reach the floor of the Senate before the end of its session. Besides, there was no intensive activity in the House of Representatives to gather support for a similar amendment.

Early in January 1973, Representative Charles A. Vanik had assembled a list of 144 representatives who agreed to sponsor in the House legislation similar to Jackson's amendment. A massive letter-writing campaign sponsored by the NCSJ and organized Jewry was to evoke a powerful response. Support for the amendment also came from other sources, including the trade-union movement and several religious groups. By early February, 238 representatives, more than a majority of the House, had decided to become cosponsors of the proposed legislation. That legislation would be designed to amend an expected administration Trade Reform Act. As important as the reaction of Jackson and Vanik was the comment of Congressman Wilbur D. Mills, chairman of the powerful House Ways and Means Committee. Approached by a prominent Jewish businessman and friend, he announced on 7 February that he had become a principal sponsor of the Vanik amendment, and

proceeded to introduce formally the legislation that linked trade concessions to the USSR with free emigration.

The Soviet authorities initially sought to meet congressional action
head-on. The major target was to be big business in the United States,
which was thought to be most susceptible to Soviet blandishment. A
high-level 15-member Soviet delegation arrived to participate in an
American-Soviet trade conference sponsored by the National Association
of Manufacturers. At the opening session in Washington on 27 February,
which was attended by eight hundred businessmen, no less than three
powerful Soviet officials served as panel members.

The Soviet panelists quickly learned where Congress stood. Senator
Edmund S. Muskie told them that Soviet emigration policy constituted a
"major roadblock" to expanded East-West trade. An official Soviet response came the next day. Georgy Arbatov, reportedly the Politburo's
principal adviser on American questions, said at a briefing session for
both press and trade conferees that if "normalization of trade relations
between the U.S. and USSR is frustrated by the Congress," it would
prove "a harmful thing for Soviet-American relations" as a whole.
Should the Jackson-Vanik legislation be adopted, Arbatov warned, it
would, among other things, "revive anti-Semitism in the Soviet Union."
Arbatov's threats evoked an outraged response from Senator Ribicoff,
who received word of them while holding hearings of the Senate Subcommittee on International Trade, of which he was chairman. "I am using
this platform to tell Mr. Arbatov to mind his own damned business," he
said.

The Russians by no means relied exclusively on the Arbatov-type
threats. They also focused the softer line of economic inducements on
congressmen, with NAM providing the required link to the Hill. On 12
March, Deputy Trade Minister Alkhimov and two Soviet Embassy economic officials met with fifteen congressmen, among them key Republicans, at a luncheon requested by the Soviet Embassy and arranged by
NAM officials to explain the advantages of increased U.S.-Soviet trade.
They were told that members of Congress are "much concerned with Soviet emigration policies, and that we tend to link them with the granting
of the most-favored-nation status."

Alkhimov was told by Mills in a private meeting that 350 House members would vote to block the trade measure if the exit tax was still in
force. On 15 March 1973, Senator Jackson bolstered the Mills warning
by formally reintroducing his amendment on the Senate floor. In intro-
ducing his amendment, Jackson said its "heart" was the provision making MFN status and credits contingent on periodic presidential reports to
Congress on compliance with the free emigration requirements by the
country in question. Senator Ribicoff put the issue sharply, warning that
Congress was not "bluffing," and that "the next move is up to the Soviet

Union." Moscow no doubt got the "message" when large majorities in both houses of Congress—75 senators and 272 congressmen—agreed to co-sponsor the amendment. Clearly rejected was an appeal by Secretary of State William P. Rogers on the television program *Face the Nation* that no "conditions" be attached to the trade legislation to be introduced by the administration.

Washington must have received assurances that the USSR would alter, at least in some degree, its emigration procedures. Secretary of the Treasury George P. Shultz had met on 14 March with President Brezhnev and spoke of Soviet leaders showing "willingness to tackle [the emigration problem] in very real terms." Indeed, only four days after the Shultz visit, Moscow signaled a clearly positive, if limited, response to the pressure of Congress. On 19–20 March 1973, the USSR allowed forty-four Soviet Jews who had obtained a higher education to leave without paying the diploma tax. On 21 March, the Israeli daily *Yediot Aharonot* published an article by Victor Louis, a Soviet journalist with close KGB connections, which said the diploma tax "will no longer be enforced." Acknowledging that the Soviet decision was the result of congressional pressure in the United States, he observed: "It seems that the Soviet citizens who have decided to emigrate from the Soviet Union have won a victory in the six-month war against the education tax."

Anxious to deepen the détente to which it was committed, Washington reacted quickly. At the very moment the exit-visa tax waivers were disclosed, the U.S. Export-Import Bank extended to Moscow the first grant of sizable credits—$200 million—for the purchase of industrial equipment. The Soviet concession did not elicit so enthusiastic a response from Senator Jackson. Speaking at the National Press Club in Washington, he welcomed the Moscow developments as "encouraging signs," but also made it clear that he would continue to press for his amendment to ensure that Moscow did not "relapse into the old patterns" of harassment and taxation to limit emigration. The issue, it was clear, remained the right to leave a country. So long as harassment and intimidation of would-be emigrants continued in the USSR, the fundamental problem was by no means resolved.

The Nixon administration now shifted to the political offensive that would in part seek to neutralize or weaken the Jewish community's support for the amendment, thereby isolating congressional opposition. The offensive was launched on 29 March by Deputy Secretary of State Kenneth D. Rush in an address to six hundred leaders of the American mass media attending a State Department foreign-policy conference for editors and broadcasters. He indicated the Kremlin had displayed "commendable flexibility" on the issue of emigration, implying that progress was achieved by "quiet diplomacy." On 10 April, President Nixon sent Congress a comprehensive Trade Reform Act with the stated goal of "creating a new international economic order" by "building a fair and open trading world." It would enable him to grant MFN treatment to the USSR and other nonmarket countries.

However, Congress continued to be the obstacle. On 18 April, Nixon called in six key senators. Kissinger attempted to persuade them not to impose restrictions on Soviet trade, arguing that the administration's "quiet diplomacy" was proving productive. To indicate the effectiveness of the Nixon approach, Kissinger read from two unsigned Soviet "communications," which indicated that the exit taxes had been waived. Ribicoff, a prime mover of the Jackson amendment, was said to have shocked the president by telling him bluntly: "Mr. President, there's nothing new in this. We have known about the suspension for several weeks. But that in no way diminishes the need for passage of the Jackson amendment." While the prime movers of the amendment in the Senate could not be budged, a key figure in the House was won over. On the day the president met with the senators, one of his assistants showed Congressman Mills the two Soviet "communications," which persuaded Mills that "any number [of Soviet Jews] will now be able to leave the Soviet Union, except for national security reasons."

The administration now followed up with an approach to the Jewish community. At Nixon's invitation, fifteen prominent Jewish leaders who had long sought a meeting with the president to discuss the totality of the Soviet Jewish problem, but with one exception had been unsuccessful, received invitations from the White House. Now it was the president who sought the meeting, which lasted seventy minutes and ranged over central aspects of the Soviet Jewish problem. Inevitably, the impact on the Jewish participants was powerful, especially since Nixon showed sympathetic understanding of the problem. He asked Kissinger to share with the leaders the contents of the "communications." Most important, he explained to them the profound moral dilemma in which he found himself. On the one hand, he had made a commitment to the Kremlin on MFN status that was perceived as integral to his search for détente. On the other hand, there was the Jackson amendment, which would negate that commitment.

Delivered in a delicate manner, the message was clear. The White House hoped the Jewish community would reconsider its adamant support of the Jackson amendment. The strategy appears to have temporarily succeeded. After the meeting, Jacob Stein, chairman of the Conference of Presidents of Major American Jewish Organizations; Charlotte Jacobson, vice chair of the National Conference on Soviet Jewry; and Max Fisher, former president of the Council of Jewish Federations and Welfare Funds, issued a statement on behalf of all participants that was as revealing for what it did not say as for what it said. It noted the contents of the Soviet documents read by Kissinger, and "asked the help of the president for the 100,000 Soviet Jews who had been refused exit visas." Finally, it reaffirmed "the commitment to Soviet Jews and our determination to continue maximum efforts in their behalf." The statement's failure to include any reference to the Jackson amendment raised doubts on Capitol Hill about the firmness of the Jewish community's position. The very ambiguity of the statement stirred a grassroots backlash. Pressure for clarification rapidly mounted among the organizations composing the NCSJ. Parallel and interlocked with this pressure were demands by the amendment's leading sponsors for a strong statement of support, without which their ability to hold congressional supporters in line was open to question.

Jewish leaders were faced with a dilemma that they had sought to avoid. Until their meeting at the White House, they had made every effort to present publicly their support of the Jackson amendment as in no way directed against the president. On the contrary, they had argued, support of the amendment aided the president's "quiet diplomacy" by strengthening his hand in negotiating with the Russians. Now, the leaders felt, they were being pressured into making a choice between support of the White House and support of the Jackson amendment. They were keenly aware that Nixon had been a friend of Israel and continued to aid the Jewish state.

A decisive consideration in resolving the dilemma was the attitude of Soviet Jewry. Just as Soviet Jews had played the key role in sparking the extraordinary American Jewish mass movement in late 1970 on behalf of their emigration rights, so, too, was their opinion key at this juncture. When reports about an apparent ambiguity concerning American Jewish support for the Jackson amendment reached Moscow, Soviet Jewish activists decided to intervene directly. On 23 April 1973, they sent an appeal bearing more than one hundred signatures to American Jewish leaders, urging them to continue backing the amendment. Their language was strong and designed to remind American Jewry of the Holocaust. The closing paragraph was particularly poignant: "Remember, the history of our people has known many terrible mistakes. Do not give in to soothing deceit. Remember, your smallest hesitation may cause irreparable tragic results. Remember, your firmness and steadfastness are our only hope. Now as never before, our fate depends on you. Can you retreat at such a moment?"

Clarification of the Jewish community's position was pressed at an enlarged executive committee meeting of the NCSJ on 26 April. It reached the decision that a prompt public statement of support for the amendment was essential, but implementation had to wait for endorsement by the Conference of Presidents, scheduled to meet the following week. (The understanding between the two organizations was that major policy questions required approval by both.)

That meeting was marked by much tension. Stein resisted a renewed endorsement of the Jackson amendment lest the links of the group with the White House be compromised. This perspective was not supported by the overwhelming majority of the representatives of Jewish organizations. A clash bordering almost on insurrection developed as one organizational leader announced his intention to keep the meeting in continuous session unless a statement responsive to grassroots demands was accepted. The chair finally capitulated, and a statement of reaffirmation, hammered out after the meeting, declared the Jackson amendment had "contributed" to the "effort to alleviate the plight of Soviet Jewry, and we continue our support for this legislation." It also expressed "appreciation" for the "initiatives of President Nixon." The text was to be released to the press on 2 May because it was thought appropriate to advise Kissinger, with whom Jewish leaders were to meet on 1 May, of the planned release.

At the meeting, Stein, Fisher, and Richard Maass, chairman of NCSJ, frankly told Kissinger that the organized Jewish community stood solidly behind the amendment, but that, at the same time, they welcomed the maintenance of "the channel of communication" between the White House and the Jewish community. They then spoke of the Kremlin's cruel harassments of Soviet Jewish activists and asked Kissinger to intercede on behalf of some eight hundred hard-core cases whose applications for exit visas had repeatedly been refused. While Kissinger was "sympathetic," he also made it clear that granting MFN status to the USSR was essential for détente.

While the administration was unable to sway Congress, Leonid Brezhnev thought he might try during a scheduled trip to the United States in mid-June. Two days after his arrival, he met with seventeen members of the Senate Foreign Relations Committee and eight members of the House, and outlined the prospects for vast Soviet-American trade. After some time, he emphasized rather vigorously that the condition for such trade was MFN status for the Soviet Union. Expecting questions on emigration, he came fully prepared. He pulled from his pocket a red notebook and ran through emigration data that showed, he said, that 97 percent of all exit visa applicants were allowed to leave. One Jewish leader called the figures "make-believe." But it was not only the accuracy of Brezhnev's data that was central to the issue. There was the prolonged torment would-be emigrants knew they would have to face: ostracism, discrimination, job dismissal.

Brezhnev received a far more enthusiastic reception from forty of America's top industrial and banking executives, invited by Secretary Shultz to a meeting at Blair House on the morning of 22 June. They were enormously impressed by the broad picture Brezhnev painted of the potential of trade relations between the two countries. Yet, for all his lobbying, Brezhnev failed to achieve his primary objective of winning over Congress for the administration's trade bill. The large majority in both the Senate and the House had not retreated from support of the Jackson amendment. The amendment now had 77 sponsors in the Senate and 285 in the House. The legislative session, which resumed in September 1973, was marked by an intensification of the struggle between the White House and Congress over the trade bill. The locus of the conflict was in the House.

A new factor in the debate was Andrey Sakharov's decision to enter directly into the controversy. His "open letter" to the Congress, dated 14 September, appealed for support of the Jackson amendment. Its passage, he said, was an indispensable first step to assuring détente. In his view, the "minimal right" of emigration is essential for "mutual trust" and, therefore, détente. To reject Jackson-Vanik would be nothing short of "a betrayal of the thousands of Jews and non-Jews who want to emigrate, of the hundreds in camps and mental hospitals, of the victims of the Berlin Wall."

The appeal had especially powerful overtones in view of the extraordinarily vicious propaganda campaign the Kremlin had unleashed against Sakharov in late August and early September. That campaign coincided with a general KGB crackdown on Soviet dissenters, nonconformists, and critics. The response of the American scientific and intellectual communities was one of enormous concern. The result was an unexpected broadening of the Jackson coalition. Many militant doves who had been suspicious of Senator Jackson's hawkish record now urged support of his amendment.

The immediate test of strength between the administration and the Jackson coalition was in the House Ways and Means Committee. The 25-member panel had been under pressure from business circles, including Donald M. Kendall, chairman of the newly formed Emergency Committee on American Trade. But the charged moral-political atmosphere flowing from the Sakharov issue all but neutralized that pressure. The House committee voted on MFN status on 26 September. By a voice vote, it agreed to deny MFN status to nonmarket countries restricting emigration. However, the administration succeeded in seriously weakening the bill through an unexpected parliamentary maneuver. Before the vote was taken, the ranking Republican member of the Ways and Means Committee suddenly, on a point of order, asked that the provision barring credits and credit guarantees be eliminated. He contended that this section fell under the jurisdiction of the House Banking and Currency Committee. The chair ruled in his favor.

The committee decision on the bill, while not completely to the liking of the Jackson coalition, was an important setback to the administration. Even before the House committee action, the administration indicated that it was determined to reverse it. Kissinger deliberately chose the hour before the vote to hold his very first press conference as secretary of state.

The expected committee vote, Kissinger said, would raise "the most serious questions," not only by Soviet Russia but by other countries as well, about the ability of the United States to fulfill its pledges. The day after the committee action, the administration openly launched its campaign to overturn the decision. President Nixon, with Kissinger at his side, met at the White House with the Republican leaders of Congress and urged a determined effort to eliminate the restrictions placed on granting MFN status to the USSR.

The Jackson coalition was equally determined to restore the provision on credits. In a speech on the Senate floor on 27 September, Jackson called the House committee vote "a most welcome affirmation of the commitment of this country to the cause of human rights," but expressed regret that "a vital part of the Jackson amendment" had been dropped on grounds of "a jurisdictional question." Bank credits were far more crucial than Soviet manufactured goods, which, in the immediate future, were most unlikely to find a market in the United States for a variety of economic reasons. Credits, on the other hand, involved the very hard reality of trade. Because the Soviets were anxious to import quantities of American products, including advanced technological equipment, credits through the U.S. Eximbank were essential. By October, Eximbank had already extended to the USSR several hundred million dollars in credits. Estimates of credits to be extended were in the billions.

Before the bill came up for final vote in the House (scheduled for 17 or 18 October), fighting had broken out in the Middle East. The Yom Kippur War significantly affected the character of the debate and the strategic maneuvering behind the scenes. For one, the Jewish community, the principal public backer of the Jackson amendment, was now chiefly concerned with Israel's survival. At the same time, a major objective of American foreign policy was to bring about a cease-fire in the Middle East, which required the cooperation of the Soviet Union.

Kissinger felt that the time was not opportune for a House vote on the Trade Reform Act, and that passage of the Jackson amendment would jeopardize Soviet cooperation in ending hostilities. On 11 October, he urged the House leadership to postpone the vote in "the best interests of the country." The request was approved by House leaders. Consideration of the trade bill was rescheduled for 24 or 25 October. But as the time for the vote approached, Middle East tensions had not been resolved. The two cease-fires reached on 22 and 24 October appeared threatened. Kissinger again sought delay.

At this point, a curious episode took place. On 23 October, Kissinger, who had just that day returned from his whirlwind trip to Moscow, Tel-Aviv, and London, met at the White House with Stein, Maass, and Fisher. Toward the end of the meeting, which mainly focused on Middle East matters, Kissinger raised the issue of the Jackson amendment. He reiterated that the president favored its elimination from the Trade Reform Act, and then surprised his listeners by asking whether, in the event Jackson and Vanik agreed to the elimination of the amendment, the Jewish leadership would condemn them. Since the Jewish leaders did not know whether Jackson or Vanik had been approached by the White House, their answer was evasive. If indeed Jackson or Vanik agreed with Kissinger, they said, they would have to ask their constituency for instructions on how to proceed.

The White House reinforced the Kissinger tactic. Peter Flanigan, its chief adviser on international economic policy, told Jewish leaders that the interests of Israel required the elimination of Title IV (Jackson-Vanik). He proposed on 2 November that the leadership meet with Vanik and Jackson concerning this objective. Jewish leaders had been scheduled to see Jackson on 5 November. During the preceding weekend, word of the administration proposal leaked out and quickly generated a chorus of anger and concern. The executive committee of the NCSJ rejected the Kissinger and Flanigan proposal. Instead, Maass was instructed to report to Jackson on the White House position, and to seek his counsel.

The 5 November session with Jackson was the turning point in the yearlong campaign. The senator chose to invite to it, in addition to Maass, Stein, and Jacobson, his principal legislative partner, Senator Ribicoff, and B'nai B'rith president David Blumberg. After Maass reported on the conversations with administration officials, Jackson and Ribicoff addressed the source of the Jewish community's anxiety: that continued support of the amendment might undermine or weaken U.S. support of Israel. In their view, the linkage was spurious; indeed, enactment of Title IV would not only serve to ameliorate the condition of Soviet Jewry, but would also provide the United States with an effective lever in negotiations with the Soviet Union on the Middle East.

After the meeting, Stein and Maass immediately went to the White House to advise Flanigan that the organized Jewish community would continue to back the Jackson amendment. The following week, Maass issued a public statement to this effect. It made clear that backing the amendment did not mean the Jewish leadership had cut its ties with the Nixon administration, or did not appreciate its massive aid to Israel. What the leadership rejected, Maass emphasized, was the attempt to use that aid to weaken or remove the Jackson amendment. On 10 December, the trade bill was finally called up for action. The key vote came a day later on a motion by Vanik to refuse credits, credit guarantees, and investment guarantees to nonmarket countries denying their citizens emigration rights. The overwhelming 4 to 1 ratio in the voting (319 to 80) testified to the massive support enjoyed by the Jackson coalition in the House. Then, by a ratio almost as large (298 to 106), the House defeated an administration-sponsored motion to delete Title IV from the bill.

The collapse of Nixon's strategy compelled the administration to shift in 1974 to a new approach. Kissinger had to recognize the political reality that more than three-quarters of the Senate supported the House-approved legislation. He therefore, for the first time, entered into negotiations with the principal sponsors of the amendment, Senators Jackson, Ribicoff, and Javits. The purpose of the negotiations, which continued throughout the spring, was to find a formula to make the Jackson amendment acceptable to the administration and to the Kremlin. Ineluctably, the administration was compelled to conduct parallel and interlocking discussions with Soviet officials to determine what concessions the Kremlin was prepared to make to satisfy the Senate. Kissinger frequently met with Soviet Ambassador Anatoly Dobrynin, and saw Soviet Foreign Minister Andrey Gromyko at Geneva in April and at Cyprus in May, to discuss the matter.

Two aims were central to these discussions: ending the harassment of Soviet Jews who applied for exit visas, and raising the level of Jewish emigration. (The rate of Jewish emigration during the first half of 1974 had declined by 40 percent.) Concerning the first point, Gromyko at Cyprus was prepared to acknowledge that such practices were "inconsistent with Soviet laws." With reference to the level of emigration, he proposed a figure of 45,000. The three senators suggested 75,000 as a desirable number.

The accession of Gerald Ford to the presidency on 9 August was a decisive development. Not only was Ford, in the calculations of the Kremlin, an uncertain factor as far as détente was concerned, he had also committed himself, in his first public act, to a "marriage" with Congress. The Kremlin moved rapidly. Three days after Ford's inauguration, Dobrynin interrupted his vacation to fly to Washington, and the two met on 14 August to discuss the trade measure. The discussion was clearly encouraging. The president called the three senators to the White House the following morning and offered them his personal guarantee that the Kremlin was prepared to end harassment of Jewish applicants and to raise significantly the level of emigration.

The administration-Senate negotiations now entered their final stage, with the NCSJ playing a valuable role. It spurred the opposing sides to reach agreement, a task that was complicated by personality clashes. Initially, the negotiators agreed that Kissinger would write a letter spelling out the Soviet commitment on eased emigration procedures. Upon the insistence of Stanley H. Lowell, new chairman of NCSJ, it was agreed that the letter would refer to "assurances" rather than a vaguer term. Jackson would then respond by giving his interpretation of the agreement, indicating a precise figure of 60,000 as the emigration rate—a compromise between the earlier figures. A third letter from Kissinger to Jackson, accepting Jackson's interpretation, was later dropped.

As the negotiations proceeded, the Soviet Union was kept apprised of, and appeared to accept, the understandings that were being reached. Indeed, on 20 September, President Ford met successively with Jackson and Gromyko on the basic content of the proposed exchange of correspondence, and later that day, Kissinger and Gromyko talked about it at length. In essence, the Kremlin had become a "silent partner" to an administration-Senate understanding.

Announcement of the understanding was made by Senator Jackson on 18 October. Kissinger's letter stated that "punitive action" against would-be emigrants and "unreasonable impediments" would no longer obtain. Only in the case of persons holding "security clearances" would "limitations of emigration" be imposed, and then only for a designated time period. Senator Jackson's response translated the assurances into specific terms. With respect to "security clearance" cases, he set a date of three years from the time they had been exposed to sensitive information. As a "benchmark, a minimum standard of initial compliance," Jackson set an emigration figure of 60,000 per annum. He added that "we understand that the president proposes to use the same benchmark." On the basis of these understandings, Jackson agreed to propose an additional amendment that would authorize the president to waive, for a period of eighteen months, Title IV restrictions with respect to MFN status and credits. Thereafter, the presidential waiver authority could be extended, on a one-year basis, by concurrent resolutions of both houses of Congress.

Excessive optimism was dispelled when, during the autumn months of 1974, the level of emigration of Soviet Jews remained low and harassment continued. On 21 November, nine prominent Soviet Jewish activists, in an open letter to President Ford, extensively documented cases of harassment. More important, the activists warned, the Kremlin was taking steps to reduce the number of possible applicants for emigration. The concern of the Soviet Jewish activists, which was echoed by the American Jewish leadership, only testified that Soviet "good faith" had yet to be fully tested.

A week after the Kissinger-Jackson exchange, Gromyko handed Kissinger, who was then in Moscow, a letter dated 26 October, which complained that the letters presented a "distorted picture of our position." It stated that "we resolutely decline" the interpretation of "elucidations that were furnished by us" on emigration practices as involving "some assurances and nearly obligation on our part." The Gromyko letter was kept from the Senate—and the public. Kissinger made no reference to it during his crucial testimony in support of the Trade Reform Act before the Senate Finance Committee on 3 December. He nonetheless insisted that "assurances" on emigration had been given by Brezhnev, Gromyko, and Dobrynin.

On 13 December, the Senate, by a vote of 88 to 0, approved the waiver provision, with the proviso that the president certify to the Congress that "he has received assurances that the emigration practices" of the USSR will "lead substantially to the achievement of the objectives" of the Jackson amendment. But on the morning of 18 December, Moscow suddenly decided to react publicly to the trade measure. Its comments were unusually negative. The official Soviet news agency, Tass, asserted that "leading circles" in the USSR flatly reject as "unacceptable" any attempt to attach conditions to the reduction of tariffs on imports from the Soviet Union, or otherwise to "interfere in [its] internal affairs." The statement denied that the Kremlin had given any specific assurances on emigration procedures. To support its contention, Tass released the Gromyko letter of 26 October.

The Tass release revealed a totally new Kremlin attitude. Prior to 18 December, the Kremlin failed to indicate publicly that it had second thoughts about the understandings reached between the White House and Senator Jackson, to which it was a silent partner. What brought the changed perspective? Analysis suggests that it was triggered by another congressional action completely unrelated to the Jackson amendment.

By 16 December, it had become clear to the Kremlin that the Senate was about to approve an amendment to a bill that extended the life of the U.S. Export-Import Bank for four years. The amendment, sponsored by Senator Adlai E. Stevenson III, would place a ceiling of only $300 million on credits to the USSR over the entire four-year period. It had been initially voted on favorably by the Senate on 19 September. As the House version of the Eximbank bill contained no similar amendment, the issue went before a Senate-House conference committee, which adopted the ceiling on 12 December. The Senate then began considering the conference report, and after several sessions—the last on 16 December—appeared almost certain to adopt it.

As Kissinger later indicated, the amount of credits permitted the USSR under the ceiling was "peanuts in Soviet terms." As compared to more than $1 billion in credits it sought for the next three years, the proposed $75 million per annum was a severe disappointment. From the Kremlin's perspective, the bargain that had been struck involving an agreed-upon exchange of money credits for emigrants had been unfavorably altered.

Significantly, Ambassador Dobrynin met with Kissinger on 18 December and, in a reportedly stormy session, lashed out at the credit ceiling and warned that the October 1972 trade agreement would thereby be placed in jeopardy. At the same time, Tass had issued its statement denying any assurances on emigration. The connection seemed clear. Moscow was saying that if the ceiling on credits was imposed, the trade deal with the United States and, most recently, incorporated in the Kissinger-Jackson exchange was jeopardized. The linked Soviet actions of 18 December were clearly designed to stir State Department lobbying in the Senate. But the last-minute lobbying, if intensive, proved unavailing. On 19 December, the Senate approved the conference report even as the State Department denounced the Stevenson amendment as "most unwise and unfortunate."

The puzzling question is why the administration failed to alert public opinion and the Congress as to what the Stevenson amendment involved in relation to the understandings reached on the Jackson amendment. Strikingly, Jewish organizations, which had a great stake in the emigration issue, were totally unaware of the Stevenson amendment and its potential consequences. Kissinger was reported to have admitted to his aides that he failed to focus on the Eximbank bill and the Stevenson amendment when he should have done so.

An attack would now be mounted by the Kremlin against the entire Trade Reform Act. On 20 December, both the Senate and the House approved the act by large majorities. The very next day, Tass unleashed the new propaganda offensive, denouncing both the Trade Reform Act and the Eximbank legislation as "attempts at interference in the internal affairs of the USSR." Several weeks later, the Kremlin formally scrapped the October 1972 trade agreement.

The Trade Reform Act, with its historic Jackson-Vanik amendment, became law on 3 January 1975, when President Ford signed the legislation. The amendment was among several human rights enactments that were adopted at the time by a Congress infuriated with an "imperial presidency" that seemed to be indifferent to burning human-rights issues. As the very first piece of legislation that drew its inspiration consciously from the Universal Declaration of Human Rights, the amendment was to ultimately serve as a powerful lever on Soviet emigration practices.

Even before Jackson-Vanik became law, it had compelled the Kremlin, in an unprecedented act, to nullify an education tax on exit visas. During a seven-month period while the tax was applied, 1,450 Soviet Jews had to pay approximately $7 million to emigrate. How many were kept from applying because of the tax is not known. But never again would Soviet Jews be required to pay an exorbitant ransom tax. The same leverage would be used by the United States with Communist Romania. Granted MFN in 1975, the Ceauşescu regime sought suddenly to impose a huge education tax on would-be emigrants in November 1982. After Washington warned that MFN status and Eximbank credits would be withdrawn by June 1983, Bucharest relented. The exit visa tax was canceled.

Nor would Moscow choose to disregard the message of Jackson-Vanik, even after its vehement media outbursts of December 1974. After 1975, the annual emigration rate of Soviet Jews rose, jumping to 28,000 in 1978 and an unprecedented 51,000 in 1979. During 1978–79, a draft strategic arms limitation agreement (SALT II) occupied a key place on the American-Soviet agenda, and Moscow sought to win support for Senate ratification of the treaty. Preliminary discussions concerning trade and credits were also taking place at the time. There was little doubt that the Carter administration was prepared to show flexibility in applying the waiver provision of Jackson-Vanik should an agreement be reached.

Strikingly, in 1978, the United States reached a trade agreement with the Soviet satellite state of Hungary. That agreement was preceded by written exchanges in which Budapest gave assurances on its emigration practices. Had Moscow continued to have strong objections to the amendment as an intrusion into domestic affairs, it would no doubt have pressured Hungary to reject the agreement.

The Soviet invasion of Afghanistan in December 1979 brought an end to the warming trend with the West. The resumption of an even more frigid cold war ineluctably followed, with a concomitant plunging downward of Jewish emigration rates. By 1986, the figure had reached the lowest level since the sixties.

With the emergence of glasnost and perestroika following Mikhail Gorbachev's coming to power, a new era in East-West relations appeared on the horizon. It found expression in the Helsinki process talks held in Vienna, especially during 1987. Moscow would commit itself to free emigration and the removal of virtually all obstacles to it. Even on the core issue of the national security device designed to inhibit emigration, Moscow was prepared to impose "stringent time limits" on the "state secrets" obstacle. Gorbachev himself made this commitment in an address to the United Nations General Assembly on 7 December 1988.

Central to Jackson-Vanik was less the commitments, but rather the actual flow of emigrants. Implementation constituted the heart of the amendment and explains why Senator Jackson insisted a "benchmark" of 60,000 emigrants per annum as essential for determining whether a waiver of his statute was to be granted. From 1989 onward, that "benchmark" was annually reached and, indeed, exceeded. In 1989, it was 72,000, and then jumped to 213,000 in 1990 and 180,000 in 1991. Since 1992, the annual emigration rate has been more than 75,000 and is expected to continue at that level for the immediate future.

Appropriately, the waiver was granted, and the Soviet Union and its successor states, most notably Russia, were extended MFN status and Eximbank credits on an annual basis. The very existence of the Jackson-Vanik amendment, together with the annual review, provided the leverage for assuring continuing compliance. President Boris Yeltsin, in view of Russia's positive record and eager to remove any obstacles to American investment and trade, sought to have Jackson-Vanik entirely revoked. When he met with President Bill Clinton in Vancouver, Canada, in April 1993 at their first summit, he vigorously pressed the issue.

At the press conference that climaxed the meeting, Yeltsin observed that the two leaders had "decided to do away with the Jackson-Vanik amendment." The comment was hardly accurate. Clinton, in his press comments, had merely indicated that, only after the White House is certain that restrictions on emigration are no longer implemented, would he then be prepared to recommend to Congress that the legislation be reconsidered. As it happened, the administration learned from the NCSJ that the number of refuseniks was disconcertingly sizable: 252.

Given these facts, Clinton was hardly in a position to ask for a change in the status of Russia under Jackson-Vanik. Moscow had to do better and knew it. The next year, Russian Prime Minister Viktor Chernomyrdin came to Washington armed with positive details. It was on 21 June 1994 that he met with several Jewish leaders brought together by the NCSJ. Besides noting the continuing high level of exodus, Chernomyrdin could call attention to the sharp decline in the number of refuseniks. A specially created commission in Russia, headed by Sergei Lavrov, had reviewed 139 key refusenik cases and approved 135. When the NCSJ indicated that it had a list of new cases, totaling approximately fifty, the prime minister offered to arrange for the Jewish leadership to meet with Lavrov himself in Washington. He proved most cooperative, promising to examine the controversial cases and to expedite solutions. Since then, the refusenik category plunged downward, laying the groundwork for a change in Russia's MFN status.

But that change would not and could not mean that Jackson-Vanik no longer applied to Russia. That is precisely what Chernomyrdin sought (as had Yeltsin in Vancouver). Enlightenment was provided by the late Senator Jackson's collaborator, former Congressman Charles Vanik. As an invited member of the NCSJ delegation, he told the Russian prime minister that the Jackson-Vanik amendment was "firm as concrete" in both American law and the American mind. Besides, only Congress, not the president, can remove Russia from the Jackson-Vanik rubric, and that is most unlikely. In view of Russia's (and the Soviet Union's) past record on Jewish emigration, as well as the continuing instability of authority in Moscow, Congress could hardly be certain about future Kremlin conduct.

Still, a significant step under Jackson-Vanik could be taken in recognizing Russia's compliance. President Clinton, with the support of NCSJ, formally affirmed on 21 September 1994 Moscow's "full compliance" with Jackson-Vanik. This affirmation permitted Russia to obtain MFN status and Eximbank credits without an annual review (by both the administration and the Congress). The removal of the burdensome annual review was strongly welcomed by President Yeltsin when he arrived in Washington shortly after Clinton's announcement.

Sakharov's "policy of principle" has come full circle. More than a million and a quarter Jews have emigrated from Russia and the former Soviet Union since Jackson-Vanik was first introduced, a testament to its power, as Yeltsin himself indirectly recognized. But it was also a testament to the determination of American Jews to stand firmly behind the legislation in the vigorous struggle on behalf of their beleaguered Soviet Jewish brethren.

Marshall I. Goldman

Jackson-Vanik
A Dissent

The Jackson-Vanik amendment (JVA) has proved to be one of the most effective policy weapons ever wielded against the Soviet Union. The amendment decreed that unless the Soviet Union liberalized its emigration policies, it would be denied MFN (most favored nation) status. Despite warnings that it was a proud and strong country and not vulnerable to threats or pressure from the West, Soviet authorities nonetheless eventually found it in their interest to accommodate themselves to demands from the United States to liberalize emigration of Soviet citizens. Using the lever of MFN status, the United States pressured the Soviets eventually to allow the emigration of more than one million Jews, along with tens of thousands of Germans and Armenians. However, despite the evident success of such a measure, a case can be made to show that as effective as MFN status was as a diplomatic weapon, there were limits to its effectiveness, and that the rigid and unwavering support for the JVA ultimately proved to be counterproductive. (For a slightly different interpretation, see J. J. Goldberg, *Jewish Power* [Reading, Mass.: Addison-Wesley, 1996], 173. Goldberg looks at the JVA as a case study of how the American Jewish community came to develop its political clout, even if somewhat reluctantly. Although he does not explain why, he does assert, as I shall argue in this essay, that "since the passage of the JVA in 1974, Jewish activists in America and the Soviet Union alike have never stopped hailing it as the weapon that turned the tide in the freedom struggle of Soviet Jews. The truth is very nearly the opposite.")

I became involved early in the effort to bring the JVA into being. *The Advocates*, a program featured on public television at the time, decided to devote its program on 6 December 1973, to a debate on pressuring the Soviet Union to allow the emigration of minority groups such as Jews with the threat that if it did not, it would not receive MFN status. An effort was being made at the time by the Ford administration to pass a trade bill that included measures to normalize some of our trade relationships with the Soviet Union. I was in the process of completing a book on American trade with the Soviet Union at the time, and so I was asked to participate in the *Advocates* program in support of the JVA. It was my task, along with Dimitri Simes, to support the proposition that the United States should withhold MFN status from the Soviet Union until it liberalized its emigration policies.

As was the custom with the *Advocates* program, viewers were asked to send in their votes as to which side of the debate they had decided to support. Much to the surprise of the television staff, our side prevailed. We were helped in making our case because of the arrest and death sentences imposed on a small group of Jews caught attempting to hijack a plane in Leningrad in 1970. Our case was further strengthened by reference to the emigration tax passed by Soviet authorities in August 1972. The show trial and the emigration tax certainly provoked anger. But our case on the televised debate was markedly strengthened when we were able to show that linking trade to an improved human rights posture in Russia, despite strong protestations by Soviet leaders, could nonetheless produce results. The Soviet reasoning seemed to be that doing away with the tax would head off the passage of the JVA.

Much the same reasoning seemed to explain the sudden and remarkable widening of the emigration doors. Allowing more than 30,000 Jews to leave in both 1972 and 1973 was all the more remarkable given that since the time of Stalin, no group, certainly not the Jews, had been allowed to leave in such large numbers. The fact that this policy was changed was evidently a response to criticism in the West, and especially the strong possibility that Congress would ultimately pass the JVA.

That the Soviet leadership could alter its rigid position when there seemed to be something in it for them eventually caused me to reconsider my own tactics in dealing with the USSR. I concluded that the best way to pry open Soviet concessions was to find a continuous stream of goodies to tempt them. Rather than cutting economic and political ties or adopting an unyielding stance on existing disputes, it seemed to make more sense that, wherever possible, we should seek to whet Soviet appetites. We should continually seek to hold out the promise that if they behaved, we would offer them "something new." Moreover, we should take our time in implementing our promises. We should try to hold out the bait as long as possible. Similarly, we should hold out the promise of such concessions as MFN status, but never actually provide it, or for that matter, never pass the JVA which, if passed, would deny them something they wanted. Similarly, we should debate participating in the 1980 Olympics in Moscow, but seek to avoid a decision as long as possible.

I described this at the time as a policy of "linkage interruptus." Always be on the verge, but don't deliver. Indeed, when the Congress did pass the

JVA in late December 1974 and early January 1975, the Soviets evidently concluded that they no longer had anything to gain by being responsive to American pressure (at least until the issue would be reconsidered). As a result, emigration, which had risen to 34,733 in 1973, fell to 20,628 in 1974.

There was no doubt in my mind that support for the JVA was the proper strategy at the time, but once it was adopted, what then? I became more and more convinced that the time had come to adopt a more responsive and flexible policy. The American Jewish Congress asked if I would make a presentation to them in November 1975. There had been some in the organization who had opposed the JVA from the beginning, and others (including me) who had supported it from the beginning. Whatever the prevailing view in 1973–74, by late 1975, the circumstances had changed significantly. The JVA had become law, and the Soviet economy had begun to develop some serious problems. In particular, its grain harvest had fallen about a quarter from 1974, and it was in desperate need of foreign grain imports.

Still angry over what had come to be called the "Great Grain Robbery" of 1972, when the Soviets had availed themselves of large quantities of American grain at bargain prices, many in the United States were calling for a halt to any further grain exports to the Soviet Union. Others would allow the sale of grain, but only in exchange for wide-ranging political concessions. My own attitude was that the Soviets had serious needs, but that bad as it was, the situation was not serious enough to spark a collapse of the Soviet Union or the Soviet economy. Instead, the Soviet need for grain presented the United States with an opportunity to engage the Soviets once again on the assumption that the better state of U.S.-Soviet relations, the better it would be for Soviet Jews seeking emigration.

Admittedly, the 1970s era of détente was far short of a normal political relationship between the United States and the Soviet Union. But disappointing as the emigration figures were for 1974 and 1975, it was necessary to remember that in the earlier era of the cold war, there was virtually no emigration. It was only when the Soviet leadership wanted something from the United States or the West, and thus was at least partially concerned about its outside image, that it even contemplated being responsive.

Whether or not the Soviet Union was in a mood to make political concessions in exchange for more economic interaction (including subsidized grain sales) became moot. By 1976, the approach to U.S.-Soviet relations had become so polarized that it would have come close to heresy if the Jewish community had adopted a more conciliatory attitude in dealing with the Soviet Union, or if it had backed away from support for the JVA.

To appreciate why, we must recall how the coalition supporting the JVA came into being. However natural it seemed at the time, the groups advocating the adoption of the JVA were as unholy a political alliance as existed in the United States. To begin with, there were the supporters of human rights, liberals for the most part who, were it not for the Soviet disregard of human rights, would be among the strong supporters of a better U.S.-Soviet relationship. They normally favored a policy of détente. Some even supported certain of the social and economic policies that Soviet leaders espoused, if not always implemented. They were joined in their support of the JVA by what can be called hard-liners. As these hard-liners saw it, any policy that resulted in a bashing of the USSR warranted their support, even though a liberal might be holding the other side of the banner. The hard-liners included representatives from the trade unions, especially among the leadership of the AFL-CIO, along with other traditional opponents of Soviet policies from the military and conservative sectors of American society. As far as these groups were concerned, there had not been and never would be any redeeming value to support for the Soviet Union.

Against this background, no subtle analysis was needed for the American Jewish Congress to recognize that it would not be easy to turn its back on such an influential grouping of supporters. Moreover, given the pattern of Soviet behavior, you did not have to be a hard-liner to be tough on the Soviet Union. The Soviet policies at the time were universally condemned. To have offered kind words about the Soviet Union would have meant a breaking of ranks, and that might mean a loss of support for Israel and other agenda items not having to do with the Soviet Union or emigration matters. And of course, no one wanted to embarrass Senator Henry Jackson; his support was crucial on a whole range of other issues important for the Jewish community.[1]

Despite the hazards associated with any deviation from the anti-Soviet coalition, concern about the drop in the number of Jews emigrating precipitated a reexamination of the Jewish stand on the JVA. Bertram Gold of the American Jewish Committee and Phil Baum of the American Jewish Congress were two of the first to go public.[2] Even then, however, they sought to keep the discussion within the Jewish family. There was a hesitancy to be seen as a breaker of ranks.

One of the first to break out was the American Jewish Congress. On 1 June 1978, in testimony before the House Committee on International Relations, the AJCongress offered its support for a bill that would have allowed the Commodity Credit Corporation to extend credits to the Soviet Union for the purchase of U.S. grain. Even though it was not a direct assault on the Jackson-Vanick amendment, if adopted, the extension of credit would contravene the terms of the JVA. The amendment outlawed "any program of the U.S. government which extends credit or credit guarantees or investment guarantees directly or indirectly." In any event, the AJCongress testimony amounted to a clear break in ranks within the

National Conference on Soviet Jewry, the umbrella group to which the organization belonged.

There was considerable criticism of the AJCongress position, particularly from the Student Struggle for Soviet Jewry and the Union of Councils for Soviet Jewry.[3] While the AJCongress was not eager to distance itself from these two hard-line groups, the fact that they were so unyielding and so uninhibited in their protests served to prevent the more moderate National Conference from being more flexible. This was clearly a source of concern for those seeking a more responsive strategy.

While the debate among Jewish groups over continued support for Jackson-Vanik in Congress seemed to be the main forum for policymakers concerned with such matters, some of the leaders of the movement were also invited by Soviet diplomats to private and off-the-record discussions. Given the heat of the rhetoric used by both the Jewish community and the representatives of the Soviet government, the willingness of Soviet officials to engage in such back-channel talks came as quite a surprise. On occasion, the Soviet ambassador to the United States, Anatoly Dobrynin, was a participant.[4] It was also suggested that the JVA had served a purpose and that the Soviets were eager to find some way to remove the sanctions. As they promised, beginning in 1978, Soviet authorities began to increase the number of emigration visas. From the Soviet point of view, this was a clear demonstration of good faith. Having met their promises, Ambassador Dobrynin returned to the Jewish leaders, noting, "We responded; we gave you the sign. Now what is your counter-response?"[5]

The timing of the back-channel discussions and the increase in the number of visas were not random acts. The Soviets sensed that the time was ripe to be responsive. Not only was there the discussion about the possibility of Commodity Credit Corporation credits; the Soviets were also well aware that in 1979, the U.S. Congress would again debate the extension of MFN status. This time, however, Congress would examine not only whether MFN status should be extended to the Soviet Union, but also to China. It was important, therefore, for the Soviet Union to show that it could be flexible on the question of emigration.[6]

Unfortunately, the reaction of the vast majority of Jewish groups was anything but forthcoming. On the contrary, most critics pointed to the rising numbers of emigrants as proof of the effectiveness of the JVA. As they saw it, this was not the time to break ranks. Eugene Gold, chairman of the National Conference of Soviet Jewry, sent an angry letter to Howard Squadron, president of the American Jewish Congress. He complained that the AJCongress action would be, "seized upon . . . as an opening wedge in a campaign to eliminate the JVA."[7]

Similarly, Stanley Lowell, representing the New York Conference of Soviet Jewry, made a personal plea to representatives of the AJCongress not to take independent action. He reported that he was meeting with Soviet representatives, and that a deal was in the works. It was important, therefore, to maintain a united front until such an arrangement was publicly announced. Even within the AJCongress there were complaints that the leadership lacked the authority to act as it did in coming out in support of loans for the Soviet Union from the Commodity Credit Corporation.[8]

Most painful of all, the AJCongress representatives were continuously reprimanded for seeking concessions for the Soviet Union at a time when "at the very moment," refuseniks such as Anatoly Sharansky, Vladimir Slepak, and Ida Nudel faced trial and severe punishment."[9] I personally received phone calls and visits to my home from recent Soviet émigrés pleading with me not to do anything that might jeopardize the emigration prospects of their relatives and friends left behind in the USSR.

Undeterred, the AJCongress decided to hold to its strategy and to seek accommodation. It returned to Washington on 24 July 1979 for hearings before the Subcommittee on Trade, Investment and Monetary Policy of the Committee on Banking Currency and Housing of the House of Representatives. This time, in light of the increased outflow of Soviet Jews, the AJCongress announced its support for issuing a one-year waiver of the JVA.[10] I went so far as to ask for a three-year waiver. This time, the AJCongress expected that it would not be alone because the National Conference itself, at a spring 1979 meeting, had also decided to support a more flexible policy. At the congressional testimony, however, despite some change in language, the new National Conference position in effect varied only slightly, if at all, from its earlier stand.

Naturally, all of this was viewed as a disappointment, if not a broken promise, by Soviet authorities. To make matters worse, the U.S. Congress did vote to extend MFN status, but to the Chinese and not to the Russians. This decision seemed to be part of Zbigniew Brzezinski's (chief adviser of President Jimmy Carter's National Security Council) strategy. Unlike Secretary of State Cyrus Vance, Brzezinski seemed intent on isolating the Soviets. By providing support for China, whose human rights policies at the time were certainly no better than those of the Soviet Union, and denying it to the Soviets, Brzezinski sought not only to embarrass Vance and his adviser on Soviet matters, Marshall Shulman, but also to tease the Soviets into action on a whole variety of fronts. It was clear that if the Soviets were not going to be cooperative, the United States and China would gang up on the USSR as the United States played its "China card."

Whatever the success of this policy on American-Chinese relations, it sparked a massive setback in American-Soviet relations. Of course, there were issues involved other than the Soviet treatment of Jews. One of the most important was how, if at all, to resolve American-Soviet differences over arms control. Nonetheless, the decision to give MFN status to China and not to Russia was viewed by the Soviets as a clear signal that there was no point in moving to accommodate or seek compromise with the United States. The decision to continue the denial of MFN status may even have removed a major restraint Soviet leaders might have had about their December 1979 invasion of Afghanistan. The possibility of an American boycott of the 1980 Olympics in Moscow also was not enough to deter the Russians. In any case, by the end of 1980, it was clear to the Soviet leadership that there was nothing to be gained by facilitating the emigration of Soviet Jews.

Almost immediately, OVIR, the Soviet immigration agency, stopped issuing visas. During 1983 to 1986, the rate was slashed to pre-1971 levels and effectively curbed the flow of emigration. It was no surprise that American-Soviet relations hit their lowest ebb since the days of Stalin. President Ronald Reagan likened the Soviet Union to an evil empire and joked about dropping nuclear bombs on the Kremlin's men's room. For their part, the Soviets fully expected that the United States would launch a preemptive strike. Through it all, supporters of the JVA refused to acknowledge any need for change. If anything, the increased intransigence of the Soviet Union in Afghanistan, and in Europe over arms control, not to mention the treatment of refuseniks, convinced them that the Soviets could not be trusted, and that a hard-line response was the correct course to pursue.

A retrospective look at the impact of the JVA indicates that within limits and for an initial period, it was highly effective. By extension, the Jewish community deserves enormous credit for lobbying Congress and other human rights groups and for mounting massive demonstrations in support of their cause. It was clear that the American Jewish community was determined that never again would there be a repeat of what happened to the Jews of Germany. It mattered not that the Soviet Union banned all emigrants, not just Jews. They could be and were pressured into making an exception. There was no better proof of the wisdom of such a strategy than that by 1979, more than 50,000 Jews a year were being allowed to leave, and that by mid-1995, more than one million visas had been authorized. This was one of the largest emigrations of the twentieth century.

What this look back ignores, however, is that while tens of thousands of former Soviet Jews owe their exodus to the JVA, there is good reason to believe that if Jewish groups and other supporters of Jackson-Vanik had shown more flexibility, the Soviets would have allowed even more Jews to leave sooner. The JVA was not a tool for all times and all purposes. If the last twenty-five years demonstrate anything, it is that Jewish groups must learn to be flexible. In the case of the JVA, Jewish groups were too rigid and held out too long. It was clear by 1984 that the JVA had become counterproductive and was hurting, not helping, the cause of Soviet Jewry.

Admittedly, it would have been awkward to advocate a policy of better relations and more concessions with and for Russia when its policies warranted just the opposite. But then again, it is conceivable, although certainly not inevitable, that more flexibility shown earlier might have led the Soviet Union down a different international path. There were ample demonstrations that the USSR was prepared to be pragmatic and would have no trouble scrapping its principles so that it might continue to receive flows of financial and other forms of material support from the West.

As useful as the JVA was initially, by the mid-1980s it had become a barrier, in effect a lost opportunity. For those unwilling to acknowledge such a counterintuitive assessment, it is essential to realize that while 260,000 Jews were allowed to emigrate from 1971 to 1986 in what might be termed the fifteen-year heyday of the JVA, it is the period 1987 to 1995 when the real and massive emigration took place. But this change had nothing to do with Jackson-Vanik, which had rejected Mikhail Gorbachev's effort to win acceptance in the West. For that matter, in his first two years in power, emigration remained at a low level. It was Gorbachev's belated perception that the Soviet Union must be accommodating in all respects, not only in arms control but also in human rights, that by late 1987 produced his change in policy. Thus, beginning in 1987 and the eight years that followed, approximately 750,000 Jews, three times as many as in the earlier period, were allowed to leave.

In evaluating the total experience then, it was not the JVA that made the major difference, but Mikhail Gorbachev and his valiant, if imperfect, effort to liberalize the Soviet Union and reshape it into a hybrid democracy. In sum, one cheer for the JVA; two cheers or more for Mikhail Gorbachev, and no cheers for the latter-day efforts of the Jewish community.

Notes

1. Baum, Phil. "Rethinking Jackson-Vanik: A New Approach to Soviet Jewish Immigration?" *Congress Monthly* (June 1976), 8.
2. Ibid.
3. *Jewish Advocate*, 15 June 1978, pp. 1, 15, 23.
4. *New York Times*, 1 June 1986, p. 1. Phil Baum, Marshall Goldman, Henry Rosovsky, "Statement of the American Jewish Congress on Proposals to Alter the Charter of the Commodity Credit Corporation," submitted to the Subcommittee on International Economic Policy and Trade of the House Committee on International Relations, 1 June 1978, p. 6.
5. Phil Baum, Marshall Goldman, Henry Rosovsky, p. 6; Marshall I. Goldman lecture to the Leadership Assembly of the New York Conference on Soviet Jewry, 20 November 1978.
6. Robert O. Freedman, ed., *Soviet Jewry in the 1980s: The Policies of Anti-Semitism and Emigration and the Dynamics of Resettlement* (Durham: Duke University Press, 1989), 224.
7. Letter, Eugene Gold to Howard Squadron, 20 June 1978.

8. Minutes of the executive committee of the American Jewish Congress meetings, 18 June 1978, p. 5.

9. Letter, Eugene Gold to Howard Squadron, 20 June 1978.

10. See letter to Steven L. Neal, chairman of the Subcommittee on Trade, Investment and Monetary Policy of the Committee on Banking, Currency and Housing, from Howard Squadron, president of the American Jewish Congress, 8 August 1979.

From Helsinki
A Salute to Human Rights

Initial leverage offered by the valuable Jackson-Vanik Amendment was inevitably limited in consequence of Moscow's unilateral repudiation in January 1975 of the October 1972 trade agreement between the United States and the USSR. Because that agreement had provided for the granting of MFN (most favored nation) tariff benefits to Moscow, its rejection, for the moment, made moot the applicability of Jackson-Vanik to the Soviet Union. But the gap in applying pressure upon the USSR to permit Jewish emigration would soon be filled by another development in 1975 in which Moscow had the strongest possible interest: the Helsinki Final Act.

The Final Act, signed on 1 August 1975, by thirty-five states of Europe and North America (only Albania refused to participate), offered Soviet Jews as well as dissidents in the USSR and throughout its East European empire an extraordinary banner and forum in which to raise issues of human rights. The American Soviet Jewry movement would now concentrate around the so-called Helsinki process, extending it a very high priority. Augmenting the efforts of the American Jewish movement would be Soviet Jewish activists, as well as a newly created World Conference on Soviet Jewry, coordinated by the Liaison Bureau in Tel Aviv. Virtually no one in a leadership role in the Jewish world had foreseen the potential power and significance of the Helsinki process.

Yet, by 1990, fifteen years after the Final Act was signed, the Helsinki process had become what one perceptive Washington foreign affairs analyst called the "premier post–Cold War political forum." It helped, in a major way, to facilitate a vast exodus of Soviet Jews even as it sparked popular revolutions throughout Eastern Europe that torpedoed the hated symbol of Soviet dominance: the Berlin Wall.

Ironically, the Helsinki Final Act was primarily an outgrowth of Soviet aspirations to freeze the post–World War II borders in Eastern Europe and, thereby, assure its military and political domination of the area. Ever since 1954, Moscow had been pressing for a security conferences—eventually called the Conference on Security and Cooperation in Europe (CSCE)—that would sanction the "inviolability of borders." During three years of negotiations leading up to the Final Act signing in Helsinki, the West, mainly the European democracies, insisted upon a modest human rights quid pro quo. Among the ten fundamental principles to regulate interstate relations (the so-called Decalogue) would be recognition of "human rights and fundamental freedoms." This Principle VII was to constitute a mild form of balance for Moscow's major achievement of "inviolability of borders" in Principle III.

The quid pro quo was extended from the Principles to three major sections of the Final Act, called "Baskets." If Basket 1 focused on security issues, largely a Soviet concern, and Basket 2 dealt with trade matters, also primarily a Moscow aspiration, Basket 3 concentrated upon limited and rather vague "humanitarian" aims. Still, the language here was pregnant with possibilities. Included was a demand that the Helsinki signatories "facilitate" and "expedite" the approval of exit visas for achieving "reunion of families." If Soviet Jews were perceived as aspiring to reunite with families in Israel, a doorway to emigration could be opened. Basket 3 also spoke briefly of religious and cultural rights, along with an easing of contacts and communications between East and West. The phrase "freer movement of peoples and ideas" summed up what Basket 3 meant.

Even as Moscow registered strong support of the Helsinki Final Act (with the understanding—only later disclosed—that it would simply "pigeonhole" and avoid acting upon human rights matters), deep skepticism existed in the United States about its ramifications. Secretary of State Henry Kissinger saw U.S. participation, at best, as only "damage control," to prevent Western Europe from dealing directly with Moscow.

U.S. involvement in the negotiating process leading to the Final Act was negligible. Right-wing and conservative forces in America saw it only as a betrayal of Western democratic interests. Governor Ronald Reagan of California joined Senator Henry Jackson in supporting the *Wall Street Journal* editorial calling upon President Gerald Ford not to go to Helsinki to sign the Final Act. In their shortsightedness, they were echoing the view of the most prominent Soviet exile in America, Aleksandr Solzhenitsyn, who sharply condemned the Helsinki accord.

Soviet Jewish activists saw the Final Act in a very different way. Three weeks after it was signed, Jewish applicants for exit visas to emigrate to Israel appealed to the document and its specific reference to "reunion of families." Helsinki, for them, provided a "legal framework for aliyah" [emigration], as noted by a specialist on international law who served as an adviser to Soviet Jewish activists. The Final Act was perceived by him as a most "useful mechanism." Strikingly, during the balance of 1975 and throughout 1976, more than one-third of the total number of available petitions and appeals sent by activists to the Kremlin or abroad framed their arguments for exit visas in the context of Helsinki.

Even more perceptive about the implications of Helsinki was Yuri Orlov, a prominent Russian physicist and member of the Armenian Academy of Sciences. Already a dissident who had helped organize in 1975 a branch of Amnesty International in Moscow, he saw in the Final Act's Principle VII a potentially powerful lever for change in the USSR. "It was the Soviet government itself that gave us something to work with," he later noted. He was referring to the fact that the government newspaper *Izvestiia* published the entire text of the Final Act in September 1975, so proud was the Kremlin of its achievement. "If the Soviet government said [Helsinki] was important, it was, in fact, important," said Orlov. A chronicler of the dissident movement observed that many of the democrats and activists in the USSR, after reading the Final Act's text in *Izvestiia*, "were stunned by its humanitarian provision."

Working with Orlov to give Helsinki a concrete human rights application to the USSR was Anatoly Sharansky. The latter, a committed Zionist, recognized the ramifications of the "reunion of family" phrase; at the same time, however, he welcomed the broader aspects of Principle VII. Sharansky would help Orlov create a Helsinki monitoring group—the Moscow Helsinki Watch Group—comprising a dozen Russian democrats, including two other Zionists, Vitaly Rubin and Vladimir Slepak. The group formally came into existence in August 1976, and began its preparation of valuable documentation on human rights compliance by Moscow with the Final Act. Details about emigration abridgments of Jewish applicants, along with other Jewish cultural and religious rights abridgments, were included. The first Final Act review conference in Belgrade, Yugoslavia, in 1977–78 received twenty-six documents from the Moscow Group. To the later Madrid conference in 1980–83, it sent a striking 138 documents.

As significant as his contribution to human rights developments in Moscow was Orlov's indirect impact upon the Washington scene. This came about quite accidentally through contact with an extraordinary congresswoman from New Jersey, Millicent Fenwick, who was serving on a delegation of high-level legislators to Moscow in August 1975. Fenwick met with Orlov and was encouraged by him to recognize the potential great value of the Helsinki document. Present at this meeting was a prominent Jewish refusenik-scientist, Veniamin Levich.

More important in affecting Fenwick's thinking was a profound experience with another refusenik, Lilia Roitburd of Odessa. That meeting had been set up by the National Conference of Soviet Jewry, whose officials had briefed the congresswoman before the congressional junket. Roitburd told Fenwick how her husband had been fired from his engineering job and publicly denounced as "an imperialist puppet" simply because he sought an exit visa for himself and his family. Fenwick recalled that she was overwhelmed by the "ravaged face" of the refusenik pleading her family's case. Back in Washington, she told herself: "We've got to do something for Lilia. We've got to do something."

That "something" would fundamentally reshape America's negative perception of Helsinki and help set Washington on a course of using the Final Act for promoting Jewish emigration, as well as other Soviet Jewish rights. In this initiative, the NCSJ would play both openly and behind the scenes a vital, if not decisive, role. Fenwick introduced legislation in September 1975 that was designed to create a U.S. commission comprising mainly congressional members (but with several persons from the executive branch added) that would monitor implementation of Helsinki's human rights provisions by East European governments. Her New Jersey colleague, Senator Clifford Case, introduced similar legislation in the upper chamber.

Although Fenwick's bill had picked up 96 cosponsors, it languished until the end of the year in the House Committee on International Affairs. What was needed, as two leading specialists on international politics—Madeleine Albright and Alfred Friendly, Jr.—noted, was special energy "to breathe fresh life" into the congresswoman's idea. The "resuscitator," in the language of the specialists, was the director of NCSJ's Washington office, Jon Rotenberg. A highly skilled political operative who had served on the staff of Congressman Thomas (Tip) O'Neill, Rotenberg delivered crucial legislative support to activate strong interest in the proposed statute.

Hearings on the Fenwick bill were held in November 1975 by a key subcommittee of the House International Affairs Committee, which was chaired by the powerful veteran congressman from Florida, Dante Fascell. Testimony in favor of the legislation by Jerry Goodman, director of NCSJ, elicited a strong response from Fascell. The NCSJ testimony, he said, "provides the reason for the legislation that is now before us." What that testimony documented was the drop in Jewish emigration from the Soviet Union since 1973. Spelled out was the host of harassments imposed by the Kremlin to intimidate exit-visa applicants, deprive them of jobs, and cast them into a pariah status. Fascell, who would become chairman of the Helsinki Commission once the legislation was enacted, lauded Goodman and the NCSJ for "the excellent work you have done" in creating "a sensitivity and awareness" about the Soviet Jewish problem. The later relations between the Florida congressman and the commission's staff with NCSJ officials would remain close. Indeed, a key staffer of NCSJ, Meg Donovan, who was well versed in all aspects of the Soviet Jewish issue, moved over to the commission staff and became a repository for the flow of NCSJ documentation.

Adoption of the Fenwick-Case legislation did not come quickly. Secretary of State Kissinger regarded it as an intrusion into the domain of the executive branch and bitterly fought it. What clearly concerned him was the certainty of the commission's raising of human rights issues, which he saw as jeopardizing his special relationship with the Soviet Union. He regarded Fenwick as his "tormentor" and charged that she was setting "a dangerous precedent." But support for the legislation in both houses of Congress was overwhelming. Lobbying for the legislation came from the Jewish community, as well as various American ethnic groups—Balts, Poles, Czechs, and Hungarians.

The timing of the vote in the House in May 1976 synchronized almost precisely with the creation of the Helsinki Moscow Watch Group. Fenwick, noting the timing, commented that "they and we are hoping that this international accord will not be just another piece of paper." Kissinger sought to restrict the commission's activity from the very beginning, but to no avail. The commission was off to a fast start, with its initial interest focused upon Soviet Jewish emigration. After Moscow rejected the commission's request for a formal visit, its staff creatively pursued research in Israel. The staff's director said: "The Soviets wouldn't let us in, so we decided to go to Israel and interview the émigrés in the absorption centers."

A long questionnaire was prepared in Russian, asking how many times the emigrant had to apply before being allowed to emigrate; how long he had to wait for approval; how long before he actually left; and what other difficulties he had experienced, such as loss of an apartment or a son drafted into the army. These questions were, of course, central to NCSJ inquiries. Commission staff director Spencer Oliver, with whom NCSJ closely collaborated, brought eight researchers fluent in Russian. What emerged from this imaginative project was a mass of statistical data providing valuable insights into the innumerable obstacles to "reunion of families," even if such reunion was authorized and legitimized by Basket 3 of the Final Act. That the commission would quickly become, with the encouragement of NCSJ, a repository of documentation on emigration violations was certain. Its case list ultimately numbered 3,500, a huge resource of fully documented items.

After the new Democratic administration of Jimmy Carter was installed in late January 1977, a crucial initiative was undertaken by the commission. Former NCSJ staffer Meg Donovan, now in charge of the growing commission case load, recommended to Spencer Oliver that the emigration issue be given a high priority in official U.S. efforts concerning Helsinki. Shortly afterward, the commission's deputy director, Alfred Friendly, Jr., in a memo to Chairman Fascell, contended that the Final Act gave the United States a legitimate basis for inquiring into the status of emigration applications in the USSR and elsewhere in East Europe.

He suggested that the matter be raised with new Secretary of State Cyrus Vance.

The language of the Helsinki Final Act ineluctably posed a problem. Emigration was not mentioned at all. Instead, Basket 3 spoke only of "reunion of families." What the commission staff did was prepare a careful analysis of the act that demonstrated in a most cogent manner that free emigration was clearly implied by the Helsinki drafters. The thesis was incorporated in the commission's 194-page study of the implementation record of the Helsinki signatories issued on 1 August 1977. Moscow-imposed obstacles to Jewish emigration would now become part of the official U.S. reports on implementation without changing the far more restrictive language of the Helsinki accord.

The significance of the Helsinki Commission cannot be underestimated. It was a unique institution in the history of making American foreign policy. No such official legislative-executive body was ever created to serve American international objectives in a major way. And no other Helsinki signatory established an apparatus that even remotely resembled the commission. The delegations of all other signatories were composed exclusively of professional foreign service officers (or, in the case of the Warsaw Pact countries, several high-level security officials). Commission involvement in delegations was extraordinarily extensive. The NCSJ could take considerable pride in helping bring into existence this distinctive contribution to human rights advancement.

The commission's activist orientation on human rights generally meshed neatly with the philosophy of the new U.S. president. Secretary Vance and his deputy, Warren Christopher, gave the commission considerable, though not dominant, authority in the delegations to Helsinki forums. For the organized American Jewish community, with its emphasis placed upon Soviet Jewish emigration, it was an especially welcome development.

Central to the Helsinki process, and perhaps even more important than the banner of the Final Act, was the forum the accord provided. The signatories were to assemble in a "follow-up meeting" to discuss implementation. While only one such meeting was initially spelled out—to be held in Belgrade, Yugoslavia—it established a precedent for continuing meetings. It was at such forums that the Soviet Jewish issue could be publicly aired, along with other human rights violations. Practitioners of these violations might thereby be stigmatized before an international audience.

A fundamental obstacle, however, presented itself. West European governments, anxiously pursuing détente and vigorously urging arms-control agreements, were determined to avoid confrontation with the Soviet superpower and its allies. The public airing of human rights violations was seen as taboo. What reinforced the view of West Europe was the prevailing attitude of the State Department's career officers specializing in

European affairs, who perceived the Helsinki accord as a reflection of détente with the East, and not of confrontation.

The clash of views came to a head in behind-the-scene discussions at Belgrade from October 1977 to March 1978. President Carter chose as chief of the U.S. delegation Ambassador Arthur Goldberg, the former Supreme Court justice who was a strong human rights advocate. Goldberg was, of course, no stranger to Jewish organizational life and its concerns. But when he sought to "name names" and cite specific instances of human rights violations, he incurred determined opposition from America's NATO allies and from his own deputy, a State Department career man, as well as from other career officials serving on the delegation. Helsinki Commission staffers, on the other hand, were his vigorous supporters. Goldberg, even if the only head of a delegation at Belgrade to speak out, courageously cited eight instances of gross and egregious violations of human rights by Moscow and its allies. Included in the citations was the notorious arrest of Anatoly Sharansky on grounds of alleged espionage. While the number of cases Goldberg chose to cite was extraordinarily modest, they nonetheless set a precedent for what would become the United States's and the West's major instrument in responding to the Kremlin's ideological threat and challenge.

Non-governmental organizations (NGOs), including the NCSJ, did not play much of a role at Belgrade. The authoritarian character of the Yugoslav regime was hardly conducive for open demonstrating or lobbying. Besides, the forum character of the Helsinki process was not yet clearly understood. It was at the second "follow-up meeting" in Madrid from November 1980 to September 1983 that NGO advocacy came into its own. The resulting impact would not quickly be forgotten. How Madrid appeared on the opening day of the session was powerfully captured in *Le Monde* with the marvelously descriptive phrase "city of dissidence." The Spanish capital had become a magnet for dissidents and democratic activists from every part of Eastern Europe, along with their human rights champions and advocates in the West. Wives and relatives of Soviet "prisoners of conscience" (like Avital Sharansky) and refuseniks mingled with NGO representatives in rallies, demonstrations, press conferences, and mini-review sessions. Displays and leaflets, films and posters, books and recordings—all produced by NGOs—were everywhere.

NCSJ gave its lobbying a high priority. It helped in a most significant way to prepare a major and detailed document of the plight of Soviet Jews for the World Conference on Soviet Jewry—severe emigration obstacles, religious and cultural discriminatory patterns, and overt anti-Semitic practices in the official media. Copies were made available to every delegation and were distributed at a specially held press conference. Addressing the press conference were the top officials of NCSJ and experts from the key Jewish organizations in the United States and the

West. A reception room was rented by the NCSJ for purposes of lobbying, and its specialists, drawn from the separate organizations that composed it, were asked to stay in Madrid, on a staggered basis, to press every delegation, whether friend or foe. The Union of Councils for Soviet Jewry was also extremely active in Madrid and maintained a full-time office.

Carter's appointee, first as deputy chief of the U.S. delegation and then as chief, was Max Kampelman, who would be reappointed by President Ronald Reagan following the 20 January 1981 inauguration. No one was better schooled and determined on the subject of Communist totalitarianism and its various manifestations, including anti-Semitism, than Kampelman. In contrast, however, to his equally knowledgeable predecessor, Arthur Goldberg, Kampelman was naturally gifted in the art of diplomacy. His persuasiveness won over or neutralized the resistance of Western allies in naming names and citing egregious violations of human rights. During the first six weeks, Ambassador Kampelman and his staff publicly cited in the Madrid sessions sixty-five instances of human-rights violations, including almost all of the major refusenik cases. In the course of the next two years, the U.S. delegation cited an additional 250 cases. What Goldberg had established in a modest manner was now transformed into a potent weapon of what Kampelman called "shaming."

The United States was no longer alone in this endeavor. No doubt encouraged by the lobbying and documentation of NCSJ and the World Conference of Soviet Jewry, nine Western delegations—especially Canada and the United Kingdom—raised various aspects of the Soviet treatment of Jews. One small NATO country—Belgium—took the risk of openly accusing the Kremlin of engaging in anti-Semitism. Of course, stigmatization was enormously enhanced by the technological revolution in the electronic field. In the USSR, as of 1980, there were more than 168 million radios, and radio broadcasts, especially foreign ones, were quite popular. Voice of America and Radio Liberty (even when heavily jammed), along with BBC and Deutsche Welle, carried details of what transpired at the Helsinki forum, whether in Belgrade or Madrid or at later meetings. The "shaming" of the Kremlin's conduct on Jewish emigration, for example, became a source of major embarrassment to the USSR even as it strengthened the morale of the refuseniks.

Similarly, these foreign broadcasters, especially Radio Free Europe, as they carried the news of Helsinki forums to the publics of Eastern Europe outside of the USSR, reinforced the hopes and aspirations of democratic activists. Lech Wałesa, Vaclav Havel, and Yuri Orlov have all spoken glowingly of the impact of the "voices" of the West. A leading Swiss scholar on Communism, Ernst Kux, wrote that "the modern electronic media" were critical in spreading the ideas of the Helsinki accord. He echoed the view of a leading Moscow sociologist who observed in a Soviet newspaper in 1990 that "the information revolution" had a potent effect in revealing "the unseemly aspects of life."

At subsequent Helsinki conferences, whether at Ottawa, Canada, in the summer of 1985 or in Bern, Switzerland, in the spring of 1986, or at the major "follow-up meeting" in Vienna from November 1986 to January 1989, the experience of Madrid was recapitulated. The World Conference on Soviet Jewry prepared and distributed detailed documentation, relying heavily upon the research work of NCSJ. Intensive lobbying was conducted by the professionals of NCSJ and of some of its constituent groups, or by trained lay leaders. Several professionals (and later lay leaders) were even selected as "public members" of the U.S. delegations and, thereby, participated in official activity. Close cooperation with the Helsinki Commission proved most productive. Especially important was the Vienna meeting, which coincided with a significant advance in Mikhail Gorbachev's policy of glasnost and openness. This policy, to a certain extent, as Gorbachev himself acknowledged, had been affected by the Helsinki process. Agreements reached in the latter part of Vienna and incorporated in its concluding document constituted historic breakthroughs in the human rights field generally and in the Soviet Jewish area specifically.

The right to leave a country—free emigration—was now formally assured. Secretary of State George Shultz, keenly interested in ending the refusenik plight and advancing free emigration, authorized Ambassador Warren Zimmermann, his chief of delegation in Vienna, to link the strong Soviet desires for further arms limitations talks and for a human rights conference in Moscow to the USSR's acceptance of a positive commitment on emigration. Also included in the link was the ending of the jamming by the Kremlin of Western broadcasting, and the freeing of all prisoners of conscience in the gulag and mental institutions. A tough U.S. negotiation stance brought a significant fulfillment of these demands.

In addition to providing for the removal of virtually all obstacles to free emigration, the Vienna document elaborated in great detail on how the signatories were to assure cultural and religious rights. This, too, fulfilled the aims of the Soviet Jewry movement. And the end of jamming meant, too, that Tel Aviv's Kol Yisroel could now be heard without much difficulty in the southern reaches of the USSR.

The fulfillment of the early Helsinki aspirations of "freer movement of people" was to have extraordinary, unexpected consequences. While from 1989 through 1995 some 600,000 Soviet Jews would emigrate to Israel, and another 200,000 would go to the United States and several other Western countries, the new right-to-leave principle triggered an even more powerful reaction. Thousands of East Germans vacationing in Hungary in September 1989, several months after the Vienna document was approved, decided to move to West Germany.

Strong objections came from the Honecker regime in East Berlin. It demanded that East German tourists in Hungary be required to return home. This would be in keeping with a bilateral treaty signed by the two Communist governments—Hungary and East Germany. But the authorities in Budapest, sensitive to new liberalizing developments, of which the Helsinki process was a vital expression, told the Honecker regime that international agreements transcended bilateral treaties. It was a clear reference to the Vienna document. The resulting emigration flood of East German residents through Hungary weakened the Honecker government and set in motion popular demonstrations for democratic reforms. The consequence of the vast populist movement was the collapse of the East German regime and the crumbling of the Berlin Wall, that symbol of Soviet authority that had split Europe in two. What Moscow had hoped to achieve with the Helsinki Final Act—the freezing of the status quo and "the inviolability of borders"—was undermined precisely by the Helsinki process itself. During the following several months, democratic revolutions in Czechoslovakia and elsewhere in East Europe, spurred by the Helsinki process with its increasing focus on human rights, swept away Communist rule altogether, except for the Soviet Union itself.

But the Helsinki process was hardly at an end. While the West was still celebrating the triumph of democracy, the British philosopher, Sir Isaiah Berlin, was cautioning that not freedom, but rather nationalism and racism, "are the most powerful movements in the world today." Indeed, freedom had brought in its wake the freedom to hate. Xenophobia, chauvinism, anti-Semitism, and ethnic hostility were to be the unanticipated consequences of the unfolding Helsinki process.

Not that these threats to a stable democratic new order were altogether unnoticed and neglected. At the Copenhagen meeting on the "human dimension" in June 1990, the rising tide of anti-Semitism and anti-Gypsy actions were discussed. Ethnic conflicts in the crazy-quilt nationality pattern of East Europe could not be escaped. One nationality specialist, examining the teaching and propaganda of the various ethnic groups, concluded that "the reservoir of conflicts in Eastern Europe is immense." In his view, the psychological component of ethnicity was certain to take on a distinctly "politico-territorial aspect." Researchers at the Soviet Academy of Sciences' Institute of Geography reached a similar conclusion.

The Copenhagen document sought to cope with the emergent racism in two ways. First, it adopted an unprecedented call to action against various and specific forms of bigotry. Helsinki signatories were called upon to condemn strongly overt hate phenomena; enact or implement legislation against hate; and undertake on an educational level "effective measures . . . to promote understanding and tolerance." Especially was the act of governmental condemnation stressed. Ambassador Kampelman explained that political leaders must use their offices as "bully pulpits." In his view, "vigorous, systematic and public condemnation" of bigotry "by the highest authorities in government" was essential.

Second, Copenhagen provided the most far-reaching international statement on minority rights ever adopted. Members of minorities were to be assured of the right to express and develop their "ethnic, cultural, linguistic or religious identity." Spelled out was the right to use one's mother tongue in schools and institutions, and to maintain contacts with the same minority elsewhere in a state or in other states. Every form of discrimination against ethnic minorities was to be outlawed. Finally, governments were "to take account of the history and culture of minorities" in the educational system, and "promote a climate of mutual respect, understanding, cooperation and solidarity."

NCSJ lobbyists in Copenhagen, together with colleagues in the World Conference on Soviet Jewry, played a decisive role in having the Copenhagen document carry a specific reference to anti-Semitism. It was to be the very first international agreement that specifically required of governments that they condemn anti-Semitism and take actions to combat it. Initially, the reference to anti-Semitism was not advanced by any delegation. Then the Canadian delegation, prompted by the Canadian Jewish constituency of the World Conference on Soviet Jewry, formally proposed this reference, along with those regarding racism and similar forms of bigotry. The chairperson of NCSJ, Shoshana Cardin, sought to convince the American delegation, of which she was a "public member," to support the Canadian initiative. Her efforts at the beginning were not successful, but lobbying back in Washington by the Helsinki Commission brought about a change in the State Department's posture. After that, the U.S. delegation moved into a leadership role to have the specific reference to anti-Semitism incorporated in the Copenhagen document.

At the subsequent summit meeting of CSCE heads of state in Paris in November 1990, the Copenhagen language was included in the adopted Charter for a New Europe. Also adopted in the charter—which was dubbed the new "Magna Carta"—were a host of detailed democratic reforms spelled out at Copenhagen. The Paris charter ratified the historic achievements of the fifteen-year-old Helsinki process. For the Soviet Jewry movement in the United States, it was a moment to relish. The milestone could not but provide enormous gratification for the movement's high-priority objective.

A particularly valuable postscript for the Jewish community was added the following May in Cracow, Poland, at a Helsinki symposium on "Cultural Heritage." Helsinki signatories agreed "to preserve and protect . . . sites of remembrance, including most notably extermination camps, and related archives." The reason for the consensus decision was then made explicit: "Such steps need to be taken in order that those [extermination] experiences may be remembered; may help to teach present and future generations of these events; and thus ensure that they are never repeated."

It was the first time that an international document spoke eloquently about the Holocaust and the urgent need to take educational steps to prevent its reoccurrence. Of Helsinki's humanitarian value, there could be little doubt in the Jewish community.

American Diplomacy, 1985–1989

A few years ago, one of my daughters collected my correspondence with my parents during the years 1938 to 1941 and translated these papers from German into English. Included is the last message from my parents, dated July 1942. It came from Maidan-Tatarski, the so-called Restghetto, which, we now know, was liquidated four months later. The translations are now one family's constant reminder of the experience of millions driven into a cage from which there was no escape.

That personal history was well in my mind when, forty-five years later, it fell to me to help initiate the third major Jewish exodus from the Soviet Union, counting the exodus in the years following the revolution as the first, and the exodus of the 1970s as the second. I wanted to make sure that I would not fail as I had failed in 1939 and 1940, when I tried to extricate my parents from Europe. Here is my eyewitness account of the circumstances that brought about that third exodus, based on my experience as United States assistant secretary of state for human rights and humanitarian affairs.

As I look back at this effort, I note that my experience in representing clients before administrative agencies of the U.S. government turned out to be quite useful. In this case, my clients were the applicants for exit permits, and I was practicing before agencies of the Soviet government, dispensing advice on proper procedures. I took office as assistant secretary on 1 November 1985. By then, the Soviet Jewry movement had been in full swing for fifteen years. Authorized Jewish emigration from the Soviet Union had begun around 1970, had peaked in 1979 at more than 50,000 a year, but then had declined sharply to 1,000 per year in 1983 and 1984. It was at that low level in 1985 as well.

Although I had, for obvious reasons, a deep personal interest in the emigration issue, I want to make clear that in my dialogue with the Soviets, I did nothing other than carry out U.S. policy. Years earlier, the

American Jewish community had succeeded in placing Jewish emigration on the agenda of the U.S. government's dealings with the government of the Soviet Union. If there was ever any doubt as to the commitment of the United States, that doubt was resolved by legislative action when, in December 1974, Congress passed the Trade Act which included the Jackson-Vanik amendment.

To be sure, Jackson-Vanik and Jewish emigration were never the key issues in the relationship between the United States and the Soviet Union. Broad questions of geopolitics were always in the forefront, but Jewish emigration became an essential part of the fabric of relations between the two countries. Thus, the decision in the fall of 1979 to curtail Jewish emigration once again seems to have coincided, more or less, with the decision to invade Afghanistan and realign Soviet policy in Latin America to join Cuban dictator Fidel Castro in his efforts at subversion of established governments.

Then, after years of deep freeze in our relationship, Mikhail Gorbachev took office as general secretary of the Communist Party in March 1985. In the following month, a human rights meeting under the auspices of the Conference on Security and Cooperation in Europe began in Ottawa. Prior to the beginning of the meeting, I decided, as head of the U.S. delegation, to invite the leadership of the Soviet delegation for lunch, so as to determine whether we could make progress on any of our issues, including that of Soviet Jewish emigration. We got nowhere.

Regarding emigration, I was told that there were about 300 Jews who wished to emigrate, but had not been given the opportunity to do so. My answer was that three zeros were missing from that figure, that the number was at least 300,000. When I argued that Jews were discriminated against in education and in employment, my Soviet interlocutors were fully prepared. They told me that Jews constitute seven-tenths of one percent of the population of the Soviet Union, and then I was given the percentages of university students, lawyers, physicians, teachers, and so forth, all of which significantly exceeded seven-tenths of one percent. It was clear that there was, so far, no light at the end of this tunnel.

In November 1985, shortly after I took over as assistant secretary, the first Reagan-Gorbachev summit took place in Geneva. Our delegation to those talks came back quite enthusiastic about the Soviet Union's new leader, who was so clearly cut from a cloth different from his predecessors. There was hope for progress across the board, they believed, including progress on the issue of Jewish emigration. But as we entered 1986 and the months passed, the figures did not change. Jewish emigration remained at a level of 80 to 100 per month, suggesting that the policy of an annual quota of 1,000 was being continued. In February, one of my colleagues in the European Bureau of the State Department told me that he had called in one of the key members of the staff of the Soviet Embassy, and had said to him that there had been a great deal of expectation after Geneva that the Jewish emigration figures would increase, and that the United States would view this as a good sign. The Soviet official had merely stared, offering no comment at all.

A few months later, in the spring of 1986, the Soviets created within the Foreign Ministry a Humanitarian Affairs Administration. The head of that new entity, Yuri Kashlev, came to see me in Washington in the summer of 1986. We talked about various human rights problems. As to emigration, Kashlev told me that the matter was under study, that a new approach was being formulated, but that he could assure me that there would be no special arrangements for Jews. All applicants, irrespective of nationality, would be treated alike.

Many additional months passed before we heard any further news. Then, in November 1986, there was the announcement for which we had been waiting: A new emigration policy was to take effect as of 1 January 1987. The November 1986 release revealed that a new law had, in fact, been adopted by the Soviet Council of Ministers the preceding August. That was, presumably, the law which Kashlev anticipated when he had spoken to me. My colleagues in the European Bureau of the State Department were eager to hail the announcement of the new emigration policy. I insisted, however, that our comment merely welcome the new policy as a small step forward, but emphasize that it did not constitute compliance with the requirements of the Helsinki Final Act. The new law, I pointed out, allowed emigration only for those persons who had so-called first-degree relatives abroad, namely a spouse, parent, child, or sibling; that persons in possession of security-sensitive information would not be allowed to emigrate; and that exit permits would be denied if a prospective emigrant had an obligation to support a person, such as a parent, who remained in the Soviet Union.

Nevertheless, I also recognized that we were about to see some moderate forward movement in the field of emigration. In spite of the statements that had been made to us that there would be no preference for Jews, we noted that a policy that limited emigration to persons who had first-degree relatives living abroad meant, in effect, that only members of those ethnic groups would qualify that had benefited from the emigration policy of the 1970s. That policy had allowed only Jews, Armenians, and ethnic Germans to leave the Soviet Union. Obviously, it was for these three ethnic groups and none other that the door was being opened once again.

I won the bureaucratic fight over the character of our response. The United States's subdued and qualified comment on the announcement of November 1986 set a precedent for our response to the various changes in Soviet emigration policy that took place thereafter. Whenever a change for the better was made, the United States welcomed it, but immediately called attention to the continuing shortfalls. It is my impression that that approach did, in fact, bring about a whole series of changes that resulted, by 1991, in almost free emigration.

Subject to the three limitations cited above, OVIR, the Soviet immigration agency, began to do business under the new rules in January 1987. The notorious Samuil Zivs, vice chairman of the Anti-Zionist Committee, was trotted out to announce that long-term refuseniks would be given an opportunity to leave. We soon discovered that the first-degree relative requirement was interpreted to govern only new applicants. Those who had applications pending that had been filed prior to 1 January 1987 were required merely to produce a new *vyzov* (invitation from a relative abroad) without having to prove the closeness of their relationship to the inviter. And the number of exit permits did begin to climb. In February 1987, some 146 Soviet Jews left the USSR, a greater number than in any month in the preceding four years. The number was soon beyond four hundred per month, and then seemed to reach a plateau of seven hundred per month.

It was now clear to us that the Soviet Union had made a gesture in our direction. We, in turn, made it clear that the gesture was inadequate. At the rate at which exit permits were being issued, the 400,000 persons who, according to Israeli estimates, were interested in leaving would be strung out for up to fifty years. Some obviously would get their permits posthumously.

This first, very modest change in many years in Soviet emigration policy had come against the background of a Soviet decision to engage seriously in arms reduction talks. The discussions on that subject in Geneva were now to be supplemented by talks led by Secretary of State George Shultz and Foreign Minister Eduard Shevardnadze, so that they could move forward more rapidly. A meeting between the two ministers, accompanied by experts, was scheduled to take place in Moscow in April 1987. I suggested that I go along to discuss human rights, and Shultz fully agreed. When we got to Moscow and were ready to talk, Shultz explained to Shevardnadze that I had come along to engage in human rights discussions and urged him to appoint a counterpart. Shevardnadze agreed to do so and designated Deputy Foreign Minister Anatoliy Adamishin. Adamishin was then deputy foreign minister for African affairs, and obviously far removed from the issues which we were to discuss. Shevardnadze had picked him because he trusted him and also because he was viewed as tough, but "civilized."

On this visit, Adamishin and I had our first of what turned out to be many meetings. I laid out my concerns, which included political prisoners, abuse of psychiatry, suppression of religion, and emigration. It soon became clear that I was merely speaking to the notetaker. Adamishin had at this first meeting no real knowledge of any of the issues, nor was he authorized to make any concession on any one of them. When we got to the subject of emigration, which included my presentation of a list of about fifteen persons whose applications had been denied, I was once again told that there now was an orderly system in place for the issuance of exit permits, and that it should be clear that no nationality would be given preference over any other nationality. When we concluded our meeting, Adamishin and I shook hands. He smiled and said, "We shall meet again to continue playing this game." My response was, "This is not a game. It is serious business."

Our delegation had reached Moscow just prior to the beginning of Passover. The commercial attaché at the U.S. Embassy and his wife had organized a seder, to which about forty of the most prominent refuseniks had been invited. For me, it was a fascinating experience to meet the people who bore the names that we had known so well over the years: Slepak, Nudel, Brailovsky, Begun, Meiman, Lerner, Feltsman. Secretary Shultz had an appointment for a discussion on arms control on this first seder evening. But before going to his meeting, he stopped off at the seder. After donning a white kipah, he rose to give a talk. George Shultz is a person not usually given to the expression of emotions. But on this occasion his emotions shone through. He had no prepared text. Facing the group of refuseniks, he told them of his commitment to their cause. He ended with this admonition: "Never give up. Never give up. I can assure you: We are not going to give up."

When we left Moscow, we were given a list of about a dozen refuseniks who had recently received their exit permits. Some of them we had known about prior to our arrival. All in all, we could not point to any great breakthrough on this trip. But, as they say in diplomacy, we had left a marker. It was in the months that followed that we saw the gradual rise in exit permits which I have already mentioned. Nevertheless, the increase in the monthly exit permit figures, which soon reached a level ten times the monthly average for the years 1983 to 1986, was still far too modest. We continued to object to the disqualification of many prospective emigrants. We also complained about requirements intended to discourage applications, such as the requirement to relinquish one's apartment at the time the application was filed.

After some delay, brought about by snags in the arms negotiations, another ministerial meeting was scheduled to take place in Washington in September 1987. I decided that in order to make our dialogue more productive, I should visit Moscow prior to the Washington meeting. So, around 20 August, I traveled to Moscow, where I raised the topic once again in a meeting with Adamishin. He told me that he would not get into a detailed discussion of emigration cases, but that such a discussion would take place at the Foreign Ministry's Division of Consular Affairs.

I moved on to that office, where I began by reviewing the cases of persons interested in emigrating to the United States, but who had been denied exit permits. My Soviet interlocutors looked into their records and gave me a status report of each of the cases. Not all the answers were positive, but it could not be said that they were not responsive. When I had reached the end of the list of prospective emigrants to the United States, I turned to the list of persons who wanted to go to Israel. At that point, the responsiveness of my interlocutors ended. I was told that the case of a citizen of the Soviet Union who wanted to emigrate to a third country was no business of the United States.

It so happened that the very first case on my list of prospective emigrants to Israel was that of Professor Naum Meiman, whose daughter had emigrated to the United States and lived in Colorado. I pointed out that here we had a clear U.S. connection. I was then given a status report on Professor Meiman, who was denied permission to leave the country on the ground that he was in possession of classified information. I called attention to the fact that he had last worked on classified matters thirty-five years earlier, but that did not get me anywhere. After I had received the information about Professor Meiman, my interlocutors closed their books. It soon became clear that there was no point arguing with them. They had their instructions and were following them.

As previously arranged, I then returned to the office of Deputy Foreign Minister Adamishin. He asked me how things had gone. My answer was that they had not gone well at all, that I would report fully to Secretary Shultz, and that Secretary Shultz would be very unhappy with my report. He asked me what the problem was. My response was that the right to leave was a right incorporated in the Universal Declaration of Human Rights, which the Soviets had under the terms of the Helsinki Final Act agreed to respect. As far as we were concerned, I explained, the issue was not whether a particular person wanted to emigrate to the United States (although this was indeed of special importance to us if he had relatives in the United States), but whether the Soviet Union was prepared to abide by the provisions of the agreement that had been signed by Leonid Brezhnev on behalf of his country. Adamishin heard me out politely, but did not respond.

The following morning, a U.S. Embassy officer drove me to Sheremetyovo Airport. As I was about to enter the terminal building, I was greeted cheerfully by a junior Soviet Foreign Ministry official, who insisted on taking my bag, escorting me to the VIP lounge, and helping me get checked in. I still recall his name. It was Oleg Krokhalev. He had an excellent command of the English language. After I had settled down, he brought me a cup of tea and then, without any preliminaries, said: "That list of names which you wanted to discuss at the Foreign Ministry. Please let me have a copy." I reached into my briefcase and handed him the list, consisting of the names of many of the best-known refuseniks: Slepak, Nudel, Brailovsky, Begun. He thanked me. As he decided to stay with me until my plane left, I used the opportunity to reemphasize the importance of action regarding the names on the list. He said he understood.

As I was going to Warsaw rather than back to the United States, I composed a cable to Secretary Shultz, reporting to him on my Moscow experience. I stressed my encounter with Krokhalev at the airport, suggesting that the other side may just have blinked. When I got back to Washington, some of my colleagues who were trained diplomats suggested that as an amateur, I was reading much too much into my encounter with Krokhalev. They pointed out that he was a very low-ranking official. My answer was that just because he was low-ranking, his actions were significant. He would never have done what he did without having received specific instructions. I was convinced that Krokhalev's appearance at the airport was the direct consequence of my warning about George Shultz's unhappiness.

A few weeks later, the Soviet delegation, led by Foreign Minister Shevardnadze, arrived in Washington to continue the arms reduction talks. Significantly, one officer had been brought along to engage in discussion with me concerning human rights. It was Yuri Reshetov, a man who had been present at the meeting at the Consular Division, where I had failed to get a response to my non–U.S.-related names of prospective emigrants. Reshetov had no news for me on specific cases, but he revealed a basic change in the Soviet stance on our dialogue. "We have reconsidered our position on discussing emigration cases with you," he said. "We have decided that if a Soviet citizen wants to separate himself from his motherland and live abroad, his case is no longer a purely domestic case. It is, therefore, a case which we can discuss with you." He had not come with the documents that enabled him to discuss specific cases with me at this time, he explained. He assured me, however, that the next time I was in Moscow, all emigration cases, including those which involved prospective emigrants to Israel, would be discussed with me.

We had a number of other exchanges that also helped lay a foundation for our future human rights dialogue. The handling of human rights matters, Reshetov said, is "black work" for Soviet diplomats. Try to be friendly to them, he advised. Being harsh and critical, seeking to embarrass the diplomats, will not accomplish anything. He also suggested that we see to it that our dialogue on human rights become a two-way street, that both sides could raise human rights issues with the other side.

As to his first point, I told Reshetov that we were well aware of the fact that diplomats acted under instructions. I assured him that if we were treated civilly, we would reciprocate. I also accepted his suggestion for mutuality. It was the right decision to make; as I discovered in due time, the Foreign Ministry was out in front of the rest of the bureaucracy in its willingness to cooperate with us. Its officers had to persuade the officials of other ministries to review the files, furnish documents and, above all, act favorably on the cases we submitted. The task of the Foreign Ministry was eased by the fact that its officials could assure their colleagues from other ministries that they were doing no more than what the Americans were doing to respond to Soviet inquiries, at least when it came to the matter of transmitting documents.

And so, over a period of time, we were handed lists of persons convicted of first-degree murder or planting bombs, where the defendant was a Puerto Rican nationalist or a Black Panther or the member of another politically radical, terrorist group. We would go out of our way to collect copies of the indictment, summaries of the proceedings and judgments, and of opinions rendered on appeal. We would hand the Soviet Foreign Ministry thick folders on the various cases raised, enabling them to say, quite honestly, that our human rights dialogue was not one-sided. Of course, the point we made as we turned over the documents was that murder was murder, even if politically motivated; that we did not incarcerate people for dissenting speech or unauthorized religious activity.

When it came to emigration, to be sure, we were not able to offer a quid pro quo. The Soviet representatives were not able to come up with cases of persons denied the opportunity of leaving the United States. But that did not matter. In its totality, the claim could be made that we were responding to Soviet concerns about our human rights performance.

Following the September 1987 discussion with Reshetov, which laid the groundwork for our subsequent dialogue, I visited Moscow again in October, once again as a member of a delegation consisting mostly of arms controllers. Prior to my visit, there had been an announcement from Moscow. Exit permits were to be granted to a number of the long-term refuseniks whose names had appeared on the list I had handed to Krokhalev at the airport in August. It was against this background that I met with a group of Soviet officials who were clearly instructed to initiate a genuine dialogue, a dialogue that became increasingly cooperative as the months passed. The new head of the Soviet group was Alexei Glukhov, a friendly, soft-spoken person, who increasingly made it clear that he identified himself with the reforms that were being undertaken in the Soviet Union. As I subsequently found out, he was a close friend of Anatoly Adamishin and had been picked by Adamishin for this task because of his personality and outlook.

At this point, in October 1987, we had experienced nine months under the Soviet Union's new emigration policy. Remember that the Soviets had decided at the outset not to apply the first-degree relative requirement retroactively. Persons who had had emigration applications pending would receive a call from the local office, the OVIR, asking whether they wanted to update their application, irrespective of whether they had relatives abroad. On the other hand, new applicants had to furnish an invitation from a close relative living abroad. We assumed that this differentiated treatment reflected a policy to rid the Soviet Union of the long-term refuseniks, who had increasingly become an embarrassment, while trying to discourage new emigration as much as possible. We, therefore, bore down hard in our criticism of the first-degree requirement.

Jewish emigrants from the Soviet Union usually left for Vienna, from where a minority moved on to Israel, while the great majority opted to leave for the United States. The latter group would then be cared for by the Hebrew Immigration Aid Society (HIAS). I stayed in close touch with the HIAS office in New York, so as to get a good picture of the numbers of emigrants from the Soviet Union arriving in Vienna and to get a breakdown of their backgrounds. That is how I found out that while early in the year most of the emigrants arriving in Vienna were long-term refuseniks, by the middle of the year, some new applicants were coming through. And in September, I heard from HIAS for the first time that some of the new applicants had admitted to having falsely stated that their *vyzovs* had come from first-degree relatives and the OVIR had not bothered to ask for proof. A few others had not claimed to have a visa from a first-degree relative and had nevertheless been allowed to leave.

When I asked Glukhov about the *vyzov* policy, he smiled and said: "We are now being flexible." I asked whether this meant that the requirement to furnish a *vyzov* from a first-degree relative would simply be ignored. He shrugged his shoulders and emphasized again that the OVIRs had instructions to be flexible. The impression with which I was left, which was borne out by later data, was that the first-degree relative requirement would be waived for the nationality groups for which the emigration doors were being opened—Jews, Armenians and ethnic Germans—but would remain in place for all others.

The second barrier concerning emigration that we protested was the requirement to append to emigration applications the consent to the emigration of the applicant signed by all first-degree relatives remaining in the Soviet Union. The argument offered in support of this requirement was that every Soviet citizen had an obligation of support to his relatives. I argued that this reading of the law seemed to give the lie to a basic principle of the Communist system, namely that the state would support all persons in need. Here, too, we obtained a modification of the rules: The policy was changed so as not to require the consent of siblings. The consent of parents or spouses, including divorced spouses with minor children, continued to be required. Once the requirement to obtain the consent of siblings was removed, however, the most onerous burden had been lifted. The number of cases about which we continued to argue became relatively small. The typical remaining case was one in which a parent of a non-Jewish spouse, who had objected to the marriage in the first instance, would use this opportunity of retribution.

And then there was the problem of persons in possession of government secrets. We argued, as a matter of principle, that the state did not own any of its citizens and could not deny any citizen the opportunity of leaving. Over and over again, I explained to disbelieving Soviet listeners that the U.S. government could not stand in the way of any person, even nuclear scientists, leaving the country. I argued that that was indeed also the interpretation to be placed on the relevant provisions of international law. But it was clear to me that that argument of principle was not going to get me anywhere. My second line of attack was that many persons denied exit permits on the ground that they had secret information never had had information that was secret, or, if they did, that it was no longer secret or was obsolete. It was the secrecy barrier, involving thousands, that was for a long time the topic taking the most time in my human rights negotiations with the Soviet Foreign Ministry.

As our discussions evolved, it became clear to me that the Foreign Ministry was turning from the role of an adversary into an ally. The officials with whom I was working were clearly under instructions to resolve as many cases as possible to our satisfaction. What they needed was ammunition they could use with other agencies of the Soviet government. Thus, our task became to provide information that would demonstrate that the persons who were being denied exit permits on the ground that they were in possession of secret information did not, in fact, possess such information. What also became clear to me was that if we turned over a long list of names of refuseniks, on all of which we wanted action, we overloaded the system. They would not know where to get started. In light of these considerations, I decided to array my lists of refusals based on secrecy in the order in which the prospective emigrants had terminated their classified work.

I still recall that for quite some time my list was headed by a woman whose name was Irina Varshavskaya. She had quit her work as a secretary in an NKVD office in 1947, when she was thirty-three years old, after she had had a nervous breakdown. Forty-one years later, at age seventy-four, she was still being denied the opportunity of leaving the Soviet Union. Furthermore, it became clear to me that the Foreign Ministry was simply too scared to touch cases in which the decision had been made by the KGB, and the KGB evidently had a flat rule that anyone who ever worked for it or for its predecessor organization would not leave the country. Having found out that she was a mere secretary, I made the point in one of my talks in Moscow that this woman could not possibly be a security risk. I asked, sarcastically, "What are you worried about? Did she work for Lavrenti Beria?" At the next session at which I once again asked about her, one of my Soviet counterparts said: "I've heard it said that she might have worked for Beria." I reminded him that I had been the source and that I had meant it as a joke.

The case finally did get resolved. I recalled seeing a photograph in the *New York Times* of the new head of the Soviet KGB, whose name was Kryuchkov. I recalled that when I had represented the United States on the Human Rights Committee of UNESCO, I had encountered Sergey Kryuchkov, a member of the Soviet delegation who was generally assumed to be the KGB representative, a young man who resembled the person in the photograph I had seen in the *Times*. Therefore, at my next session in Moscow, I inquired about Sergey Kryuchkov. I was told that he happened to be assigned to the delegation that was meeting with us, that he was in the very building in which we were meeting. I asked whether he was related to the new head of the KGB and was told that, indeed, he was his son. When I asked whether I could see him, someone went to look for him.

Before long, I was talking to Sergey, reminiscing about UNESCO and Paris. I then said: "Sergey, there is a matter that I hope you will talk to your father about." And then I laid out the case of Mrs. Varshavskaya, explaining that it makes no sense from the Soviet point of view to deny her permission to leave the country. Sergey shrank back. "I am not with that organization," he said. I explained that I was not suggesting that he was with that organization, but that his father was. I said, "All I am asking you is to talk to your father. I would certainly listen if my son wants to talk to me about a matter of official concern." Sergey said he could not do that and walked away.

My hopes of a quick solution of this case evaporated. But within minutes, Sergey was back with the head of the United States department at the Foreign Ministry, whose name was Obukhov. "This is my boss," he said. "Talk to him about the case." By that time, I had for many months been talking to Obukhov's diplomatic colleagues about the Varshavskaya case and had gotten nowhere. So I repeated my story to him. "We shall see what we can do," he said solemnly. About three weeks later, Mrs. Varshavskaya got her exit permit. I have no doubt that Sergey Kryuchkov had delivered on that one.

Our next comprehensive human rights discussion was scheduled for early December, on the occasion of the Reagan-Gorbachev summit in Washington. The summit was scheduled to start on a Tuesday morning. On the preceding Sunday, 250,000 people participated in a rally in Washington on behalf of Soviet Jewry. A person present at the opening session of the summit talks told me how the talks got under way. After the formalities had been completed and the two leaders had sat down, Reagan turned to Gorbachev and said: "Have you heard about that rally on the mall last Sunday?" Gorbachev responded that he had heard about it and wanted to get on with the business of the meeting. But Reagan did not let him. He started to talk about the size of the turnout, how much the Soviet emigration issue meant to many Americans, and how important it was that the Soviet Union respond positively. As Reagan talked, Gorbachev grew increasingly impatient, but Reagan insisted on completing his presentation. What he made crystal clear was that emigration was an important issue in the relationship between the United States and the Soviet Union.

While the talks got under way at the presidential level, I met with Alexey Glukhov once again to discuss details. On the issue of emigration, we reviewed both policy and specific cases. As the first-degree relative requirement had been viewed, properly, to constitute a sharp limitation on emigration, I pressed Glukhov on the question of "flexibility." Can we assure the interested groups, I asked, that this requirement is simply no longer enforced with regard to certain nationalities? He told me that that was so. I asked whether we can assure the interested groups that this policy will remain in effect from now on. He said we could. This change in the rules was critical in that it expanded the population that was in principle eligible for emigration from a mere fraction of Soviet Jews (and Armenians and ethnic Germans) to all members of that group. Our constant harping on this issue had produced a major breakthrough.

I then discussed what seemed to me to be a quota policy. By the time of our conversation, the number of Jews allowed to leave monthly was slightly more than one thousand. There appeared to be similar quotas for Armenians and ethnic Germans. Glukhov started out by denying, for the record, the existence of quotas. Later, during a break in our talks, I showed him the month-by-month figures for each of the groups. They showed a pattern. For a number of months, the number of departures in each group had been constant. Glukhov admitted that it looked as if a quota was in place. I urged that the processing of applications be speeded up significantly. By the time Mikhail Gorbachev departed Washington, we were reasonably optimistic that the human rights situation in the Soviet Union, generally, would improve, and so would Soviet emigration policy.

We had, over the years, been so used to a monolithic Soviet system that we did not think it possible that one agency, namely the Foreign Ministry, would adopt one line, and another agency would adopt another. We may not have been aware of that fact even a month later, when word came to us from Moscow that applicants for exit permits who could not furnish a *vyzov* from a first-degree relative were once again being turned back. They were told that the waiver of the first-degree relative requirement had been good only for 1987. It had now expired, and the first-degree relative requirement of the law was once again being fully enforced. What I had viewed as a major breakthrough a few weeks earlier had turned out not to be a breakthrough after all.

I was able to deliver my protest personally. Early in February 1988, I attended an international human rights conference in Venice at which I ran into Glukhov. I immediately pulled him aside and reminded him that I had, on his recent visit to Washington, expressly asked him whether the waiver of the first-degree relative requirement would remain in place and that he had assured me it would. Glukhov confirmed that conversation. I then told him that I was truly shocked to hear that the first-degree relative requirement was once again being enforced. I added that we had passed on the assurances we had received to the interested groups. The Soviet Union's backsliding was, therefore, not only substantively wrong, but was also now a significant embarrassment to the U.S. government, which had evidently been misled. Glukhov appeared genuinely surprised. He promised to look into the matter immediately. He pointed out that I was due in Moscow later in the month and promised to have an answer for me by that time.

Later in the month, I was indeed in Moscow. On the Soviet side, my meeting was once again chaired by Anatoly Adamishin. He began the meeting with an apology. The waiver about which I talked to Glukhov, he said, had indeed been a waiver for 1987 only. It was sheer bureaucratic oversight that it had not been renewed at the end of the year. It had now been renewed, we were reassured. I asked whether it was a waiver for 1988 only or a permanent waiver. Though the response was unclear, I was left with the impression that the waiver would remain in effect for good. And it did. Our persistence had paid off.

The human rights dialogue with the Soviet Union which had begun rather tentatively in October 1987 had matured into a routine by February 1988. On emigration matters, the issue now taking most time was that of persons not allowed to leave because of their alleged possession of security-sensitive information. We also pressed the much smaller number of cases of persons with a parent who was denying consent to an application for emigration. And, of course, we were urging a step-up in the processing of cases. As to the latter, we saw movement toward 1,500 exit permits per month for Jews, and then beyond that number. The harassment of exit-permit applicants had stopped.

That the Soviet system was now opening up and allowing many new applicants and a few long-term applicants to leave had a particular depressing effect on those whose cases had been pending for a long time and who were still not allowed to depart. On my visits to Moscow, therefore, I would make it a point of meeting with these long-term refuseniks to assure them that the United States had not forgotten them. Many of them were close to despair. They had been waiting and hoping for the door to open. It had now opened, but not for them. Over and over again, I was told that now that the best-known refuseniks had left, the others were condemned to staying in the Soviet Union forever. Over time, I got to know the names and circumstances of my clients so well that I would not only remember the names, but also the places at which these exit-permit applicants had worked and the year in which they had left the classified work. In my talks with Foreign Ministry officials, I would review the names and the cases over and over again, providing more and more information about reasons for allowing the applicants to leave the country. And the system worked. After every meeting, I had a new list of names of persons to whom exit permits had been granted.

That did not mean that our overall list of refuseniks was shrinking. As the word got out that some refuseniks were being allowed to leave, others, who had given up years ago on keeping their names on refusenik lists or who had never applied, did indeed apply or reapply, were turned down, and then got themselves on our list of refusenik cases. As our work on these cases progressed, we learned more about the procedures followed on the Soviet side in granting exit permits to persons who had been involved in security-sensitive work. In each case, it was the applicant's former workplace that had to grant consent to emigration. At that workplace, the task of clearing an applicant for application usually fell to the security officer. I was told that security officers were members of the KGB. As I would explain to my colleagues in the Soviet Foreign Ministry, there would be a built-in tendency for a security officer to deny an application. First, by depicting his agency as a place in which highly secret work is being done, he enhances the importance of his agency and his own importance. Second, an affirmative decision could subject him to criticism; a negative decision never would. Third, the security officer would at any rate have no sympathy for the applicant, who was a Jew and whom he probably viewed as a traitor to his country.

The pattern we thus saw develop was one in which refuseniks who had clearly never been involved in security-sensitive work and whose denial of an exit permit had been based on subterfuge, were finally allowed to leave. On the other hand, applicants who had truly been involved in military work were turned down, even if their classified work was now either obsolete or in the public domain. One such case was that of Professor Naum Meiman. He had done the mathematical calculations for Andrey Sakharov in the construction of the first Soviet H-bomb. From the 1950s onward, he had not been involved in classified work. However, as the head of the OVIR, Mr. Kuznetsov, told me: "I am not going to let him out of the country so that he can build atom bombs for Israel."

Another case deserving special mention involved a couple whose field of specialization was tropical plant diseases. Not only were they denied the opportunity to leave, but so was their adult son. As I delved into the case, I discovered that the problem lay with the young man's paternal grandmother. Further analysis led me to the conclusion that she might have worked at an institute at which biological warfare research was done. The family assured me that the grandmother had not done such work, but conceded that work of this kind, in violation of international agreements, might have gone on nearby. I decided to present this case directly to Foreign Minister Shevardnadze, driving home the point that a woman's possible, remote relationship to a security concern had resulted in denial of an exit permit to her grandson. As my presentation was translated to Shevardnadze, he shook his head in obvious disbelief. A few weeks later, the young man had his exit permit. His parents followed six months later. And now even the grandmother, who happens to be of ethnic Russian stock, has emigrated.

While our bilateral discussions of human rights continued, the issue of human rights in the Soviet Union was also under discussion at the Vienna meeting of the Conference on Security and Cooperation in Europe. The Vienna meeting started in the fall of 1986. In 1987, the Soviet delegation had announced that it would not object to a number of meetings on human rights between the comprehensive sessions if one such meeting would be held in Moscow. There was no immediate need for the United States to take a stand on that proposal. However, a number of us in the U.S. government got together in the fall of 1987 to spell out some of the conditions we felt were necessary before we could agree to a Moscow human rights meeting. One such condition was the release of all political prisoners. We also intended to insist on substantial progress in bringing the Soviet Union into compliance with international standards in the field of emigration.

As a variety of matters preoccupied the delegates to the Vienna session, the question of the human rights meetings, and particularly the question of a human rights meeting in Moscow, faded into the background. In August 1988, however, the Soviet delegation reminded the participants of the Vienna meeting that the issue of a Moscow human rights meeting was still on the table.

The following month, in early September 1988, the United National Human Rights Center had arranged for a conference to take place in Milan on the subject of international human rights standards. I had been invited to speak at that meeting and had accepted. I then received word that Anatoly Adamishin, who had become a personal friend, had also been invited. To my surprise, I heard that he had accepted. I was, however, less surprised when I then received word that he wanted to be sure to see me in Milan. I suspected that I knew what he wanted to talk about and prepared myself, therefore, to discuss the issue of a human rights meeting in Moscow.

We encountered each other in a lecture hall at the University of Milan. Adamishin, who is fluent in Italian, delivered a ringing endorsement of the human rights cause in that language. He had written it out in longhand. It was indeed a sign of the times that a Soviet diplomat would have the courage to deliver a speech at a public event that he had personally written and that, it would seem, had not even been cleared. I spoke after Adamishin, on the subject of whether human rights constituted a uniquely Western cause.

As soon as the proceedings were over, Adamishin pulled me aside and urged that we go for a walk. We stepped outside, and as we walked around the quadrangle of the University of Milan, we turned to talks about the Moscow human rights meeting, which was the key to the conclusion of the Vienna CSCE talks,which in turn, were the precondition to the initiation of talks regarding conventional forces in Europe. Adamishin was quite direct in his approach. "Let's not haggle as if we were at an Oriental bazaar," he started out. "What will it take to reach agreement?" I was quite candid in my response. I explained to Adamishin that I did not deem the situation hopeless; that I had no doubt that George Shultz was genuinely interested in reaching an agreement; but that while there had been progress in the human rights area, it was not sufficient. I warned, in particular, that the staff of the National Security Council was still quite skeptical and needed clear evidence that the Soviet Union had really turned a corner on the issue of human rights.

For the rest of the day, as we walked along the streets of Milan, we went through all the details of our human rights dialogue: the problem of persons imprisoned for mere speech or for religious practice, abuse of psychiatry, restrictions on emigration, and so forth. Adamishin made a point to me regarding the importance of the Moscow meeting. Gorbachev, he explained, planned to convene a Party Congress in the fall of 1991 at which the cause of perestroika was to be significantly advanced. It would be helpful to hold the congress immediately following a CSCE human rights meeting in Moscow. I told Adamishin that upon my return to Washington, I would deliver a report on his statements, and that I hoped that we would, thereafter, be in touch with each other.

In the fall of 1988, in light of the progress we had made in our Soviet human rights dialogue over the preceding year and a half, and, above all, in light of the institutional changes occurring in the Soviet Union, I, a hard-liner on the issue of Communism, had come around to the view that the Soviet urging for a Moscow human rights meeting should be acceded to. Other hard-liners in the U.S. government remained, however, adamantly opposed. Moreover, some career diplomats who had been soft on the Soviet idea at the outset and whom we hard-liners had tried to hem in, had now gone the other way. Their position became particularly hard after election day. As I soon found out, the reason was that the word had gone out that the incoming Bush administration thought that President Reagan and Secretary Shultz had gone soft on Moscow. Anyone interested in positioning himself for promotion in the new administration was best advised to appear skeptical about changes in the Soviet Union.

The one person who, I was convinced, wanted to bring the CSCE meeting in Vienna to a successful conclusion as long as he was still in office, was George Shultz. Knowing where he stood, I tried to move the process toward a solution that would obtain significant further concessions from the Soviets and would thus allow the United States to support three follow-up human rights meetings, including one in Moscow. That would produce agreement on a final Vienna document. That document would, in turn, permit plans to go forward to call a conference on conventional forces in Europe, which would be a highly significant step toward ending the military confrontation on the Continent. But, as I have just noted, our bureaucracy was no longer interested in following the Shultz lead.

That became particularly evident when, in the middle of November, after the election of George Bush, but before he had taken office, a draft cable appeared on my desk containing instructions to our ambassador in Moscow as to a message which he should deliver to the Soviet Foreign Ministry concerning the Vienna agreement. I read the text and was shocked. It basically closed the door on an agreement in Vienna while the Reagan administration was still in office.

I immediately called the executive secretary of the State Department to tell him that I had just gotten this proposed text, that I was certain that it did not reflect Secretary Shultz's thinking, and that I, therefore, was opposed to having it sent out. The executive secretary told me that I was too late, that this cable had already gone through the entire process, had been approved by the secretary, and had been sent out. I was certain that George Shultz had not had a chance to read the document in detail and to see that it would undermine his efforts. I also suspected that it was no accident that the paper got to my desk when it was too late to stop it from being sent out. I, therefore, asked the executive secretary to schedule me for a meeting with Secretary Shultz as soon as possible. It was Tuesday evening, and a meeting was arranged for me with Shultz on the following Thursday morning.

On Thursday morning I went to see George Shultz. I told him that I thought I knew what his views were on bringing the Vienna CSCE meeting to a satisfactory conclusion, but asked him to restate his thoughts on the subject for me. He then proceeded to tell me what I had indeed understood his position to be, namely, that he believed that it would be in our best interest to bring the Vienna meeting to a close, so as to start the negotiations on conventional forces in Europe, but that there were certain conditions in the human rights area that needed to be met, and that he thought I had been on the right course in spelling out the conditions that the Soviets should fulfill. I then told him that I had indeed thought that that was his point of view and that I had come to see him because instructions had gone out two days earlier under which a message was to be delivered to the Soviet Foreign Ministry that would have the effect of closing the door.

George Shultz was not a person who would be demonstrative in his emotions. He simply sat there quietly, listening to what I had to say. After a pause, I said that I was scheduled to accompany a congressional delegation to Moscow and would be able to deliver a personal message from him to Shevardnadze. He responded immediately, telling me that was indeed what he wanted me to do. He reviewed the items on which he wanted to see the Soviets move, so that I was fully equipped to take action in keeping with his thinking. As he accompanied me to the door, he said, "Tell them that I, too, have problems with my bureaucracy."

It was now Thursday. I was not going to be in Moscow until the following Monday. In the meantime, I was sure, the negative message would have been delivered to the Foreign Ministry. I was concerned that by the time I got to Moscow, an adverse reaction would have crystallized in the Foreign Ministry. The question with which I now had to deal was how to get a message to the Soviet Foreign Ministry to wait for my arrival. If I tried to send the message through U.S. channels, there would undoubtedly be a lot of bureaucratic hand-wringing, and the message would not get there in time. As a result I decided to do something quite unorthodox. I called one of my acquaintances at the Soviet Embassy and told him that I had a message from the secretary of state for Foreign Minister Shevardnadze that I would deliver in Moscow the following Monday, and that before they acted on anything involving the Vienna CSCE meeting, they should hear that message.

I arrived in Moscow on Sunday and went to the Foreign Ministry on Monday morning for a prearranged meeting with Glukhov. In the course of the meeting, I was asked to step outside, where I was greeted by Adamishin. He confirmed that my message had been received and that a meeting had been arranged for me that afternoon with First Deputy Foreign Minister Kovalev, the person holding the number-two position in the Soviet Foreign Ministry.

That afternoon, accompanied by the deputy chief of mission of the U.S. Embassy, I met with Kovalev. I started out by explaining that I had received instructions from Secretary Shultz to discuss the terms on which we could agree to a Moscow human-rights meeting. Kovalev asked when I had received these instructions. I told him that it was the preceding Thursday. He then checked with one of his assistants as to when the embassy had delivered its most recent message on that subject. It turned out that it had been delivered on Wednesday. It was thus clear that my instructions trumped those delivered earlier.

I was somewhat concerned, from a purely U.S. bureaucratic point of view, not to settle in Moscow a matter that should be resolved in Vienna. I, therefore, suggested that our Moscow discussions should be subject to final ratification in Vienna. Kovalev said that that was completely out of the question. He declared that the Soviet Union was prepared to deal with the United States on what he called the sensitive subject before us, but would simply not engage thirty-three other countries in such talks. The discussion he was having with me, he made clear, was to resolve all outstanding issues between us then and there, and was not going to be reviewed elsewhere. Kovalev was so emphatic that I recognized there was no point arguing this issue further. I had climbed out so far on a bureaucratic limb that I might as well climb out further. I simply hoped that my colleague in Vienna, Warren Zimmermann, would forgive me and plunged into the substance of our discussions.

My meeting with Kovalev started at 4:00 P.M. and continued for three hours, until 7:00 P.M., covering every single one of the outstanding human rights questions in detail. The various issues posed by the emigration problem were among the most important topics of our discussion. I laid out our concerns regarding the continuing problem of parental vetoes of an emigration application; the obvious limit on the total number of exit permits issued each month; and, of course, our list of persons denied exit permits on the ground that they were in possession of security-sensitive information. We had, at that time, about five hundred such cases on our list. Including family members, about two thousand persons were affected. Earlier in the day, one Soviet official had indicated to me that perhaps six to ten of these cases could be resolved in short order. I made it clear that that would not be enough, that the number of cases to be resolved would have to be substantial.

Now I was sitting in the office of the first deputy foreign minister of the Soviet Union, and he posed the expected question to me: "When you say 'substantial,' what number do you have in mind?" I figured we had about six weeks left before a decision had to be made as to whether we would reach an agreement in Vienna while the Reagan administration would still be in office. I had the feeling that if I went too high, I would make it impossible for the Foreign Ministry to arrange for the processing of these cases within the time left. Calculating that the bureaucratic system should be able to handle twenty cases per week, I said: "120." My statement was noted. As our meeting concluded, Kovalev indicated to me that he was now off to see Shevardnadze, to whom he would report on our discussion.

The following morning, I joined our congressional delegation for a round of sessions with Soviet officials. At one of these meetings, I was called to the telephone. The message passed on to me was that I was awaited at the Foreign Ministry for a further meeting with Glukhov. I got there as quickly as I could and walked into a room in which Glukhov and his colleagues were waiting. Glukhov smiled broadly and handed me a sheet of paper, identified as Shevardnadze's response to Shultz. It was translated to me. The response was strongly positive on a number of questions I had posed the previous day. Then Glukhov said: "Now let me have the 120 names." With that statement, I knew, the back of our refusenik problem was broken. I previously had told George Shultz that my negotiations were like the operations of a dentist, pulling one tooth or just a few teeth at any one time. Now that the Foreign Ministry had clearly committed itself to a major effort to reduce the refusenik list, a precedent had been set on which we could rely in the future.

Of course, not all the questions at issue between us were resolved in this meeting with Kovalev. For example, while we had agreement for the release of all persons who had been convicted under Article 70, which made it a crime to engage in anti-Soviet agitation and propaganda, we were now raising the question of release of persons who had been convicted under a trumped-up charge of treason, under Article 64. But as for emigration, it was clear that we had reached an understanding that would, in time, go far to take the issue off the table.

The Vienna conference closed, as we had hoped it would, prior to 20 January 1989, and the year 1989 saw emigration figures climbing to new heights. The long-term refusenik cases were being resolved. There were fewer problems of parental denial of consent to emigration. That did not mean that we were now entirely out of business. As it was clear that Jews had the chance to leave the Soviet Union, persons holding jobs in defense industries started resigning from these jobs and would, in due course, apply for exit permits. Some of them really were in possession of fairly recent defense-related information. We, in turn, kept our lists up-to-date and continued to press our cases, meeting after meeting.

While we continued to argue that there should be no restriction whatever on emigration, we continued to help prospective emigrants who contended that their allegedly classified information was no longer a secret. The Soviets had established an appellate process in which decisions were made in individual cases, and we advised all those who came to us with their emigration problem to make full use of this process. If necessary, we put them in touch with the proper personnel in the Soviet bureaucracy. By 1990, it was clear that there were no limits in place on the number of exit permits issued each month and that no case need be deemed hopeless. If one pressed hard enough and long enough, each case could now be resolved. The long struggle had been successfully completed. Those who wanted to leave the Soviet Union were, basically, free to go.

And now to sum up. The Communist system might sooner or later have collapsed. A new regime might sooner or later have introduced democratic freedoms into the Soviet Union. In that context, later rather than sooner, the emigration policy might also have been modified. I don't think there is any doubt, however, that the engagement of the United States in the democratization effort speeded the process and caused the issue of emigration to be placed high on the agenda for bilateral discussions.

What caused the Soviet Union to respond the way it did? My own impression is that, given different agencies involved in the decision-making process, the policy changed quite a number of times. The decision taken in 1986 was to give us about 30,000 to 40,000 long-term refuseniks, but no one who was viewed as a troublemaker. When this did not satisfy the United States, the decision was made to release the troublemakers as well, to allow some new applicants to leave, but to keep the numbers down and, particularly, discourage a brain drain. When this approach, too, did not cause the problem to disappear, the policy was again modified through increasing pressure from the Foreign Ministry on other governmental agencies to move toward acceptance of international standards. This resulted in a hodgepodge of decisions, depending often on how hard the Foreign Ministry's adversary in a particular case would fight against the ministry's advocacy of the granting of an exit permit. Finally, after having spent a number of years merely trying to accommodate the United States, the Soviet leadership decided some time in 1990, as part of the democratization process, to accept the principle of a right to emigration.

Although the strongest pressure for change in Soviet emigration policy came from the American Jewish community and focused on Soviet Jewry, the U.S. government pressed for general changes in emigration policy, of which ethnic Germans and Armenians took advantage as well. However, there was also one ethnically Slav group that wanted to leave: the Pentecostals. We pressed their case as well. It appeared that the KGB came up with an idea of how they could be let out of the country without setting precedents for Slavs in general. The trick was to treat them as if they were Jews. They would have to submit invitations to come to Israel and would have to receive Israeli visas before being allowed to depart.

The Pentecostals created a *vyzov*-manufacturing establishment in Rome. By calling a number and giving the names of members of their family, a *vyzov* could be ordered. Before long, the KGB was giving out the Rome telephone number. As Pentecostals were farmers rather than mathematicians or engineers, they did not run into a refusenik problem once the government had made the basic decision to let them go. They had no secrets, not even the fact that even though they were applying for an exit permit to go to Israel, they had absolutely no intention of migrating there.

As I look back at the four years of effort that opened the Soviet Union to practically free emigration, I have no doubt that this issue would not have risen to the high place it had on the Soviet Union's reform agenda had it not been for the consistent and persistent pressure brought to bear on the Soviets by the government of the United States. Within the U.S. government I believe that the person deserving special thanks and special credit is Secretary of State George Shultz. He had met the relatives of refuseniks and then the refuseniks, and they had all, unquestionably, made a deep impression on him. This quiet, rather reticent person could also, at times, demonstrate his deep feelings. There is no doubt in my mind that the emigration issue was to him an issue of deep moral principle.

When he said to refuseniks in April 1987, "Never give up. Never give up. We will never give up," he meant every word of it. And he followed through. By setting the tone, as he did, he got the State Department to follow through. From the most junior foreign service officer at the embassy in Moscow to the highest levels of the State Department, everyone knew that the emigration issue was important, and that each of us had to do our share in advancing this cause.

One other person should be kept in mind. In Eduard Shevardnadze, we had a Soviet foreign minister who had shaken off the Bolshevik shell and whose core as a decent, honorable human being was now in evidence. He responded to our appeals and thus set a new tone for the Soviet Foreign Ministry. When we read the news from Georgia these days, let us remember that we are all indebted to him, deeply indebted.

III

Harmony and Strife

The "Noshrim" War

Dropping Out

The Hebrew word *neshira* can best be translated as "dropout." The story of the Soviet Jewish *noshrim* (that is, those who elected to drop out) represents in part an ideological conflict over the Zionist idea of aliyah (literally, to "go up"), of settling in Israel, as against opting to be relocated elsewhere in the West according to the notion that free peoples can make choices about their futures. Even the terms used in the debate over this two-decade conflict, including the very concept of *noshrim*, reflect the tenor and level of disagreement, both over policy and with regard to philosophy.

The eighteen-year war over the Soviet Jewish dropouts was actually conducted in two distinct periods. The first "battle" encompassed almost a ten-year period (1971 to 1981), while the second was waged during a briefer time of approximately two years (1987 to 1989). Yet, throughout this entire period, arguments would be formulated, policy meetings would be held, and the Jewish world on both sides of the Atlantic would remain engaged over this matter.

Beyond the "war" itself, this issue raised a profound philosophical debate around two versions of the future of the Jewish people. One reflected the rebirth of a Jewish state and the Zionist dream, bringing all Jews to the promise and prospect of a homeland, while the other envisioned the principles associated with an age where free individuals could make independent choices, allowing them to define their own destinies. American Jewish involvement and reaction reflected the respective institutional and ideological positions of the major players. The primary participants would divide into two basic camps: the Israel advocates and the "freedom of choice" proponents. The former group was composed of American Jews led by Max Fisher, representing the Jewish Agency, who, either through Zionist affiliations or personal passions, felt strongly about the Israel connection. The latter position was championed by Carl Glick of HIAS (Hebrew Immigrant Aid Society), among others.

Out of this conflict would arise two definitions for the Jewish future that would continue to have significant implications over other decisions affecting the Israel-Diaspora connection. Beyond the debate over who is a Jew, the question of whether the corporate Jewish enterprise would support and assist Jews in making national and more significantly personal choices for themselves would be a point of contention. Elie Wiesel, while on a 1965 visit to Moscow during the Simchat Torah festival, would later comment: "Where did they all come from? Who sent them here? How did they know it was to be tonight? Who told them that tens of thousands of boys and girls would gather here to sing and dance and rejoice in the joy of the Torah?"[1] In many ways, these acts of religious expression would serve as the catalyst that would later permit the Jewish communities of the Soviet Union to articulate their Zionist vision.

The seeds of this Israel connection were laid years earlier through such symbolic acts as an Israeli embassy operating in Moscow and the presence of Israeli officials visiting the few remaining centers of Jewish expression, thereby giving rise to the notion of a viable, intact Jewish presence outside of the Soviet Union. The ability of Israel to defeat its Arab enemies, who had received military, economic, and diplomatic support from Moscow, represented a tangible expression of the strength of the Zionist enterprise. These political symbols provided to many Jews a link with both their religious past and their prayers and hopes for a Jewish future. As author Ronald Sanders so eloquently noted, "These, in the metaphor of Jewish tradition, were the sparks of Jewish consciousness waiting to be redeemed."[2] Yet, for many Jews, outside of the reality that one's identity card would define their nationality status as "Jewish," there were no other symbols affirming Jewishness. It was certain, however, that many Russian students or state bureaucrats could not escape the presence of anti-Semitism that time and again would restrict a Jew's potential to excel and advance.

What, then, triggered the Soviet response to permit significant Jewish emigration in 1971? If ideology, security concerns, and political control defined Soviet behavior prior to 1971, then a different set of internal and external factors would reshape the Kremlin's policy choices. Zvi Gitelman, director of the Frankel Center for Judaic Studies at the University of Michigan, pondered these issues: "What made them respond in a different way in the case of the Jewish movement in the West—the linkage of trade and emigration by the U.S. Congress, the external pressure generated by the Soviet Jewry movement in the West?"[3]

Whatever the rationale, the Soviets, according to Gitelman, may have made a serious miscalculation. "Unfamiliar with emigration as a 'snowballing' problem and quite possibly unaware of the depth of alienation . . . , the authorities may have believed that they need only open the gates temporarily, that once they permitted a small number of noisy malcontents to leave, the emigration movement would die" (27). In many ways for the Russians, the idea of emigration was "a concession to reprehensible people, not a legal or natural right" (28). For Moscow, this was a political game, with those involved at each stage being perceived as "pawns." This can best be observed by noting that when emigration was rapidly expanded, as in the case of the SALT treaty process (1979), a correspondingly significant downturn in departures would occur (1980–81) following a series of internal and external events involving the Afghanistan invasion, the U.S. boycott of the 1980 Olympics, and the Reagan presidential victory, framed in part by an anti-Communist rhetoric.

The results of this outmigration of Jews during the 1970s was a natural counterresponse within the Soviet Union to deny educational and career opportunities, especially within the party and government hierarchy, to a people whose loyalty to the society was being directly brought into question. The results would become obvious. "For the more the opportunities are closed, the more potential émigrés are created." The legal devices introduced at various times included the "diploma tax" (1972–73), and complex provisions associated with family unification for first-degree relatives (1980–82). In addition to imposing a wide range of bureaucratic maneuvers to curtail the pace of emigration, the Soviets framed a public relations campaign in which they characterized the émigrés "as naive fools, at best; or traitors and opportunists, at worst" (Gitelman 27).

The data confirmed that prior to 1974, nearly 100 percent of the emigrants entered Israel. By the late 1970s, those numbers would drop significantly, with only one in three choosing the Jewish state over the United States. Gitelman concluded that this change was linked to the "decline in the attractiveness of Israel after the 1973 war, and even more, to the changing make-up of the emigrant population" Gitelman's findings reflected that while Jews from Georgia and central Asia selected Israel as their first choice, Jews from the Russian Republic or the Ukraine opted for the United States. The so-called Asian group were drawn by their more intact Jewish traditional roots to Zion, while those from the heartland of the USSR, second- and third-generation citizens from the Marxist enterprise, were removed emotionally and intellectually from their Jewish origins and accordingly opted for the West. The only Jewish legacy would be the insults and pain of anti-Semitism. "They are 'pushed' from the Soviet Union more than they are 'pulled' by Israel" (Gitelman 90).

The basis of legal emigration was set in this century with the passage of the Universal Declaration of Human Rights (1948). The Helsinki agreements (1975) provided that every person had the right "to leave any country, including his own," in order "to go to any country." For the Soviets, who were original signatories, participation in this accord offered a series of security and trade opportunities with the West. Yet Soviet concern regarding the issue of "dropouts" was linked to several factors, with ideological and economic considerations being primary. As Yakov Rabkin, author of an article on the Soviet Jewry movement, wrote, "Emigration to the United States goes against the fundamental premise of Soviet ideology, that is the superiority of socialism/communism over capitalism."[4]

Family reunification served as the justification of the USSR's emigration policy. "As long as Jews who left the USSR with Israeli visas continued on to Israel, Jewish emigration was in accordance with the accepted principles of family reunification and repatriation. This created no precedent for a claim of free emigration on the part of other national groups who had relations in the United States and Canada," said Rabkin (49).

The economic issues represented a second factor. As more Jews left the Soviet Union, Rabkin writes, the "brain-drain" argument took on greater importance. "Almost 12,000 Soviet Jewish professionals arrived in the United States from 1974 through 1980. One-third of them were in humanities, one-quarter in medicine, and nearly one-fifth in arts and entertainment. Together with the engineers and technicians, they made up half the working immigrants" (50). Soviet reluctance over the dropout issue may have been focused, in part, over their concern that these emigres provided "a source of information or intelligence about Soviet life."[5]

In the second half of 1979, despite significantly higher numbers of émigrés (51,547) than in prior years, the Soviets began to limit the number of new permits. Among the reasons cited by some analysts was the significant increase in the "dropout rate." The Israelis attempted to use this argument as a basis for proposing new procedures designed to discourage those who were opting for North America. However, there appeared to be little reliable evidence that Russian policy was in fact dictated by the *noshrim* situation.[6]

The dropout pattern involved a fairly consistent procedure. Upon their arrival in Vienna, the Soviet emigrants were met at either the airport or train by Jewish Agency representatives, who were there to arrange their temporary accommodations in Vienna before placing them on planes to Israel. As increasing numbers requested to be sent to destinations other than Israel, transportation was arranged by HIAS (Hebrew Immigrant Aid Society) and JDC (American Jewish Joint Distribution Committee) to lodgings, also in Vienna. These "defectors" were brought to HIAS–Joint Viennese offices in order for agency officials to offer one "final appeal." When such efforts failed—and they usually did—these families and individuals were then relocated to Rome.[7]

As early as 1972, a number of Soviet émigrés (251) declared themselves "political refugees," and as a result sought and received asylum in the United States.[8] The basis of U.S. policy in this area was established by Attorney General John Mitchell, who had issued a parole authority "allowing political refugees to come to this country without a specific quota, provided that the sponsoring agency in the United States assumed responsibility for the newcomers."[9]

The Israelis' response, which would set into motion this debate over *noshrim*, was based on two considerations. First, they would argue that Soviet Jews applying for emigration to Israel were in fact not political refugees, and therefore did not qualify for parole status. "The interpretation is that a political refugee is a person who, because of his political views, has no country to go to after he leaves the land where he has been persecuted."[10] The Israeli argument further suggested that Soviet Jews were religiously persecuted, and were not political victims. In addition, Jews from around the world, including the Jews from Russia, were returning to their own land, and Israel had borne the burdens of sponsoring them and providing arrangements for their departure.

"In general, the percentage of dropouts continued to climb, from the beginning of 1980, when it hovered about 55 to 60 percent, until October 1980, when it ballooned to 78 percent," noted Jerry Goodman, then the director of the National Conference on Soviet Jewry. Various rationales for "dropping out" were offered by the Soviet Jews arriving in Vienna. Goodman identified a number of factors that contributed to this phenomenon.[11] First, because there were many mixed marriages among the Soviets, the potential religious issues faced by these couples in Israel represented a specific concern. Second, career opportunities for academicians and certain other professionals were more problematic in an Israeli economy with its limited options. Third, the different social and political cultures of Israel "were often at variance with self-created images or expectations" of the Soviet Jews. And fourth, the economic resources being made available by competing Diaspora Jewish organizations made the prospects of "dropping out" that much more attractive.

As the volume of "dropouts" expanded, the level of tension between Israeli officials and representatives of the American Jewish relief and rescue efforts intensified, and the search for creative solutions accelerated. Each side would offer justifications for its positions on the question of *noshrim*. The proponents of "choice" put forth a set of arguments that encompassed three core positions. First, why should we establish a different standard of expectations or behavior for Soviet Jews than for ourselves? Second, is it not true that if Soviet Jews elect to immigrate to the United States or elsewhere, their options remain open at a later time to make aliyah? And third, if we, the organized Jewish community, failed to welcome and assist those Jews who opted to become "dropouts," would they nonetheless enter the United States, or another Western nation, under either non-Jewish auspices (such as the Tolstoy Foundation) or through Chabad, thereby being further alienated from the mainstream of the Jewish community?

The Israeli case was based on several principles presented as justification for American Jewry, in particular, to cease all or most relief assistance to the Soviet Jews. First, for Israel, the issue of aliyah was paramount to the idea and reality of a Jewish homeland. Second, the use of an Israeli visa with the intent of "dropping out" could jeopardize or even curtail emigration from the Soviet Union. Third, the Israelis always believed that the financial costs of absorption and resettlement elsewhere were significantly greater. Fourth, the Israelis argued that if given an adequate opportunity in Vienna, and later elsewhere (including Rome), they could effectively make the case for aliyah. And fifth, if the Jewish communities in the United States and elsewhere failed to absorb and integrate Soviet Jews effectively, they could be lost forever to the Jewish people.

In 1979, Phil Baum, associate director of the American Jewish Congress, defined the case against the *noshrim* in a 22-page document entitled "Noshrim—the Current Dilemma." Baum presented a methodical argument consisting of eleven distinct principles confirming his position. Acknowledging the emotional context in which this debate was framed, however, he noted: "This is an issue, after all, that not only engages our hottest passions. It is one that also demands our coolest reason."[12]

As one observer recalled, communal activist Max Fisher attempted, on a number of occasions, to persuade the federation system to close down resettlement options for Soviet Jews in this country, thereby in reality giving the prospective "dropouts" no choice but to accept the Israeli invitation. Clearly, this view was preferred in Jerusalem as well by successive prime ministers, whether from Likud or Labor (right-wing and centrist political parties, respectively). Another activist described the intensity of the meetings between the Israelis and their American Jewish counterparts by citing a situation in the early 1970s when then Prime Minister Golda Meir requested that HIAS cease its activities in Vienna. Following her request, it was reported that Max Fisher, turning to his American colleagues, pleaded, "Give Golda what she wants."[13]

The entire Israel operation, outside of the role played by the Jewish Agency, was handled by a little-known office operated out of the prime minister's office. It was identified only as the "office without a name," and Nehemiah Levanon was its primary operative. Controlling the flow of information on the state of Soviet Jewish refuseniks and potential émigrés, this office worked closely over the years with establishment groups in Europe and North America, while at the same time seeking to isolate what the Israelis perceived as counterestablishment elements.

The importance of the Israeli liaison office rested with its access to intelligence on Jewish life in the USSR, and its control over the lists of Jews applying to leave. The office served to blunt efforts elsewhere to direct the political strategy in dealing with advocacy and attempted to ensure that as many Russian Jews as possible opted for Israel. Carl Glick, HIAS president from 1972 to 1979, noted that negotiations over the *noshrim* issue occurred over a number of years without resolution. As Glick described it, the alignment of assorted JDC, CJF, and UJA lay and professional leaders would challenge the HIAS position and its support as manifested in Jewish communities across the country.[14]

During this most critical period of the late 1970s, Theodore E. Mann, then chair of the National Jewish Community Relations Advisory Council, recounted that the Israelis had proposed in 1977 to shut down the HIAS offices in Vienna, thereby denying any direct services to those Jews opting for the United States. This recommendation was opposed by many national Jewish organizations, including the Council of Jewish Federations and NJCRAC (National Jewish Community Relations Advisory Council). Two years later, Mann offered a "compromise suggestion," whereby HIAS would only serve those *noshrim* with first-degree relatives in the United States. The policy would be announced some months in advance of its implementation, so as to prepare the Soviet Jews for such new realities. Mann admitted in a letter to Albert Chernin, executive vice chairman of NJCRAC, that this change in procedure "will produce, at best, only fairly modest changes in the *olim* (Soviet Jews who in fact go to Israel) to *noshrim* ratio."[15] As Mann noted, "I think that the value of the new proposal is largely in its symbolism: It says to Soviet Jews that the Jewish community is not indifferent or neutral about their choice." Acknowledging that the Israelis could refrain from providing affidavits to Jews, Mann contended that Israeli officials "feel as strongly as all of us that the first and foremost obligation is to get Jews out of the Soviet Union."[16]

In 1981 Arieh Dulzin, chairman of the Jewish Agency Executive, warned that "if the competition did not cease, he and his associates would simply decline any longer to turn over the names of arriving Soviet Jews to HIAS and Joint representatives."[17] This threat created even among Israel's friends in the United States a great deal of discomfort, and a counterthreat by American Jewish leaders was issued, warning Dulzin not to proceed on this course.

Following a series of urgent meetings in Jerusalem (December 1981) among the leadership of the Jewish Agency, the Joint, and HIAS, a new formula was introduced. The "Naples Agreement" provided that HIAS and the Joint would offer services to those dropouts with first-degree relatives in the United States, along with Soviet Jews opting for the West. These persons would be moved directly to Naples from Vienna, where for a two-week period, the entire group would be "educated" as to the advantages of the Israel option by representatives assigned by the Jewish Agency.[18] Dulzin believed that this arrangement would, in fact, solve the two primary concerns in Israel: cut the rate of defections and effectively respond to Soviet complaints regarding the misuse of exit visas. At the end of a brief three-month period, however, the HIAS board on 26 April 1982 voted to disengage that agency from this understanding, arguing that the actual numbers of dropouts who changed their destinations "simply did not justify the heartache inflicted on those who were left in limbo" (Sachar, *History*, 461).

It ought to be noted that there were other avenues by which Soviet Jews could immigrate to the United States, involving both Jewish (the Satmar chasidim) and general (the Tolstoy Foundation) relief agencies. For the anti-Zionist Satmar movement, this mission had other ideological purposes, "performing a mitzvah by keeping Jews away from Israel." As Lydia Slovin reported, "The dropouts couldn't care less, of course. By the time they clear out of the Soviet Union and reach Vienna, they've already memorized the address of the good rabbi—the Satmar organization."[19] Israeli official reaction saw the actions of HIAS in part as a conspiracy by the professional elites who "induced the lay boards . . . to veto continuation of the three-month experiment." Dr. Baruch Gur, who served as deputy director to the Liaison Office of the Israel Foreign Ministry, commented that "it represented the decisive triumph of Jewish federation leadership over United Jewish Appeal leadership" (in Sachar, *History*, 462).

The battle over the *noshrim* now shifted to the Third International Conference on Soviet Jewry. The conclave was originally scheduled for Paris, but due to Israeli concerns that such a gathering convened in Europe "would have given the appearance of more universal support for the cause of Soviet Jewry," it was held in Jerusalem in March 1983 (Freedman, "Soviet Jewry," 80–81). Despite a prearranged agreement between the Israelis and leadership of the National Conference on Soviet Jewry that the issue of the "dropouts" would not be raised, in order to ensure Jewish unity, Dulzin did, in fact, raise the matter. What resulted was a highly charged debate that reaffirmed the strong divisions of opinion.

Correspondingly, the Soviets reacted negatively to the conference, and possibly as a countermeasure, established an "anti-Zionist" committee designed to attack the emigration movement and the credibility of the Jewish state. Emigration patterns fell throughout the following eighteen months to their lowest levels in fifteen years. In October 1984, only twenty-nine émigrés were allowed to depart.

In a related development, following Yitzhak Shamir's assuming the office of prime minister in October 1986, he pursued, as had his predecessors, an active effort in seeking to curtail the number of dropouts. In February 1987, for example, during the prime minister's visit to the United States, he sought to gain American government support "to deny refugee status to Soviet Jews" as a means of deterring them from considering the United States as an option (Freedman, "Soviet Jewry," 80–81). Correspondingly, several prominent American Jewish officials interviewed concerning the *noshrim* issue reported that not only did Israeli officials attempt to secure U.S. government intervention to restrict Jewish immigration, but also there was some evidence that certain American Jews may have entertained such a notion.[20]

Peter Golden, author of *Quiet Diplomat*, the biography of Max Fisher, addressed the period of 1988–89, when the number of "dropouts" once again increased substantially. Fisher noted: "We weren't able to get anyone to focus on the situation until January 1989, when the Bush administration came in. Thousands of Soviet Jews were stuck in Rome; it was costing American Jewry $8 per person—over $300,000 a day.[21] As Martin Kraar of CJF confirmed, "We ended up with 35,000 people stacked up in Rome. . . . The Jewish Agency was yelling at the federations, and the federations, upset about the cost of maintaining Rome, were yelling at the Jewish Agency because they weren't in Rome trying to convince people to come to Israel" (in Golden 471).

In response to this emerging crisis, Fisher convened the "No Name Committee," consisting of representatives from the CJF and the National Conference on Soviet Jewry, in order "to talk with the American administration about clearing the Soviet Jews through the bureaucracy" (in Golden 472). Shoshana Cardin, then president of the National Conference on Soviet Jewry, recalled: "The administration offered us 25,000 slots . . . we told them that we needed 40,000 so we could reunify families, and the Jewish community could afford to pay for that number and keep the immigrants from becoming wards of the state. . . . Then we pressed the U.S. government to press the Kremlin to let Soviet Jews apply for exit visas to either America or Israel" (in Golden 472–73). Cardin, commenting on Fisher's pro-Israel perspective on the *noshrim* issue, concluded that "Max was convinced that, first of all, Israel needed the immigrants, while the American Jewish community did not; two, that the Soviet Jews would be lost if they came here, whereas in Israel they would be returned to the Jewish people" (in Golden 473).

Several developments would bring to an end the *noshrim* conflict. First, the Bush administration agreed to extend the refugee slots for Soviet Jews from 25,000 to 40,000. Second, in 1990, the Russians adopted a dual-track system permitting Jews the opportunity to choose between applying for a visa to the United States or Israel. In February 1990, the Council of Jewish Federations convened a special general assembly in Miami Beach, at which time the federated system agreed to undertake a special fund-raising appeal, Operation Exodus, for the specific task of resettling Soviet immigrants in Israel. This $420-million effort was launched one month later (Golden 473).

The *noshrim* issue offered some fascinating insights into the patterns of behavior that have shaped the Israel-American Jewish connection. This would represent the first major issue of conflict in which a broad range of Jewish interests and institutions in both societies would be affected. The entire framework of Jewish organizational life was to be directly or indirectly caught up in this policy conflict, with profound financial and service implications for local as well as national structures.

The debates surrounding the dropout issues created alliance groupings that did not necessarily follow traditional positions. Even within institutional constellations, there were divergent positions. An excellent example can be seen within the Council of Jewish Federations as one compares the views of former CJF executive vice president Carmi Schwartz with those of his successor, Martin Kraar. In addition, a study of CJF's role offers some additional insights into the intensity of the positions and the differing perceptions held by various players.

The debates within the chambers of the Council of Jewish Federations could be seen as a test of that system's capacity to deal with a crisis-management situation. Schwartz commented that in accordance with the council's mandate to preserve institutional consensus, there were no efforts to impose a majority-minority position on the policy outcomes. Contrary to Carl Glick's perception that the freedom of choice option had "95 percent"-level support within the federation and community system, Schwartz believed that the case "for Israel" held the majority ground. He felt that the Chicago federation's leadership on behalf of the *noshrim* proved to be a significant factor in sustaining the policy of choice. Schwartz contended as well that to suggest, as the proponents of choice attempted to do, that this debate was focused around the freedom-of-choice issue represented a "serious delusion" of reality. Soviet Jews, he asserted, did not really have a choice. Certain American Jews and the organizations they represented had arbitrarily created a policy option that may not have had any real standing.[22]

The federation position as framed by Kraar, who assumed the executive vice presidency of CJF in 1989, projected a different version from that of Schwartz: "The position that the majority of us took was that the Soviet Jews were entitled to decide where they wanted to live, but we were not going to rescue them from an oppressive society, bring them into a free one, and then make their first personal decision for them. Nor, once they were in the United States, were we going to allow them to become destitute. Our mandate is to help Jews, and so our services were made available to them" (in Golden 470).

In general, many American Jewish leaders were torn about publicly declaring their positions. As a result, outside of the primary players, few institutions formally weighed in on this controversial matter. The Union of Councils for Soviet Jewry joined the "free-choice" camp, arguing that the human-rights agenda defined this cause. Similarly, the American Jewish Committee, as early as 1976, endorsed the HIAS position based on three premises: (1) that there must be freedom of choice for Jews wishing to leave; (2) that nothing must be done which would threaten to cut off Soviet Jewish emigration; and (3) that Soviet Jews ought to receive assistance in any country for which they receive a visa.

The scope of this absorption and settlement effort, both for Israel and for the American Jewish community, would represent the single largest investment of resources, and the most extensive mobilization of personnel and institutions, since the days following the end of World War II, when the world had to confront the realities of the Nazis' war against the Jews. Clearly, the memories of a people powerless and homeless did evoke a profound sense of responsibility for ensuring the future well-being of Jewish life and culture.

The *noshrim* issue introduced a series of Jewish conflicts over political behavior and practice. First, the ideas of Zionism as played out in the Israel experience were seen in conflict with the democratic consensus models of decision-making found in the American Jewish tradition. Second, the dilemma of achieving a sense of Jewish discipline around policy and practice were also played out. Third, the issue raised definitional questions regarding Jewish "citizenship" and the transnational nature of Jewish authority and action.

The caliber and intensity of the discourse over resettlement reflected the increased levels of Jewish power and influence, the presence of a modern Jewish state, and the perceived political strength of the American Jewish community, with each grouping able to articulate its unique vision for a Jewish future. The conflict over the status of Soviet Jewry exhibited in many respects the renewal of Jewish options and possibilities. The depth of passions that came to be identified with the personalities who participated in this exchange, and the impact of this drama, testified to the distinct philosophical arguments that emerged.

The "war of the *noshrim*" framed two visions regarding the Jewish future, placing the position and role of the Diaspora in a state of tension with the idea of the centrality of the Jewish state. In some measure, this represented a healthy challenge to both parties to ensure that their respective ideas for the Jewish future could be sustained.

Notes

1. Elie Wiesel, *The Jews of Silence: A Personal Report on Soviet Jewry*, trans. from the Hebrew with a historical afterword by Neal Kozodoy (New York: Holt, Rinehart and Winston, 1966), 59.

2. Ronald Sanders, *Shores of Refuge: A Hundred Years of Jewish Emigration* (New York: Henry Holt, 1988), 601.

3. Zvi Gitelman, "Why Are Soviet Jews Choosing America?" *Jewish Spectator* 43 (Fall 1978): 27; hereafter cited in text as Gitelman.

4. Yakov Rabkin, "The Soviet Jewish Revival," *Midstream* (October 1982): 49.

5. John P. Hardt and others, abstract, "Soviet Emigration" (1988): 41–42.

6. Ibid.

7. Howard M. Sachar, *Diaspora: An Inquiry into the Contemporary Jewish World* (New York: Harper and Row, 1985), 460.

8. David Korn, "The New Russian Jewish Immigration to America," *Jewish Digest* (June 1979): 49.

9. Ibid.

10. Ibid.

11. Jerry Goodman, "The Jews in the Soviet Union," in Robert O. Freedman, ed., *Soviet Jewry in the Decisive Decade, 1971–80* (Durham: Duke University Press, 1984).

12. Phil Baum, "Noshrim—the Current Dilemma," manuscript (24 August 1979), 22.

13. Interview with Carl Glick, February 1996.

14. Ibid.

15. Theodore E. Mann's correspondence with Albert Chernin, 19 September 1979.

16. Ibid.

17. Howard Sachar, *A History of the Jews in America* (New York: Vintage Books, 1993), 924; hereafter cited in text as Sachar, *History*.

18. Robert O. Freedman, "Soviet Jewry as a Factor in Soviet-Israeli Relations," in Freedman, ed., *Soviet Jewry in the 1980s: The Politics of Anti-Semitism and Emigration and the Dynamics of Resettlement* (Durham: Duke University Press, 1989), 80–81; hereafter citted in text as Freedman, "Soviet Jewry."

19. Andrew Sklover, "The Noshrim, A Jewish Tragedy," *The American Zionist* 70, no. 1 (Nov.–Dec. 1979): 11–12.

20. Based on a number of interviews with key players, who reported this possibility.

21. Peter Golden, *Quiet Diplomat* (New York: Cornwell Books, 1992), 469; hereafter cited in text as Golden.

22. Based on an interview with Carmi Schwartz, February 1996.

Myrna Shinbaum

Mobilizing America
The National Conference on Soviet Jewry

The American Jewish community made the decision that the stakes were too high for the fate of Soviet Jewry to be left to an ad hoc group. As more and more Jews in the Soviet Union demanded their right to be Jews and join their people in the Jewish state, Soviet leaders, like Pharaoh, became adamant that the Jews would stay and be punished. The leaders imposed severe sentences at the first Leningrad trial on 25 December 1970, against nine Jews who had attempted to steal a plane in order to get to Israel; the sentences imposed death on Mark Dymshitz and Eduard Kuznetsov. A stunned world, mobilized by the Jewish community, issued an outraged outcry. On 31 December, the sentences were commuted to fifteen years under the harshest of conditions.

What was needed was an entity representative of the entire organized Jewish community, staffed by professionals, whose sole mandate would be to advocate on behalf of Soviet Jews, and ultimately win their freedom. Thus, in June 1971, the National Conference of Soviet Jewry (NCSJ) was created. Its founding members were twenty-seven national Jewish organizations including the American Jewish Committee, American Jewish Congress, American Zionist Council, Anti-Defamation League, B'nai B'rith, Conference of Presidents of Major American Jewish Organizations, Hadassah, Jewish Labor Committee, National Jewish Community Relations Advisory Council (NJCRAC), Synagogue Council of America, and the rabbinic and synagogue bodies of the Orthodox, Conservative, and Reform movements. The coalition represented nearly all affiliated Jews, secular and religious alike. It would prove to be a unique coming together with one goal—freedom for Soviet Jewry.

Jewish community leaders believed that with a concerted effort, the problem could be solved in a couple of years. There was never any consideration given to a long-range plan, or to long-range funding. A start-up sum of money was transferred from the ad hoc American Jewish

Conference on Soviet Jewry, administered by NJCRAC. Each organization agreed to pay dues (though many fell short of their commitment), and, through an arrangement made with the Council of Jewish Federations and Welfare Funds (CJF), local federations were to make allocations to the new and presumably temporary organization. Officers were chosen, with Richard Maass serving as the first chairman and a representative board of governors appointed (subsequent chairmen were Stanley H. Lowell, Eugene Gold, Burton Levinson, Theodore R. Mann, Morris B. Abram, and Shoshana Cardin).

In August 1971, the National Conference on Soviet Jewry began its work in a small office suite in midtown Manhattan. Jerry Goodman was named executive director, on loan from the American Jewish Committee, where he was director of the Foreign Affairs Department. Goodman asked me to join him as assistant director. I had worked with him at the AJCommittee and held a degree in Russian Area Studies. He told me the job would be for two years, but could be extended a few more. Our collaboration was to last sixteen years. Joining the staff in the following months were Carol Richman (Savitz), as researcher and writer, and Sheila Woods, a public relations professional.

Our single purpose was to support Soviet Jews in their effort to be reunited with their relatives and the Jewish people in Israel, their historic homeland. Others had attempted to do this through means the organized Jewish community rejected, most notably the Jewish Defense League (JDL) led by the militant Rabbi Meir Kahane. We would not throw bombs or engage in violence or scare tactics.

We would need to mobilize the Jewish community, American public opinion, and the American government. Our first task, therefore, was to embark on an education and information program to make our target audiences aware of the problem. To do so, however, we needed to gather information about Jews inside the Soviet Union. This was no easy task. In 1971, there was minimal telephone and mail contact; travel to the USSR was limited and tightly controlled. We had to rely a great deal on the families of Jewish prisoners and activists living in Israel, as well as journalists and others who were in the USSR and could get information out.

On 29 October 1971, the first issue of NCSJ's *Newsletter on Jews in the Soviet Union* was distributed. It would be the forerunner of many publications issued by the NCSJ, including its newspaper-format *Outlook*, and booklets and monographs on Jewish Prisoners of Conscience and refuseniks. We understood almost immediately that we had to present the human face of Soviet Jewry; that three million Jews in the USSR were an abstract hard to grasp. So we embarked on a campaign to personalize Soviet Jewry—to bring the names and faces, and their stories, to the public.

Our first big test came in August 1972. A Soviet law was passed stipulating that persons with permission would have to repay the state for their education. A sliding scale from a high school degree to a professorship was issued. Many Soviet Jews were highly educated and held advanced degrees. They would have to pay huge sums before they could leave for Israel, being "taxed" for each degree received. The progressive "tax" made the amount due the state astronomical and outside the realm of reality for Soviet Jews. News of the "ransom tax" was received with outrage in the West.

NCSJ began a campaign to pressure the Russians to rescind the tax, enlisting the support of academics, scientists, those in the arts, religious leaders, as well as government officials. The noted author James Michener, having read about the "tax" and the efforts of NCSJ, called us to ask what he could do. We urged him to write about his moral indignation; to let the Russians and the American public know that he was furious with a country he had visited and about which he had written favorably. He came to our office, sat down at a typewriter, rolled up his sleeves, and wrote what was to be an important op-ed in the *New York Times*. It became the impetus for similar pieces appearing in newspapers across the country, penned by scientists and academics on behalf of their Jewish colleagues in the USSR.

Our next step was to bring official U.S. government pressure on the Soviets. After much consultation and discussion on strategy and tactics, the idea of linking Soviet emigration practice to their desire to receive Most Favored Nation trading status was conceived, resulting in the Jackson-Vanik Amendment, born as a direct response to the "ransom tax." While it took more than two years for the amendment to be enacted into law, the campaign surrounding it mobilized the community and the Congress, forcing the Russians to drop the "tax." They never officially rescinded it, but they refrained from implementing it. The issue of Soviet Jewry found a priority place on the government's agenda and in the media, a place it was to hold throughout the 1970s and 1980s.

It quickly became evident that the New York staff alone could not manage the efforts to involve the administration and Congress on behalf of Soviet Jewry. An office was needed in the nation's capital to handle the day-to-day activities; to provide information and solicit supporters. There were now thirty-four national agencies in the conference, and through the NJCRAC and CJF over two hundred Jewish communities. We were their representatives in Washington, just as we were the representatives of Soviet Jews.

Such a thought had not been considered in the initial planning of NCSJ. It was envisioned that the Washington representatives of the member agencies would rotate their services to us, but that didn't work. The agencies' representatives had their own agendas to move forward; Soviet

Jewry was not their first priority. The member agencies, however, were supportive, especially those with offices in Washington, including the AJ-Committee, AJCongress and ADL. They understood the need for an NCSJ Washington office. Only the executive director of the Conference of Presidents, Yehuda Hellman, balked at the idea. He was eventually persuaded by the national agencies, and an agreement was reached that when NCSJ met or communicated with top administration officials—the president, vice president, or secretary of state—the Conference of Presidents would be included.

NCSJ's presence in Washington was vital in securing freedom for individual Soviet Jews and for Soviet Jewry as a whole. The talented professionals who led the NCSJ effort—June Rogul, Jon Rotenberg, Marina Wallach, David Harris, Billy Keyserling and Mark Levin—all contributed in their own way. During their tenure, the Jackson-Vanik amendment was enacted into law; the U.S. Commission on Security and Cooperation in Europe—the Helsinki Commission—was created; the bipartisan Congressional Wives for Soviet Jewry, the first such group of its kind, and the Congressional Coalition for Soviet Jews were formed; hundreds of members of Congress and administration officials were briefed and invited to meet with former Prisoners of Conscience and refuseniks, as well as relatives of those incarcerated or denied permission to leave. Rallies were organized, culminating in 250,000 people rallying on the Mall on 6 December 1986, the largest demonstration to that date.

It was always our belief—and our strategy—that the road to Moscow was through Washington; that the Soviet Jewry issue could only be resolved by government to government intervention. History has shown that strategy was correct. We determined early on that the best way to publicize the plight of Soviet Jews was to personalize it, to present the cases of each Prisoner of Conscience (sometimes referred to as Prisoner of Zion) and individual refuseniks. To get each individual known, we published monographs, marked birthdays and arrest and trial dates via advertisements and posters, held vigils and rallies, created POC bracelets, and brought relatives and former POCs from Israel for speaking tours across the United States. The most well-known relative of a POC was undoubtedly Avital Sharansky, wife of Anatoly, known as Tolia, today Natan and minister of trade in the Netanyahu government.

The most poignant, however, would have to be the mothers of Mark Nashpitz and Boris Tsitlyonok. The two young men had been arrested and tried for a silent protest on behalf of the Leningrad trial prisoners. Their mothers were coming to the United States in hopes of gaining support for their sons. What they didn't know as they flew from Israel was that the sentences had been handed down. It was left to me and Abraham J. Bayer of the NJCRAC to tell them the news: their sons were sentenced to years of exile. It was heartbreaking. Their first instinct was to return to

Israel to be with their families. After crying together, they understood the need for them to criss-cross America on behalf of their sons.

The most unexpected and wonderful event surrounding Prisoners of Conscience occurred on Friday, 27 April 1979. Late in the afternoon, I took a phone call from President Jimmy Carter's national security adviser, Zbigniew Brzezinski. He asked that I get a message to Jerry Goodman. He told me that the United States and the USSR had exchanged prisoners and that "two are yours." I immediately tracked down Jerry, and we learned that of the five Soviet prisoners expecting to land at Kennedy International Airport at any moment were Mark Dymshits and Eduard Kuznetsov, the two Leningrad Trial defendants originally sentenced to death and now serving fifteen years. After nearly nine years in custody, they were taken from their prison cells, put on an Aeroflot airplane and told nothing of what was happening or where they were going. They had no idea where they were, until Brzezinski met them on the tarmac and welcomed them to New York, the United States, and freedom. At this point, the news had just broken that a prisoner exchange had taken place.

Goodman had been meeting with Nehemia Levanon, the man behind the Israeli effort to return Soviet Jews to their homeland. He immediately reached Kuznetsov's wife, Sylva Zalmanson, who herself had been sentenced to ten years at the Leningrad Trial and then released early. Sylva was in London, campaigning for her husband's freedom. She would take the first plane out on Saturday and arrive that afternoon for the reunion with her husband.

The former prisoners were brought to the U.N. Plaza Hotel. They were wide-eyed. In twenty-four hours they went from the Soviet gulag to a luxurious hotel in New York. Escorted by State Department staff, the five men entered the first room, thinking they were all to sleep in one room. They were pleasantly surprised that they would each have their own room. Before meeting them on Saturday, I purchased underwear, shirts, and ties for Kuznetsov and Dymshits and the other released prisoners (dissident Aleksandr Ginsberg, Ukrainian nationalist Valentin Moroz, and Pastor Grigori Vins). Following a press conference, we moved Kuznetsov and Dymshits to another hotel, away from the crush of media, where Sylva and Eduard could have a private reunion. In just two days, we learned much about life in the Soviet gulag. Kuznetsov spoke English, but Dymshits spoke only Russian. He did manage a few words in Hebrew, telling us he studied in the labor camp. Forty-eight hours after being in prison, Mark Dymshits, the pilot who had tried to fly a Soviet plane to Sweden and then on to Israel in 1970, was invited into the cockpit of the El Al plane taking him home to Israel.

What we did for POCs, we did for refuseniks. We urged American Jews to "adopt"—to write, telephone and give support a refusenik family—and we arranged Bar/Bat Mitzvah "twinnings." We encouraged

Jews to travel to the USSR to meet refuseniks personally. In the early 1970s, this was still a difficult undertaking; tourism was minimal, although "exchange" travel was increasing. The Soviets were hungry to meet with Western, and especially American, scientists, doctors, academics, and educators.

My first trip in 1974 was with an educational association. The Soviets showcased schools and institutes for us on a tightly controlled schedule. Nevertheless, I managed to break away to meet refuseniks, despite KGB surveillance. I traveled again in 1977 and 1979 as a member of the American Association of Jewish Book Publishers' delegation to the first and second Moscow International Book Fairs. By then, the authorities identified and exposed me as a "troublemaker." For the next ten years I was denied permission to visit the USSR.

They didn't want me, but they needed hard currency, and tourism seemed the way to get it. NCSJ encouraged Jewish community leaders to travel. We encouraged members of Congress to travel. We encouraged businessmen, attorneys and jurists, city and state officials, religious leaders, and prominent personalities to travel. We prepared them with extensive and intensive briefings and role-playing: from the first encounter with Passport Control and Customs at the airport, to dealing with taxi drivers, hotel staff, tour guides, and the KGB, to departure. We developed a cadre of briefers across the country and conducted "train the briefers" sessions. What began with a few people evolved into a steady flow of "tourists" whose primary goal was to reach out to refuseniks, providing encouragement and support for their struggle to be Jews and to live in Israel.

The State of Israel held primacy, if not public prominence, in the campaign to secure redemption for Soviet Jews. It was Israel that first reached out to Soviet Jews in the years it had diplomatic relations with the USSR (1948–67). Israel planted and nurtured the seeds that grew into the demand of Soviet Jews to be returned to their historic homeland and reunited with their families and their people. Israel was prepared to accept three million Soviet Jews. And Israel recognized the need for a National Conference on Soviet Jewry. Without diplomatic relations with the USSR, Israel turned to the American Jewish community to spearhead the effort for Soviet Jewry. It facilitated our work by providing information garnered from former Soviet Jews lucky enough to have been allowed to leave, and from relatives of POCs and refuseniks.

Israel initiated the First Brussels Conference (1971) and created the World Conference on Soviet Jewry, with representation from Jewish communities in North and South America, Europe, and Australia. Most of the countries developed active Soviet Jewry committees for ongoing advocacy modeled after NCSJ. At each succeeding World Conference (Brussels in 1976, Jerusalem in 1985), more and more Jewish communities were represented. For many Europeans and South Americans, travel to the USSR was easier than for Americans, and their involvement, while not on the scale of ours, was instrumental in the overall campaign. Many emulated the NCSJ as best they could, given their particular governmental situation.

One program unique to America was adopted by some: Congressional Wives for Soviet Jewry. The American women, many who traveled on official business with their husbands decided to engage their counterparts in education and advocacy. This resulted in the International Conference of Parliamentary Spouses for Soviet Jewry, held in Washington, D.C., 2–4 April 1984, with participants from Great Britain, Canada, the Netherlands, and Israel.

A benchmark date for the Soviet Union and for Soviet Jews is 11 March 1985. On that date, Mikhail Sergeevich Gorbachev was elected general secretary of the Communist Party. He and the Soviet Union were placed on a trajectory course that would result in their own demise but freedom for Soviet Jews. But there was a long way to go to get there. What Gorbachev inherited from Yuri Andropov remained in place. Sharansky and Yuli Edelstein and others were languishing in Soviet prisons. While tens of thousands of refuseniks had been allowed to leave, thousands remained, denied permission by a precarious emigration policy. Anti-Semitism was still state-sponsored, and anti-Israel propaganda was prevalent.

Gorbachev was a Communist through and through, but he recognized the need for change in order to make the USSR more competitive in the world marketplace; to bring in much needed hard currency to revitalize the disastrous Soviet economy. His policies of glasnost and perestroika— openness and restructuring—were meant to give the Soviets some breathing room, some choice, some new thinking. Gorbachev never meant them to bring about a fundamental change from Communism to democracy as we know it.

Nonetheless, his policies unleashed the worst in the Soviet Union. Taking the cue that they could speak freely, chauvinists and ultranationalists let loose a vicious anti-Semitism that had been pent up for decades. As Gorbachev slowly acceded to American and Western pressure for an end to Soviet human rights abuses, for freedom for Andrey Sakharov, Anatoly Sharansky, and others jailed or in exile, for an unrestricted emigration policy, for freedom of religion and speech, and for an end to state-sponsored anti-Semitism, the extremists mounted a counterattack. They wanted a return to the past, not a new future. Gorbachev maintained to the West that with openness comes the bad as well as the good. Pamyat and similar anti-Semitic groups were private organizations, uncontrolled by the state. What could he do? He wasn't responsible; he was told what he could do—by Secretary of State George Shultz and by President Ronald Reagan at their three summit meetings. He was told to exhibit leadership, to prosecute those in violation of Soviet law, and to speak out against the ultra-nationalist extremists and anti-Semitism.

As Gorbachev's regime progressed, his enemies were preparing to put an end to it and return the country to hard-line Communism. As we know now, that was short-lived and not meant to be. The trajectory path allowed for no turning back. Communism and the Soviet Union crumbled. Jews were free to leave or free to stay and practice Judaism. By 1988, indeed, it was evident that what the NCSJ had set out to do was mostly accomplished. Emigration from the USSR to Israel was virtually open and constant. The Prisoners of Zion were free. Some long-term refuseniks remained, but their cases would soon be resolved. Communication was open and travel was unfettered—in both directions.

Nothing made this new freedom clearer than a Soviet Jewry meeting held in Jerusalem in November. For the first time, the NCSJ and other advocacy groups took a back seat to Soviet Jews. They no longer needed us to speak for them. They were free and empowered; they spoke for themselves. They either now lived in Israel or were visiting from Moscow and Kiev. Those still in the USSR participated by telephone. By February 1989, the Soviet Jewish community was hosting us at the opening of a Jewish Cultural Center and at the Moscow Choral Synagogue. Even I was granted a visa after a decade of refusal. An era had ended and a new one began.

The return of Soviet Jewry to the Jewish people was a miracle and more. The National Conference on Soviet Jewry was a unique experiment that worked. Like the great American experiment with democracy, we had our ups and downs. There were some who never believed it could work. There were many who wanted it fashioned in their own image. There were those who sought to amend the mandate. There were issues of turf and issues of ownership. Yet NCSJ achieved the goals it set out to achieve precisely because of its makeup. It was the support of the national agencies that proved to be its strength. The Anti-Defamation League undertook to publish material, convene seminars, assist with the Moscow Book Fairs, and publish advertisements for NCSJ and Soviet Jewry. Hadassah and its cadre of volunteers embarked on letter-writing campaigns. The American Jewish Committee involved Christian religious leaders in the cause. The synagogue movements championed Bar/Bat Mitzvah twinnings and brought out their congregants to the rallies for Soviet Jewry.

Untold numbers of Americans—Jews and non-Jews—have had a personal encounter with Soviet Jewry. All were made possible because there was a National Conference on Soviet Jewry; because there was a cadre of dedicated, hard-working professionals and volunteers, driven by the belief that the redemption of Soviet Jewry could be realized. Many have told me we changed their lives profoundly. If that be the case, we accomplished even more than we set out to accomplish.

Advocacy on the Community Level
A Personal Perspective

"We are well aware of the irrational, vicious, and pervasive nature of anti-Semitism. The horror of six million Jews murdered by the Nazis still burns in our memory. We remember, too, that world response (including Jewish response) was feeble and disorganized.

"Today in the Soviet Union, anti-Semitism is deliberately cultivated as an instrument of state policy. The situation of the Soviet Jew is desperate. He is allowed neither to live as a Jew nor to leave; he is made the scapegoat for Soviet economic and political failures. To ameliorate this situation, world concern must be focused on the plight of the Soviet Jew and continued protests made to the leaders of the USSR. It is our responsibility to cry out for justice; it is our task to redeem the captive. We dare not fail again" (from the introduction to A Handbook on Soviet Anti-Semitism [1965], by Dr. Louis Rosenblum, founder of the Cleveland Council on Soviet Anti-Semitism). Within a short time, similar sentiments were expressed in communities throughout the country, and the rallying cry of "Let My People Go" provided grassroots activists around the world with the will to challenge the mighty Soviet empire.

It was a classic David and Goliath battle, with few oddsmakers giving David (Soviet Jews and their community activist allies) a chance. It was probably chutzpah to believe that an organized protest movement could force one of the world's most powerful nations to open its doors to Jewish emigration, but that belief would ultimately be vindicated.

I am one of thousands of people with a similar story in dozens of communities around the United States. My story is representative of American Jews from San Francisco to Philadelphia, Miami to Seattle, who implemented one of the most effective grassroots movements in the history of the Jewish people. This is not a comprehensive piece about the San Francisco campaign for Soviet Jewry nor an analysis of politics outside or inside the movement. It is intended to be a portrait of one community's activities, as seen through the eyes of an activist who was lucky enough to be in the right place at the right time. That time was the aftermath of the 1967 Six-Day War when Soviet Jews, who had previously been described as the "Jews of Silence," began to reveal their Jewish identities publicly and heroically along with their yearning for Israel. Their remarkable courage inspired the campaign for their freedom.

I attended my first Soviet Jewry event on 12 October 1969: a major rally in San Francisco's Sigmund Stern Grove attracting thousands of people, most of whom were hearing for the first time about the plight of Soviet Jews from compelling speakers such as John Rothmann, a college student and brilliant orator, who had recently returned from the Soviet Union. I was a sophomore at the University of California at Berkeley. Before long, I would be alternating between participating in anti-Vietnam protests and pro–Soviet Jewry rallies.

I came to that first rally more interested in the social scene than a social cause about which I knew almost nothing. By chance I met the main organizer, a charismatic man who gave anyone within his line of sight an instant assignment. The late Harold Light's organizing genius was that he did not ask you if you would be willing to help. He told you what you needed to do. My assignment was to make protest signs somehow depicting the rallying cry of the nascent movement, "Let My People Go." Light, founder of the Bay Area Council for Soviet Jews (BACSJ), had rightly assumed that by telling people what needed to be done in an immediate and practical way—and then explaining why later—there would be a warming to the cause. He would become known as argumentative and aggressive by those he challenged for not doing enough; warm, innovative, and a bold leader by the activist corps that surrounded him.

In the decades following San Francisco's first major Soviet Jewry rally, I attended and organized dozens of events, first as a lay activist with BACSJ and later as a professional with the Jewish Community Relations Council (JCRC). My interest in Soviet Jewry was fueled by a sense of anger about the response of the American Jewish community to the Holocaust. I understood that the circumstances for Soviet Jews were completely different from the experience of Holocaust victims—cultural genocide was now the danger, not physical genocide—but what was similar was the extent to which Americans, and particularly American Jews, had the ability to choose between ignoring or facing the reports of what was happening to several million of our people. I was determined that some day I would be able to look my children in the face and say, "I did what I could."

My rationale was but one of many that brought people together in so many cities to fight on behalf of freedom for Soviet Jews. Motivations varied: a determination to prove that the lessons of the Holocaust had been learned, a passion for human rights, fierce anti-communist feelings, a deep commitment to the Jewish commandment and value of *pidyon shvuyim* (redemption of the captives), identifying with Russian Jews because their families came from Russia, and Zionist ideology.

For me, traveling to the Soviet Union to meet the refuseniks was an essential part of solidifying my commitment. The year was 1971. Shaul Osadshey, a fellow Berkeley student, and I spent two weeks in Moscow, Kiev, Lvov, and Odessa meeting with refuseniks. We had been very well briefed by Colin Schindler of the World Union of Jewish Students in London. Twenty-six years later, I remember every encounter as if it were yesterday. In Moscow our primary contact was a red-haired young man named Gavriel Shapiro who vividly described the underground life of Soviet Jewish refuseniks: suspended between the country that would not let them leave, but made their lives miserable, and the country of their dreams that sustained their hope and faith. We also spent an afternoon walking up and down the street outside the Choral Synagogue with refusenik leader Vladimir Slepak, discussing our concerns about the counterproductive role of the Jewish Defense League and the fact that the group's contribution to the movement appeared to be overrated by some Soviet Jews.

In Kiev, we met with a refusenik leader, Boris Krasny, and a group of Jewish activists who had just surfaced after being imprisoned for fifteen days on a hooliganism charge because they organized a memorial service on the thirtieth anniversary of the massacre at Babi Yar, where tens of thousands of Jews were slaughtered over the course of several days in September 1941. And in Odessa, our main contact was Katya Palatnik, a young woman whose sister Raiza was then serving a harsh prison sentence for "anti-Soviet activity." In reality, Raiza was a Jewish activist and a librarian imprisoned for her Jewish and pro-Israel sentiments.

Each of the people we met had a unique and yet similar story, including multiple denials of their request to emigrate to Israel, loss of jobs, children expelled from prominent universities. All were gracious and generous hosts despite the poverty that was often forced upon them. We met a young teenager in Kiev who showed us where he and his friends went to explode firecrackers as part of their dream of fighting in the Israeli army one day. We met a famous writer, Grigory Svirsky, in his home in Moscow, and while there, welcomed the first Israeli delegation since the Six-Day War—a group of cardiac surgeons attending an international conference. Our conversations lasted well into the night. And we met Israel Sivashinsky, a well-known mathematician whose Russian-language mathematics textbook I have on my shelf but cannot comprehend in any language. We also met his daughter, who had been expelled from the Lenin Youth Organization because the family wanted to make aliyah (emigration). I still keep the pin she gave me from the Lenin Youth Organization in a little jewelry box.

We had been briefed to be discreet about our activities. Discretion meant the Soviet secret police, the KGB, would feel less compelled to stop us. The code of conduct was simple: It was up to the refuseniks to determine the level of risk they were prepared to incur, including meeting with foreigners. It was up to us to minimize their risks by not acting stupidly. We noticed the KGB twice: once when we went to Babi Yar, we were followed by five or six well-dressed men with newspapers neatly tucked under their arm, watching our every move. They fit every stereotype. And once, when walking back to our hotel with a refusenik, a car drove alongside us at the same speed as we walked. Our refusenik contact told us that he knew this particular KGB agent because he always followed him; sometimes he even asked the agent for a ride. Retaining a sense of humor was a survival strategy for many refuseniks. Neither time did we exchange words with the agents. They just wanted to let us know they were watching us. It was, on the scale of possibilities, quite benign.

Jewish educational materials came in with us. Letters to the world pleading the refuseniks' case came out with us. Two or three years later, I met many of these refuseniks again, this time in Eretz Yisrael as free people. Traveling to the USSR and suddenly being in the midst of a modern Jewish resistance movement was a life-changing experience. By the time the mass advocacy movement ended, thousands of American Jews had similar dramatic, life-changing experiences meeting Jewish refuseniks. To get the names of refuseniks from one of the local community groups, prospective travelers had to agree to a minimum of four to five hours of briefing prior to their trip. Briefings covered how to carry addresses of refuseniks and contact them once in the USSR; bring in Jewish articles; learn the Cyrillic alphabet; study city maps in advance. In short, the emphasis was on how to minimize risk and maximize opportunity. Travel was a serious commitment. Each briefing in which I participated over the next twenty years—I did many with David Waksberg who became director of the BACSJ after Regina Waldman, Harold Light's long-time associate—had a vicarious effect.

During the school year following Shaul's and my unforgettable trip, I was involved in spreading the word—slide presentations to countless groups about my experiences, two-way weekly phone calls to refuseniks to tell them that they were not alone—sometimes packing my dorm room with friends and neighbors to give their greetings, planning a wide array of public events, collecting Judaica in special synagogue drives to send into the Soviet Union with travelers and even planning my next summer's Soviet Jewry activity.

I had decided that a more systematic approach to travel was necessary, so that when travelers came back, they could help prepare the next group and there would be a constant flow of timely information. It was an idea whose time would come, but it did not run so smoothly at first. I called the program for the summer of 1972 "Have Guts Will Travel," and received modest financial assistance from the BACSJ and the Cleveland Council on Soviet Anti-Semitism. I was twenty-one years old, ready for the ultimate experience of my life, traveling to London with my girlfriend to be based there since travel to and from the USSR was much cheaper than from the United States.

Some unsavory characters in London who presented themselves as secret agents professionally skilled in travel to the USSR entered the picture and did their best to scrap the program. They succeeded only in part. Mainly they succeeded in helping to break up our relationship and scaring a number of people, including myself, with threats of physical violence. To this day I am not certain of whom they worked for, and what they really wanted. At that moment, I learned the hard way that true commitment to a cause involves personal sacrifice.

Three more times during the Soviet Jewry advocacy era I obtained visas to visit the former Soviet Union to meet with refuseniks. But I only went once more. The first time, in September 1983, I was to accompany several U.S. congresspersons, including now U.S. Senator Barbara Boxer of California. The day before we were to depart, a Korean airliner was shot down by the Soviets, killing 269 passengers. The U.S. State Department, unsure of how the U.S. government would respond, asked us not to go. The second time, in 1986, a top-level leadership mission from the Jewish Community Federation in San Francisco was set to go, and I was to accompany them. Two days prior to departure, the horrible nuclear reactor accident in Chernobyl occurred, and, uncertain of the magnitude of the nuclear fallout, the trip was canceled. With trepidation I tried again in June 1989. This time JCRC and BACSJ had organized a group of seven rabbis and seven ministers to participate in an interfaith conference with activists in the Soviet Union on the subject of human rights. "Human Dignity in the Jewish and Christian Traditions" was the thinly veiled title of the conference.

By now, it was the glasnost era, and Soviets who previously carried out the oppressive policies of one Communist regime after another no longer knew what the rules of the game were. None of our luggage was searched; nobody appeared to be followed; we even called refuseniks from our hotel rooms. Our whole group met with several refuseniks in a meeting room at the Leningrad hotel, with drinks arranged between refuseniks and the hotel catering services. Refuseniks joined us on our tour bus after a brief protest by the driver. Our human rights conference was public, held in a government agency conference hall. What an astonishing contrast from the earlier days. The Soviet empire was in the beginning of its death throes, but refuseniks' lives were still turned into hell.

One of the refuseniks whose home Lucie Ramsey, Rabbi Richard Block, and I visited in Moscow was Malka Prilutskaya, a gutsy activist who had demonstrated in public for her family's permission to emigrate. She and her daughters, Masha and Vicka, had been subject to continuous harassment. Within about a year of our trip, they were allowed to leave. I saved the letter I received from her when she arrived in Israel:

> Dear Rabbi, we wish you a happy and kosher Passover from Jerusalem. Do you remember our family in Moscow? At last in the long run, we are in Jerusalem, home. We are so happy here. The country is wonderful. The city is magic and unbelievably beautiful, its ancient holy places, streets, people—warm, hearty and friendly. We love the country more and more every day. We can't help admiring everything around.
>
> We love freedom. . . . Dear rabbi, dear friends, all who helped our family tell everybody that only thanks to all of you, your help, endless tolerance, support, encouragement, love, we managed to escape to emigrate from this awful nightmare called Soviet Russia. We owe you freedom and happiness. God bless all of you.

Interestingly, the most dramatic recollection of the last trip was not in any of the planned meetings with refuseniks but the totally unexpected encounter with our tour guide, Lucy. Lucy, a veteran Intourist guide, met our group without any sense that we were different than any other group of tourists. She proceeded to tell us of the sights we were going to see and appeared to fit the Soviet model of inflexible tour guides.

It turned out that she was not only Jewish, but had strong Jewish feelings she had never allowed to come to the surface for fear of losing her position. Suddenly, by absolute chance, she was guiding a group that included not only seven ministers, but seven rabbis—all of whom were dedicated to meeting with refuseniks and fighting for Soviet Jews. With each passing day, the impact of what we were doing, of our deep conversations with her about Jewish identity, of her sharing feelings which she had suppressed for decades, began to have a profound effect. By the third day, she was bringing her college-age daughter with her to be with us all day as we engaged in nonstop conversation about Judaism, the Jewish people, and Israel. By then, Lucy had figured out that we didn't care at all about sites off to the left and the right side of the bus. When she took us to the station for the late-night train from Moscow to Leningrad, she said a goodbye I will never forget. For twenty minutes she spoke spontaneously from the bus microphone about how this chance encounter had touched her soul and how proud she now felt to be a Jew. She thanked us from the bottom of her heart for changing her life. For years, Lucy had expended energy to shield her Jewish identity. No more.

Travel to meet refuseniks was, in my opinion, the cornerstone of the personal lifeline and the most critical component to the success of sustaining the struggle for Soviet Jews for such a long period of time. Each time community activists met refuseniks in Moscow, Kiev, Leningrad, Odessa, Kishinev, Minsk, Kharkov, Vilna, Riga, and many other cities, it had a multiple effect. The ongoing travel program organized in every major American Jewish community bolstered the spirits of refuseniks, brought Judaica and tangible material items to refusenik families, resulted in bringing out dramatic appeals from Jews (appeals that increased pressure on the Soviet government), led to a vow by those who met refuseniks never to forget their plight, and ensured a constant renewable energy source as travelers inevitably came back ready to assume leadership roles in the activist movement.

If travel were the heart and soul of the community-based Soviet Jewry program, then community educational and advocacy events were the lungs—providing both the voice and the relentless pressure of the movement. Here, communities displayed their unique creativity. In each community, the strategy was based on similar objectives: (1) present a multi-faceted activist approach because we could never be certain which kinds of activities would have the greatest impact on the Soviet government, and (2) direct our protests at the Soviet government, but make certain the U.S. government hears them loudly and clearly because ultimately governmental pressure will provide the greatest leverage.

Key ingredients in the education and advocacy program beyond travel included demonstrations aimed at embarrassing the Soviets, adaptation of Jewish symbols for the cause of Soviet Jewry, visiting Soviet refuseniks, and increasing American governmental pressure on the Soviets. Virtually all activities reflected one or more of these strategies. Whether Soviet government officials were based in the U.S. or came to visit—Soviet scholars, musicians, religious delegations including the state-appointed chief rabbi, hockey players, ballet dancers, or other dignitaries—they were met with protests in every city where Soviet Jewry activity took place. Soviet professors visiting counterparts on campuses, city officials from Moscow and other cities were not to find a moment's rest. Their presence was a moving target to dramatize the plight of Soviet Jewry with dignified and almost always lawful, but visually effective protests. I remember several times when dignitaries visited the Berkeley campus, and a friendly source in the university administration provided the confidential itinerary so we could organize properly—outside lecture halls and outside the president's home. Upon their return home, they no doubt reported to Soviet authorities that Americans everywhere appeared to be greatly concerned about Soviet treatment of the Jews—and once again the Soviet government had to ask itself, was it worth the price.

In the area of demonstrations, San Francisco was truly fortunate. We had a specific target for our protests: a Soviet consulate whose address, 2790 Green Street, was well known to the entire Jewish community. The Soviet consulate was opened at the beginning of the 1970s. (New York has a United Nations mission; Washington has the Soviet Embassy. No other American city had a Soviet government presence.) A large nondescript apartment building set in one of San Francisco's most fashionable residential neighborhoods, it became so frequent a focus of our protests that we kept an address list at the Jewish Community Relations Council office entitled "Green Street Neighbors." That way we could inform the neighbors of upcoming events, explaining that we regretted any inconvenience.

For nearly twenty years, rallies were held on every aspect of Soviet government policy toward the Jews, and in support of numerous individual families. Visiting national Jewish organizations regularly built into their busy convention schedules time for a rally at the consulate, often organized by our local groups. The Soviet government, shaken by the huge crowds and consistent protests right outside their door, regularly complained that the American government was obligated to enforce the "100-foot rule," a federal law forbidding intimidation, harassment or threats directed against consular officials within one hundred feet of their place of work. And we regularly convinced the San Francisco Police Department and other officials that our demonstrations were very respectful, even when they involved thousands of people. As we did not intimidate, harass, or threaten consular officials, the law was not applicable. From 1982 until 1990 a daily vigil was held in front of the consulate; a similar vigil was held in front of the Washington Embassy.

While most of San Francisco's protests took place in front of the Soviet consulate, the entire city was utilized: Union Square, City Hall, the Opera House, even San Francisco Bay. An impressive variety of events included the following: a "Stalin is Alive" protest with a Stalin look-alike in front of City Hall (1973); billboards throughout the city with the words "Help Free Russian Jews: Write Your Congressman"; an Underground Jewish Art Exhibit (1975) featuring the work of twelve Soviet Jewish artists (the works had been secretly smuggled out); an international tribunal focusing on the case of Natan Sharansky (1983); a Helsinki Accords funeral procession in front of the Soviet consulate (1985); a Union Square wedding by proxy featuring BACSJ Executive Director David Waksberg and his wife, Ellen Bob, on behalf of the Tarnopolskys in Moscow (1983); a hunger strike in front of the consulate by a young activist, Reuben Haller, on behalf of the Bogomolny family (1986); two youngsters surprising Soviet dignitaries at the airport with a bouquet of flowers, only for them to discover a "Let My People Go" message attached to the bouquet; an unexpected encounter with a Soviet ship captain when his ship suddenly had "Let My People Go" painted on it in San Francisco Bay (1970); the attempted delivery of a Torah to the Soviet Union by former San Francisco Mayor George Christopher (1971); and a BACSJ picket line outside I. Magnin's Department Store in Union Square to protest the sale of Russian furs (1973).

A particular challenge was the frequent appearance of major Soviet cultural groups in San Francisco. In these settings, several thousand local attendees generally paid to see the performance. We needed a method to raise the issue without antagonizing the audience. While a "Let My People Go" banner was occasionally unfurled at a large sporting event involving a Soviet team, the San Francisco cultural audience required a different, more dignified, approach. Typically, demonstrators dressed up as ushers would stand as close to the auditorium doors as possible and hand out glossy-looking programs. The cover would read, for example, "The Bolshoi Ballet. We agree it's worth waiting a few minutes for this Soviet event." The name was changed to fit the billing. Inside, the text would read, "But some people have been waiting years for another. That event would be an exit visa from the Soviet Union, where nearly 400,000 Jews have been waiting, some for more than 15 years, for their freedom. . . . It is one thing to wait in line for a cultural event. But one should not have to wait in line for freedom." A list would follow of the longest waiting families. On the back was a postcard to be sent to the Soviet president.

In August 1987, the BACSJ and JCRC organized an alternative cultural event outside the auditorium where the Bolshoi Ballet would be performing. The *San Francisco Examiner* headline the next day read, "Rally for Soviet Jews at Bolshoi Opening Draws Supportive Audience." The article started, "The sold-out Bolshoi Ballet at the War Memorial Opera House shared center stage Tuesday night with a performance staged by more than 100 demonstrators calling on the Soviet Union to allow Jews to leave that country. The rally, accentuated by its poetry and musical performances, was intended to be an alternative cultural event to the ballet." One of the performers was Opera House violinist Leo Igudesman who left the Soviet Union in 1978, but whose sister and mother were still there. As soon as he finished performing for us in his tuxedo, he ran inside with his violin to play for the ballet.

In August 1989, we finally changed tactics. We issued a press release in advance of the Kirov Ballet with the astonishing headline, "No Soviet Jewry Protest During Kirov Ballet Performances." The decision was based on recent improvements under glasnost in the areas of emigration and cultural expression. In place of the usual handouts, JCRC and BACSJ paid for a large advertisement in the ballet program.

The most ambitious demonstrations were probably the annual Simchat Torah rallies and street fairs, when we closed Green Street and drew thousands of people to express solidarity with Soviet Jews. Typically, the rally began with a procession of rabbis carrying Torah scrolls down the steep San Francisco hill facing the crowd. On the day of our Simchat Torah rallies I would typically arrive by 8:00 A.M., before the 22-foot flatbed truck that served as our stage made its noisy way down the street and stopped in front of the consulate. Before our set-up crew arrived, I would invariably see the Soviet diplomats and their families board the bus for an annual sports day or similar outing aimed at taking consular officials out of earshot for the day. Even behind the darkened windows of the consulate, we could see one or two individuals peeking out, assuring us that our message was, in fact, being heard and seen.

The last three years of the Simchat Torah rallies provided a remarkable glimpse into the changes in the USSR. In 1986, the rally culminated, as it had every previous year, with a delegation of three people walking to the front door of the Soviet consulate bearing thousands of signatures calling on the Soviet government to open the doors. And, as had always been the case, when the delegation rang the front door, no one answered, and they left the petitions under the gate on the doorstep. One year later, the ceremonial delegation, along with the entire crowd, watched in shock as the door opened and the delegation was invited inside the consulate. Inside, JCRC leader Michael Jacobs, carrying his young daughter; BACSJ president Sheldon Wolfe; and another BACSJ activist were berated by the Soviet consul for the anti-Soviet behavior of the crowd. That rally was even covered by the Soviet Union's news agency, which began its report as follows: "A noisy Zionist gathering was held outside the USSR's Consulate General here on Sunday," and proceeded to criticize American officials for permitting the demonstration. And the next year, 1988, the delegation was let in, presented its petitions, and was told by the Soviet consul, "We know your rally is not anti-Soviet, but rather pro-Soviet Jews. We will convey your concerns to our government." Times had changed on Green Street.

One year later, in 1989, plans were in place for one last Simchat Torah rally. A major earthquake two weeks prior to the event resulted in tremendous damage not far from the consulate. We decided to cancel our rally so that city officials and neighbors were not distracted from their cleanup work. That was the last major Soviet Jewry event ever planned in front of the consulate (although during the coup attempt in August 1991, the BACSJ organized, in coalition with other groups, a major pro-democracy demonstration there). It is remarkable that of all the demonstrations I attended and helped organize in front of the consulate, only a handful received less than adequate press coverage. That the press did not lose interest over twenty years is remarkable, particularly given the peaceful, even tame by some standards, nature of our demonstrations.

In the last years prior to the collapse of the Soviet Union, the national Jewish community organized an event that like the Jackson-Vanik amendment (discussed below), became a defining moment for the movement. On Sunday, 6 December 1987, the eve of Soviet President Mikhail Gorbachev's visit to Washington, D.C., a march and rally for Soviet Jews were planned on the Capitol Mall. The hope was that Gorbachev would get the message. There can be little doubt that he did. Some 250,000 people, in a dramatic outpouring of solidarity, gathered on that clear and brisk day.

Indeed, the turnout was testimony to the role of the communities in the Soviet Jewry movement, and to the leadership of Al Chernin and Abraham Bayer of the National Jewish Community Relations Advisory Council, who played key roles in making the event happen. While San Francisco's delegation was by no means one of the largest, 130 people flew to Washington on the red-eye flight and returned the next night after an exhilarating experience. Back in San Francisco, despite a torrential rainstorm, more than five hundred people gathered for a simultaneous event.

Of all the rallies I helped organize, one stands out as the most memorable. On 1 February 1987, approximately a year after Natan Sharansky was released from a Soviet prison, he paid a visit to San Francisco to thank the BACSJ and the local community for their support. The BACSJ and JCRC organized a rally in his honor on Green Street. Prior to the rally he attended a reception in a friendly home directly across the street from the consulate. At the appointed time, Sharansky left the home and made his way, serpentine style, through the throng of several thousand people, onto the stage directly next to the Soviet consulate.

He spoke eloquently. The song "I am leaving Mother Russia" was played. All of San Francisco officialdom was there. The *San Francisco Chronicle* article began with the words, "In the cool shadow of the shuttered and silent Soviet consulate, Natan Sharansky glowed with righteous exuberance yesterday and sang a song of freedom with other San Francisco protesters." The news report continued, "We gathered here so often to protest for his freedom," said Meyer Rosen, a man in his sixties and quite close to tears. "And now he is here, helping us to protest for the others. Such a day."

One of the main strategies for keeping the issue of Soviet Jewry alive was the adaptation of Jewish and other symbols. Postage seals reading, "Protest oppression of Soviet Jews," originating in Cleveland, ultimately adorned millions of envelopes. Communities sold thousands of "Prisoner of Zion" bracelets with the names of those Soviet Jews in the gulag at the time. In Washington, huge signs were placed outside every synagogue and major Jewish institution with the theme, "Let My People Go."

A description of the use of Jewish symbols from the Detroit Jewish Community Council is representative of the approach taken throughout the country in connecting Soviet Jewry with Jewish holiday themes on a repeated basis:

We blanketed the community with dramatic ways to tie holiday observance to awareness of Soviet Jews. Examples: Rosh Hashanah cards were distributed to the community with address labels provided. Bookmarks were printed with a bio; picture and address on one side, and ways to get involved on the other. These were in the pews of all the congregations on Yom Kippur. Chanukah was the occasion for the "Unlit Menorah" ceremony. Most seder tables in Detroit talked about the "Matzah of Hope." Many set aside chairs as "The Empty Chair" at their *simchas*, and on the bima on Shabbat." (Excerpt from a letter by Beverly Yost, community liaison of the Detroit Jewish Community Council)

San Francisco also incorporated into its annual life cycle of Soviet Jewry activity Simchat Torah and the Night of the Murdered Poets, honoring the memory of twenty-four Jewish poets, writers, and intellectuals murdered in Moscow on 12 August 1952. One year, we held a Passover Freedom Seder with participants seated at tables on the street directly in front of the Soviet consulate. The following four questions were asked: Is the Soviet Union a place where Jews can live as Jews? Does worldwide protest help the condition of Soviet Jews? Is this moment a good time for saving Soviet Jews? Can we do it?

We always spoke of three or three and a half-million Jews in the Soviet Union. But early on, there was a clear recognition that it would be easier to engage American Jewish activists—and to press the Soviet government—by focusing on individual cases. Even when there were more than twenty thousand refusenik families, the thrust of advocacy was on a personalized approach. Travel, Bar and Bat Mitzvah twinning (explained below), telephone calls, "adopt a family" programs, and targeted protests were all part of this strategy. The critical factor in this approach was the desire of Soviet Jews to take the risks inherent in greater publicity. The hope was that by having their profiles raised, the level of embarrassment to the Soviets would lead to their freedom. The fear was that the Soviets would make an example of some by maintaining the number of Prisoners of Zion at a consistent level of twenty to thirty. The code of conduct was clear: no refusenik's case was publicized without it being absolutely clear that this was the desire of the refusenik.

A good case study is the plight of Valery and Galina Panov. Valery Panov was one of the world's premier dancers at the Kirov Ballet in Leningrad. After the Panovs applied for visas in 1972, they were not only denied permission to emigrate, they were also barred from dancing. The BACSJ helped mount an international campaign. The San Francisco Ballet agreed to offer Valery Panov a contract as a principal, putting further pressure on the Soviet government. In 1974, the Panovs were allowed to emigrate. They came to San Francisco soon thereafter to thank their supporters—doing a benefit for the BACSJ and dancing with the San Francisco Ballet for four performances. Over the course of the advocacy movement, American Jewish activists felt as if they truly knew Vladimir Slepak, Gavriel Shapiro, Ida Nudel, Natan Sharansky, Mikhail Zand, Alexander Lerner, Valery Panov, Benjamin Bogomolny, and thousands of others. The personalized approach was part of the genius that sustained the movement for so many years.

Of course, the travel program was the ultimate personalizing experience. But, since many people could not make such a trip, there were opportunities at home as well. Bar and Bat Mitzvah twinning was a particularly effective vehicle for personalizing the plight of Soviet Jews. The BACSJ was responsible for the twinning program in San Francisco. Several hundred families participated in it through the years. Twinning not only underscored the idea of the extended family and reached new audiences; it dramatized the fact that American Jewish children were free to get a Jewish education while those living in the USSR could not, except at great personal risk in underground activities. The inclusion in the ceremony of a Soviet Jewish twin—through the Bar or Bat Mitzvah's speech and an empty chair on the bimah with the twin's name on it—had a deep impact on many American children who became Bar or Bat Mitzvah, on their families, and on the Soviet twin whose Bar or Bat Mitzvah was celebrated in absentia.

Matthew Stein became Bar Mitzvah in Massachusetts in April 1984. His twin was Alexander Shoyket of Kharkov. His letters about the twinning got through to Alexander, and the boys began to correspond, as did their parents. The Steins moved to the Bay Area, and in 1989, the Shoykets finally received permission to leave and settled in San Francisco. When Alexander Shoyket got married in 1995, he asked Stein to be his best man. The honor that Stein had extended eleven years earlier to his twin had thus been repaid.

Also effective as a personalizing tool was the use of telephone calls to refuseniks. In the 1970s, a telephone call to the USSR typically cost around four dollars per minute and had to be booked ahead of schedule. The usual practice was to give the overseas operator three or four names in case the first was not home or the lines were jammed. Even if you got through, there was always the prospect of interference by those listening in on the conversation. Amplified telephone calls became a valuable program tool. Typically we would go to people's homes, and the people gathered there were suddenly able to converse with a modern Jewish hero or heroine about his or her plight. In every city, similar calls took place every day of the week, sometimes going through, sometimes not, depending on the KGB's whims.

My last year at Berkeley, 1972–73, I placed a weekly call to a refusenik on behalf of BACSJ, each week from a different home. My regular contact was Boris Einbinder, a mathematician and refusenik leader from Moscow. In June 1973, I told him I would not be able to continue the calls because I was moving to Israel for my first year of rabbinical school. I closed by saying that I looked forward to meeting him in Israel. Because he had just received another refusal, he despaired of ever being allowed out and said that he thought he and his family would never be permitted to leave.

In the beginning of October 1973, just days before the Yom Kippur War, I received a call at my Jerusalem apartment late at night. Not only did Boris and his family get permission, they were arriving that night. A little before midnight, Boris's feet touched the soil of Israel, the land of his dreams. As his family walked in our general direction with their luggage, I approached and said, "Boris." Before I could identify myself, he said, "Doug, I recognize your voice." We embraced. The Einbinders were finally free.

The Soviet government's harsh treatment of its Jewish population was mitigated by one factor: its interest in normative relations with the West, particularly the United States. In the early years of the movement there were limited community efforts appealing to private businesses engaged in Soviet-American trade, but it was clear that the business community was unlikely to jeopardize potential deals by raising the subject of Soviet Jewry. The real focus shifted to the U.S. Congress. There, in 1974, one of the critical moments in the history of the Soviet Jewry advocacy movement took place, the passage of the Freedom of Emigration amendment to the Trade Reform Act, otherwise known as the Jackson-Vanik amendment. It denied most-favored-nation (MFN) status and commercial credit to the Soviet Union and other Communist countries that restricted emigration and provided that the restrictions could be waived if the president and Congress concurred that there had been a significant positive change. Communities, including San Francisco, played a significant role in advocating for the amendment. In the early days, there was deep division in the American Jewish community over whether the law might have a reverse effect, but there was no division among grass-roots activists.

Congressional action for Soviet Jews hardly stopped there. In recent years, the Lautenberg amendment, which gave presumptive refugee status to Soviet Jews, has been critical to ensuring that Soviet Jews who wanted to reunite with their first-degree relatives in the United States would be able to do so—as refugees. In earlier years, the congressional record was filled with statements, letters, resolutions on behalf of Soviet Jews, and the activities of the congressional Human Rights Caucus.

Most of these actions were not unusual. What was different was the extent to which public officials became involved in personal ways: making phone calls to refuseniks from their offices; "adopting" a family to develop a close relationship with; visiting refuseniks in the USSR; and scheduling appointments with Soviet diplomats at the consulate in San Francisco to argue vehemently on behalf of a particular family. Senator Barbara Boxer wrote of her experiences on the occasion of the BACSJ's twenty-fifth anniversary, when she was still a U.S. representative: "Since coming to Congress in 1983, some of my proudest moments have come when I spoke out on the House floor, at rallies in San Francisco, and before Russian envoys at the Washington embassy, for the freedom of Soviet Jews and other political prisoners around the world."

Public officials' involvement with the issue played a key role in pressing the Soviets. The bipartisan nature of the human rights struggle for Soviet Jewry increased the pressure. Soviet officials got the message that even political adversaries joined hands in agreement on this subject. Mikhail Gorbachev became general secretary of the Communist Party of the Soviet Union in March 1985. Prior to instituting his glasnost policies, emigration rates remained at very low levels: 1,140 in 1985; 914 in 1986; and 8,155 in 1987. After the beginning of glasnost, and the dramatic summit-eve rally in Washington, emigration began to increase rapidly: 18,965 in 1988; sharply rising to 71,217 in 1989; and 213,042 in 1990.

The increased emigration, the reduction of the number of refuseniks, the freeing of Prisoners of Zion, the passage of an emigration law, and the sudden openness of Soviet government officials posed a variety of challenges to the activist movement. If the situation was improving in tangible ways, yet thousands of refuseniks still remained and Jews in the USSR continued to be the targets of discrimination, how should we respond? In San Francisco, we responded on several levels. In 1986, the JCRC, with the agreement of the BACSJ approved a short policy statement entitled "Guidelines for Measured Responses." It read:

> We endorse the concept of responses linked to Soviet behavior toward Soviet Jews. Increased Soviet persecution, harassment and imprisonment have been and will be met by increased activity on behalf of Soviet Jewry.
>
> By the same token, tangible progress would be cause for measured responses from the Jewish community. Responses should be undertaken only when there is a consensus of the organized Jewish community, including the Soviet Jewry activist community, on a particular issue.

As the situation improved, there was a legitimate concern that a breakdown in community discipline might occur as a result of a rush to embrace the new Soviet Union while refuseniks still languished behind. Thus, the JCRC, with the support of the BACSJ, also approved several new policies including the 1986 Guidelines on Cultural, Professional, Academic and Athletic Exchanges (1986). The policy was based on an anticipated significant increase in exchanges and addressed the importance of Soviet Jewry issues being raised in all appropriate settings, lest Soviet counterparts interpret silence as lack of American interest in the issue.

During this period, David Waksberg and I were invited by one citizens' exchange group to meet with a number of Soviet officials, including top advisers to Boris Yeltsin, about the subject of Soviet Jewry. Perhaps the most unusual sign of the times was when the BACSJ hosted the police chief of Moscow at a small luncheon. This mild-mannered man in his mid-thirties spoke about all his refusenik friends. Change was clearly in the air.

Along with glasnost came the opening of the Green Street fortress. Although the consulate was established in the early 1970s, the first official meeting with a delegation of Jewish community leaders was not held there until 19 May 1988. Our delegation of ten people met with Consul General Valentin Kamenev and two other members of his staff for a little more than an hour. The exchange was direct and formal. We conveyed our continuing concerns, and Kamenev spoke about the positive changes that were taking place. He also warned that it would create a dangerous situation if the Soviet government gave Jews special privileges other nationalities did not have. He indicated that we should all work to improve Soviet-American relations and find solutions to the human rights problems. He accepted our letter and concluded the meeting by saying, "Anytime we want to discuss these or other matters, I am at your disposal." From that moment forward, the San Francisco Jewish community met Soviet government representatives with some frequency—usually focused on specific refuseniks' cases.

It is hard to identify a specific date that the grassroots Soviet Jewry advocacy movement came to an end. There continue to be individual refusenik cases and specific concerns about popular anti-Semitism and the rights of Jews in the Soviet Union. But by the time the Soviet Union broke apart in 1991, public protests were already in the history books—except for two return engagements. One was the pro-democracy rally after the coup. The other was on 7 November 1994. On that day, Vladimir Zhirinovsky, the virulently anti-Semitic Russian nationalist, came to San Francisco for his only public appearance in the United States. Outside the Sheraton Palace Hotel where he spoke, two thousand people gathered to protest, including many émigrés who, by then, composed one-third of the Jewish population of San Francisco. Among the featured speakers was Theodore Bikel, who would rush from the rally to the theater where he was performing as Tevye in "Fiddler on the Roof." The rally was, in many ways, a nostalgic trip back to the height of the advocacy movement.

San Francisco's campaign for Soviet Jewry was, on one level, similar to the advocacy movement throughout the country. Each community had its charismatic leaders, creative geniuses, and core activists who shaped a strategy that was likely to resemble the approach taken in other cities, albeit with differing emphases. By way of example, one of the strongest programs in the country was Philadelphia's, coordinated by its Jewish Community Relations Council and attracting a particularly high percentage of top community leadership. This brief description captures some of the diversity of its program.

The Soviet Jewry Council of JCRC held demonstrations and torchlight marches; signed petitions; led missions to Washington; developed support from government officials and legislators, as well as non-Jewish civic and religious leaders; picketed concerts and sports events; conducted teach-ins and interfaith vigils; coordinated phone calls to Soviet Jews; sponsored freedom buses, freedom fasts and freedom runs; organized programs in synagogues and youth groups; held press conferences and action conferences; published calendars, newsletters and Action Alerts; put up a billboard; sponsored a Freedom Ship; delivered hockey pucks to TV sports editors; and mobilized more than 160 buses to the Summit Sunday demonstration in Washington in 1987.

While there were many tactics in common, as is evident from Philadelphia's description, there were idiosyncratic features in each community's Soviet Jewry effort. In San Francisco, on the external level, it was the presence of a Soviet consulate. On the internal level, it was the extent to which the "establishment" and "nonestablishment" worked closely together. San Francisco's Soviet Jewry structure included JCRC and its Soviet Jewry Commission (affiliated with the National Conference on Soviet Jewry and, of course, the National Jewish Community Relations Advisory Council); Bay Area Council for Soviet Jews (affiliated with the Union of Councils for Soviet Jews); Soviet Jewry Action Group (also affiliated with the UCSJ and publisher of *Exodus* newspaper beginning in 1969); Northern California Lawyers Committee for Soviet Jews (a group of attorneys, judges, professors, and law students); Scientists for Sakharov, Orlov, and Scharansky (independent, but led by leading scientists from Bay Area institutions); Interreligious Task Force for Soviet Jews; and a Bay Area Chapter of Medical Mobilization for Soviet Jews.

Many other organizations worked tirelessly on the issue, including the numerous women's groups that hosted the annual Women's Plea for Soviet Jewry. BACSJ was, and still is, a beneficiary agency of the Jewish Community Federation. That was most unusual for an "antiestablishment" Soviet Jewry organization. Even more unusual was that the JCRC supported this relationship because of the important role the BACSJ played in mobilizing grassroots activism, and because of the increased accountability that resulted from the BACSJ's responsibility as a beneficiary agency. In 1988–89, it received $92,000, its highest annual allocation.

Prior to the establishment of the BACSJ, the JCRC was one of the first CRCs to be active on the subject of Soviet Jewry. In the mid-1950s, it produced a thirteen-week series for local radio on the plight of Soviet Jews. Soon thereafter, annual gatherings were organized. In 1964, JCRC formed an interfaith committee on behalf of Soviet Jewry, led by key Protestant and Catholic clergy and laypeople. The focus then was on religious liberty, not emigration.

In the aftermath of the Six-Day War, the BACSJ was born in San Francisco. Relationships were not always so smooth, however, particularly in the early years. But, by 1974, the situation had improved. In that year, Earl Raab, then the executive director of the JCRC, wrote a memo entitled "Notes on Local Soviet Jewry Activity," which briefly discussed the role of the BACSJ and its importance in spurring the organized Jewish community toward bolder activism. It said in part,

The national Jewish organizations continued the slogan of internal freedom for Soviet Jews *and* emigration; the BACSJ concentrated on the emigration theme exclusively, and that was the theme which was to bear fruit. The BACSJ more boldly invented and mounted programs for direct contact with Soviet Jews; the national Jewish agencies held back out of an expressed concern for the safety of Soviet Jews. . . .

The San Francisco JCRC was less resistant to the BACSJ approach than the national Jewish agencies, but was somewhat bound by their deliberations, because of the composite nature of the JCRC. . . . Organizationally, there are no longer those same philosophic and programmatic differences between the members of the Union of Councils and the national Jewish agencies. . . . There is no basic difference in either militancy or programmatic direction.

As a veteran of antiestablishment (early years), nonestablishment (middle years), and establishment-based Soviet Jewry organizations (later years), I agree with Raab that tone and timing, not substance nor strategy, were the only real points of contention. Based on my personal experiences, I believe the antiestablishment organizations played a critical role in pushing the establishment to embrace many tactics before they otherwise would have without such pressure. But in the end, with rare exceptions, establishment organizations adopted virtually an identical advocacy program to the grassroots activist groups. That certainly was the case with the Jewish Community Relations Council in San Francisco.

Over the years, a number of Jewish communal professionals played a key role in the local advocacy campaign. The JCRC's efforts were led by Earl Raab, whose national reputation in the field of Jewish community relations was earned precisely because of his extraordinary ability to get groups with views on opposite ends of the spectrum to work together around common goals. Rita Semel, who succeeded Raab, contributed interfaith, coalitional, and media expertise. Harold Light, with support from his wife, Selma, brought charisma, passion, and vision. His successor as director of BACSJ was Regina Waldman, a Libyan Jew who had escaped with her family from Libya. She dedicated her professional career to freedom for Soviet Jews and brought unusual creativity and style to the programming. David Waksberg brought equally strong leadership skills, along with an intellectual quality that catapulted him into a key role as strategist for the national Union of Councils for Soviet Jews and as a major point of contact for Soviet Jews inside the USSR. Joel Brooks, former director of the Northern California Region of American Jewish Congress, was also an early leader of the activist campaign. And, finally, the quality of lay leadership was consistently outstanding.

I look back at those years with a feeling of great satisfaction. I feel proud to have made a small contribution to one of the great success stories in Jewish history—a Jewish resistance movement initially given little chance of prevailing. I achieved my personal goal of wanting to be able to look my children in the face and say, "I did what I could." As is often the case, I received infinitely more than I gave. I feel grateful that my wife, Ellen, was so supportive of my involvement and the cause for all these years; that our older son, Daniel, as a very young child participated in a number of major rallies; and that our younger son, Joey, never had to do so because by then we had achieved a real victory. The fruits of that victory can be seen daily on the streets of Israel and in our own institutions throughout America as 1.3 million former Soviet Jews now live in freedom.

The Role of Nonestablishment Groups

How did the so-called activist groups within the American Soviet Jewry movement—the Union of Councils for Soviet Jews (UCSJ) and the Student Struggle for Soviet Jewry (SSSJ)—define their specific role and mission in the battle on behalf of Soviet Jews during the 1970s and 1980s, the movement's most crucial decades? Why were the UCSJ and SSSJ so manifestly unwilling or unable to cooperate productively with the so-called establishment Soviet Jewry groups—the National Conference for Soviet Jewry (NCSJ), the National Jewish Community Relations Advisory Council (NJCRAC), and the Greater New York Conference on Soviet Jewry (GNYCSJ)?

I covered the Soviet Jewry movement during the 1980s as an independent journalist (specifically as the New York correspondent for the *Jerusalem Post* and several American Jewish publications), and was never a member of any Soviet Jewry organization. Therefore, my comments should not be seen as being representative either of the UCSJ or SSSJ, but rather as the observations of an independent observer who observed and wrote about the movement with no particular axes to grind. In addition to covering the international Soviet Jewry movement from New York starting in 1983, I made four trips to the Soviet Union to meet with refuseniks (in 1985, 1987, and twice in 1989) before moving to Moscow in 1990 for two years as correspondent of the *Jerusalem Post, Ma'ariv,* and the *Forward.*

I was not involved in Soviet Jewry issues at all during the 1970s. My comments concerning that period are based upon research I undertook in preparing for the June 1995 conference "The History of Soviet Jewry Advocacy in the United States" as well as upon research I did ten years ago as one of the writers of a book by the *Jerusalem Post* entitled *Anatoly and Avital Sharansky: The Journey Home.* My research on the Soviet Jewry movement during the 1970s convinced me that the seemingly intractable conflicts between so-called establishment and activist Soviet Jewry organizations upon which I focused during the 1980s had their antecedents during the 1970s and, in fact, went back to the very origins of the movement in the early 1960s.

Despite my independent perspective, however, I readily acknowledge coming to the belief as I covered the Soviet Jewry story a decade ago that the so-called activist groups evinced a more passionate concern about the often desperate plight of Soviet Jews, and appeared more emotionally and ideologically in sync with the people the American Soviet Jewry movement was supposed to help: the refuseniks, Prisoners of Zion, and other adherents of the Jewish emigration and culture movement inside the Soviet Union.

I believe that much of the seeming lack of passionate commitment to the refusenik cause on the part of some of the leaders of the establishment groups was due to their organizational constraints, rather than a lack of concern or compassion. The lay and professional leaders of groups like NCSJ, NJCRAC, and GNYCSJ were answerable not only to a wide and often contentious coterie of Jewish organizations with which they were affiliated—the Council of Jewish Federations, Anti-Defamation League, American Jewish Congress, American Jewish Committee, Conference of Presidents of Major American Jewish Organizations, among others—but, in a less obvious but very real way, to the Israelis as well. The Soviet Jewry establishment groups deferred to the judgment and sought to carry out the policy aims of the highly secretive Lishka (sometimes referred to as the Office With No Name), the department of the Israel Foreign Ministry assigned the mission of rescuing Soviet Jews. In addition, the mainstream organizations had to take into account, as they formulated policy positions, the stance of the U.S. administration vis à vis the Soviet Jewry issue and U.S.–Soviet relations in general. As a result of all of these organizational and political ties and obligations, the leaders of these groups often appeared to take a more studied and consensus-oriented line concerning the situation of Jews in the Soviet Union than did their activist counterparts, who saw their constituency almost exclusively as the grass-roots members of their own organizations and the refuseniks in the Soviet Union.

Another key difference between the activists and establishment groups was that while the latter sought to do their best for the adherents of the Jewish movement in the Soviet Union, they were not answerable to them. I recall Jerry Goodman, the longtime executive director of the NCSJ, telling me more than once during the mid-1980s, when I called him to get his response to remarks by one prominent refusenik or another criticizing the NCSJ line, "The refuseniks, heroic as they are, are stuck in Russia. They don't have the whole picture."

Goodman argued that much of the crucial decisionmaking affecting the fate of Soviet Jews was taking place within the councils of American

Jewish organizations, as well as in Jerusalem, the Kremlin, the White House, and on Capitol Hill. One had to take the generally tough-minded positions articulated by the refusenik leaders with a grain of salt, Goodman argued, since their understanding of the overall geopolitical situation was limited.

Goodman's point was well taken. The refuseniks *were* limited in their outlook, as the events of the late 1980s and early 1990s made abundantly clear. From the advent of Mikhail Gorbachev to power in 1985 almost until the collapse of the Soviet Union itself in 1991, leaders of the Jewish emigration movement in the USSR consistently argued that Western governments and Western Jewry alike should maintain the hardest possible line with the Soviets. The refuseniks insisted that the ever more dramatic manifestations of glasnost, perestroika, and growing democratization on the part of the Soviet leadership represented nothing but a sinister trick to lull the West to sleep. Once the Kremlin's goal of stabilizing the Soviet system had been achieved, the refuseniks contended, it would rapidly jettison liberalism and return to Brezhnevism or even Stalinism.

The Jewish emigration movement leaders were proved dramatically wrong in those positions. Gorbachev was for real, or at least the process he started to reform and rationalize Soviet power rapidly spun out of his control and led within the space of seven dizzying years to the dissolution of the Soviet Union and the Communist system. But virtually no one, including the most prominent Sovietologists in the West (or leaders of any of the American Soviet Jewry groups), dared predict in 1985–88 that the seemingly impregnable citadel of repression that was the Soviet Union would self-destruct so quickly, or that more than 500,000 Jews would be able leave the USSR in three years beginning in late 1989.

The only person I remember who made such a prediction was Avital Sharansky, who told me forcefully during an interview in New York during a very bleak moment in 1984—at a point during which fear for her imprisoned husband's very survival had reached a peak in the West—that not only would Anatoly soon be granted his freedom, but that hundreds of thousands more Soviet Jews would be coming on aliyah in the near future.

I asked Avital what was her basis for being so optimistic at a moment when U.S.–Soviet relations had hit a low point. She responded with evident seriousness that her study of Judaism had convinced her that the God of Israel had already preordained a great modern Exodus of Soviet Jewry to rival the biblical Exodus from Egypt. I recall feeling in awe of Avital's evident deep faith in Jewish redemption in the face of an implacable situation that appeared to be turning ever more ominous, but concluding sadly that she was engaged in willful self-delusion. In fact, Avital Sharansky's unworldly vision proved prophetic.

But to return to my point, I believed in the 1980s and continue to believe today that the fact that the political perspective of the refusenik movement was hardly infallible did not absolve the Soviet Jewry establishment of the responsibility to consult more closely with them in planning strategy and decisionmaking. Not only did the American Jewish establishment groups fail to consult sufficiently, but all too often they evinced an arrogant and paternalistic attitude toward the refuseniks, treating them like impetuous children who needed to be guided and even dictated to. I found the supercilious approach sometimes transmitted by some professionals of the American Jewish establishment toward the very people they were supposed to be buttressing and sustaining to be both inexplicable and morally indefensible.

I came to feel strongly after my inspirational visits with refuseniks in the Soviet Union that no one in the American Jewish communal leadership could hold a candle in terms of Jewish pride and constancy to the likes of Yosef Begun, Victor and Irina Brailovsky, Vladimir and Masha Slepak, Aryeh Volvovsky, Alexander Lerner, and so many other less famous refuseniks I met in Moscow, Leningrad, Kiev, Vilnius, and other cities. The refuseniks were putting their own lives and those of their loved ones on the line, surviving without jobs and income and suffering countless forms of degradation at the hands of Soviet authorities. They lived in a constant state of fear that they could be charged with parasitism or subversion and sent off to Siberia at any moment, or that they and their families could be victims of officially inspired violence.

Yet the quietly heroic refuseniks, who had thrown down a fundamental challenge to a power that held hundreds of millions of people in its clutches, were expected to sit by patiently and quietly while their fates were being negotiated by unelected Western Jewish leaders, sometimes during cozy soirees with Soviet leaders in the Kremlin. It seemed to me at the time that the establishment groups, no matter how well-meaning, exhibited gross insensitivity and a fundamental failure of *menschlichkeit* by presuming to make decisions on behalf of the refuseniks, often without even attempting to secure their agreement for a particular course of action.

The UCSJ and SSSJ leadership, by way of contrast, understood and explicitly stated that their role was to succor and support the refuseniks. As I found during my visits to Russia, key members of the refusenik leadership appeared to trust and respect their nonestablishment Western interlocutors far more than leaders of the establishment groups. Many refuseniks saw the Soviet Jewry establishment as merely carrying out the directives of the Lishka, with which they often had testy and contentious relations, both in the USSR and in Israel after they had emigrated. The refuseniks, who gloried in free expression, deeply disliked what they saw as the authoritarian, almost Soviet style the Lishka adopted in its dealings with them.

Like the refuseniks, the activists of the UCSJ and SSSJ felt undercut and belittled by the Lishka and the American Soviet Jewry establishment. The activists felt that the professional staffers at NCSJ, GNYCSJ, and NJCRAC put an inordinate amount of time and energy into trying to minimize their participation in the movement to limit the amount of recognition and credit they received in the media. This deeply felt sense of hurt needs to be understood if one is to comprehend behavior on the part of the activists that often appeared churlish and even childish.

It explains, for example, the unwillingness of the activist groups to participate in the June 1995 conference, despite assurances that their point of view would be adequately represented. Spokesmen for the UCSJ and SSSJ insisted that they could not participate in a conference where they would be given less time to speak than erstwhile representatives of establishment groups, and said they did not trust assurances that their words would not be tampered with in the book to be published from the speeches at the conference.

Such seeming pettiness and paranoia by the activists can only be understood in the context of twenty years of perceived slights and a sustained effort to diminish their role in the Soviet Jewry movement by the Lishka and establishment. The activists view this conference and follow-up book as an effort by the establishment to rewrite history in a way that will reduce their own considerable contributions to the liberation of Soviet Jewry and cover up uncomfortable aspects of history, such as the reality that the establishment and refuseniks were often at cross-purposes.

The Union of Councils for Soviet Jews was formed in early 1970 by the uniting of six grassroots Soviet Jewry organizations, and grew to twenty-two affiliated groups across North America by 1978. With a few exceptions, such as the Bay Area Council for Soviet Jews in the San Francisco area, the affiliates of the UCSJ, unlike the NCSJ and Greater New York Conference on Soviet Jews, received no funding from the United Jewish Appeal–Federation network and had to do their own fund-raising.

In a situation where accurate information about the conditions of Jews in the Soviet Union represented power for Soviet Jewry organizations, the Lishka sought to damage the effectiveness of the UCSJ and SSSJ by withholding information from those organizations that it routinely shared with the NCSJ and other establishment groups. Glenn Richter, national director of the SSSJ, noted that by the early 1970s, "The Israelis told the activists that if they pursued an independent course, they would be cut off from all Israeli information related to Soviet Jewry, including the most complete lists of refuseniks and prisoners of Zion."[1] Attorney Alan Dershowitz, who served as Anatoly Sharansky's principal lawyer in the West, noted that during the period immediately after Sharansky's 1977 arrest by the KGB, the Lishka tried to discourage advocacy of his case by withholding important information (*AAS* 192–93).

Indeed, in his classic 1979 study of the Soviet Jewry movement, *The American Movement to Aid Soviet Jews*, William Orbach notes that during a 1978 UCSJ conference in Israel, Nehemiah Levanon, who had become head of the Lishka in 1970 and remained so through the 1980s, openly acknowledged that the Lishka withheld information from activist groups. Orbach wrote, "[Levanon] deplored the publication of lists of refuseniks, [asking] 'Why the hell do you need all 800 names? Why do you make up lists? Don't make up lists and don't correct them.'"[2]

Orbach notes that Michael Sherbourne, a London schoolteacher who served for decades as a crucial telephone link between Soviet Jewry activists in the West and Jews in the Soviet Union, once wrote in sarcastic exasperation that "God Almighty in his infinite wisdom has seen fit to grant authority to Mr. Levanon, Mr. Zvi Nezer, Mr. Yehoshua Pratt and Mrs. Nann Griever (all members of the Lishka) to decide which Jews we in England can help and which Jews . . . we are not permitted to help." Sherbourne added that while the UCSJ and SSSJ quickly and reliably published information on the situation of refuseniks and Prisoners of Zion—as long as those people asked that their cases be made public in the West—the NCSJ has "ignored and suppressed (information) or it comes with long delays and much distortion" (*AM* 79).

The response of the activists to being cut off from information by the Lishka was to develop their own network of information, while bridling at what they saw as heavy-handed Israeli efforts at gaining control. The activists often had to scramble, but they were generally able to get the information they needed through their own contacts with refuseniks in the Soviet Union, through the efforts of the indefatigable Sherbourne and a few others like him who maintained constant telephone communication with Soviet Jews, and through American government and congressional sources.

While there was certainly bitterness among the activists about the attitude of the Lishka, there was also an understanding that the Israelis had a more complex set of priorities. UCSJ executive director Micah Naftalin said in a recent interview for this article, "There was an appreciation on our side that the Israelis were trying to balance several goals, including aliyah [emigration], reestablishing diplomatic relations with the USSR, enhancing trade. . . . We understood that. Our only priority was to be the voice of the refuseniks."

Naftalin further acknowledged, "There certainly was an element of good cop/bad cop in the behavior of the establishment and the activists." He explained that the UCSJ believed it was useful for the movement to have both establishment insiders who could deal in the corridors of power with the White House, Congress, and Kremlin, and the activists in the streets who provided the energy and passion to maintain the cause of Soviet Jewry in the public consciousness.

Yet Naftalin noted, "The Lishka and establishment Soviet Jewry organizations in the West made it abundantly clear that they were genuinely angered by our stance and our activities, and really went out of their way to undercut us." Indeed, the Lishka did not stop at withholding information in its campaign against the activists. Shortly after the creation of the UCSJ, representatives of the Lishka appeared determined to do whatever was necessary to destroy the new umbrella group, an aim for which they had at least the tacit support of key sectors of the Soviet Jewry establishment groups in the West.

In his book, Orbach recounts a 1970 incident in which Zev Yaroslavsky, then chairman of the California Students for Soviet Jewry (CSSJ), was fired from his paid position as a staffer of the Los Angeles Jewish Federation Council. In a letter to Dr. Louis Rosenblum of the Cleveland Committee on Soviet Anti-Semitism, Yaroslavsky recounted that

on Thursday, April 16, 1970, I had a telephone conversation with Yoram Dinstein (the representative of the Lishka in New York), at which time he informed me that he was quite concerned about the fact that the California Students for Soviet Jews appeared on the stationery of the Union of Councils. He went on to inform me that if I did not find some way to eliminate CSSJ's name from the stationery, I would no longer be working for the federation. He said that this was a "declaration of war" on my part, and that I could not expect to be working for the federation after a period of two or three weeks. He said that this was not his desire or his war, but rather that of NJCRAC and the American Jewish Conference on Soviet Jewry (AJCSJ, the precursor of the NCSJ).

Yaroslavsky said in the letter to Rosenblum that when he contacted Abraham Bayer, the Soviet Jewry point man at NJCRAC, to complain about Dinstein's threat, Bayer blandly responded that the term "declaration of war" might not be the proper choice of words, but refused to confirm or deny Dinstein's assertion that the AJCSJ was sending out directives that "all those of the UCSJ mailing list who are presently funded by the Jewish Welfare Federations around the country should be immediately cut off" (*AM* 48). Yaroslavsky was soon fired by the Jewish Federation Council.

After Rosenblum wrote to then Israeli Ambassador to the United States Yitzhak Rabin complaining of Dinstein's brutal tactics and citing in his letter an occasion upon which Dinstein warned Rosenblum, "I shall see that you are destroyed," he was invited to a meeting in Washington with Lishka head Nehemiah Levanon. During the meeting, a more conciliatory Levanon promised that his office would take "a more open view on passing information to the public." Rosenblum, in response, requested a list of Soviet Jews applying for exit visas, but the Lishka never supplied the list (*AM* 60).

Rosenblum recalls that Levanon expressed unhappiness with telephone contacts between UCSJ members and Jewish activists in the Soviet Union, claiming that such contacts endangered Soviet Jews, despite their own protestations to the contrary. In response to Rosenblum's request, Levanon agreed to send Soviet Jewish refugees to the United States, but insisted on discretion in the matter—only parlor meetings with émigrés and no publicity (*AM* 60).

The hypersensitivity and even paranoia of the Lishka and the Jewish establishment toward the activists was undoubtedly fueled by the brief but spectacular involvement of the Jewish Defense League (JDL) in activities in support of Soviet Jews during the early 1970s. Following the bitterly anti-Zionist Leningrad trial in December 1970, during which two Jewish activists were initially condemned to death for involvement in an alleged plane hijacking (the sentences were commuted to fifteen years at hard labor following an international outcry), the JDL stepped up its year-old campaign of civil disobedience and harassment of Soviet diplomats in New York. More violent tactics soon followed. Late 1970 and early 1971 saw bomb explosions at Aeroflot and Amtorg offices, and at the Soviet cultural building in Washington. The JDL actions dangerously exacerbated U.S.-Soviet tensions, leading to acts of harassment against Americans in Moscow and a decision by the Soviets to recall Ambassador Anatoly Dobrynin for consultations.

Urged on by the Jewish establishment, which bitterly condemned the rhetoric and actions of JDL leader Rabbi Meir Kahane, the FBI arrested Kahane and twelve other JDL leaders on charges of smuggling arms. But the violence did not immediately abate. In November 1971, four shots were fired into the Soviet U.N. mission in New York, and on 16 January 1972 bombs exploded at Sol Hurok Productions and at Columbia Artists Management Inc. (both of which sponsored Soviet-American cultural exchanges). The first bomb injured fourteen people, one fatally.

The JDL campaign fell off rapidly after the Hurok bombing, due in part to the mass revulsion the action wrought even among militant devotees of the Soviet Jewry cause, but also to the depletion of the JDL's funds and the arrest of many of its leaders. The charismatic Kahane soon moved to Israel, leaving many of his followers floundering.

One of the effects of the JDL campaign was to discredit and seriously weaken the rest of the activist camp, especially the SSSJ. Kahane repeatedly excoriated the SSSJ as a "dangerous group" that provided "a false sense of activism" (*AM* 55). Jacob Birnbaum of the SSSJ, who had first introduced Kahane to the Soviet Jewry cause in 1964, recalls agreeing to allow Kahane to speak for fifteen minutes at an SSSJ demonstration in 1969, but being chagrined when Kahane and his thuggish followers took over the podium and turned the event into a JDL rally. According to Birnbaum, Kahane subsequently acknowledged he had broken his word about leaving the stage after his speech, but insisted that given the holiness of the cause, no tactical agreements that he made could be considered binding. Yet while Kahane savaged the SSSJ, much of the establishment declined to see the difference between its nonviolent activism and the activities of the JDL. After the Hurok bombing, Birnbaum said, the SSSJ had to endure extensive investigations by the FBI.

Nevertheless, Birnbaum acknowledges today that Kahane made lasting contributions to the cause of Soviet Jewry. "He did heighten mass awareness of the plight of Soviet Jewry in a way that would not have occurred otherwise," said Birnbaum in a recent interview. "In the beginning, the JDL made a positive contribution, but that changed later as they began to adopt violent tactics." Birnbaum noted, too, that the JDL anti-Soviet campaign created strong feelings of pride and identification among thousands of Jews in the USSR. Richter agrees with Birnbaum's analysis, acknowledging during a June 1995 interview, "We could hold hundreds of peaceful demonstrations, but the fact was that it was the JDL that got the publicity" that made Soviet Jewry an international cause célèbre.

Nor was the split between the SSSJ and JDL the only one within the activist camp. There were, in fact, major differences between the SSSJ and UCSJ. The former group was much smaller than the latter, but given its strong presence in New York City (the nearest UCSJ group was the Long Island Committee for Soviet Jewry) and penchant for holding high-visibility demonstrations and acts of civil disobedience at Soviet diplomatic offices in New York and Washington, the SSSJ made up in noise and media savvy what it lacked in size. The SSSJ chose to stick to its student base and was particularly strong at New York City campuses like Yeshiva University, Stern College, Brooklyn College, and City College. Its adherents tended to be traditional and observant Jews, in contrast to the more secular and suburban supporters of the UCSJ.

By the early 1980s, with ascendancy within the SSSJ of Rabbi Avi Weiss, an ardent supporter of Jewish settlers on the West Bank and Gaza Strip, the politics of the SSSJ appeared to overlap more and more with the ardently nationalist thinking of Gush Emunim and other "modern Orthodox" groups that supported Jewish settlement in Israel's occupied territories. Of all the American Jewish leaders, Weiss formed the closest working relationship with Avital Sharansky, who, in the years prior to her husband's release, had become an observant Jew and ardent supporter of the settlers.

The UCSJ and SSSJ also disagreed on basic ideological issues related to the Soviet Jewry movement. The SSSJ was strongly committed to aliyah by Soviet Jews, and rejected the "freedom of choice" precept advocated by the UCSJ, which upheld the right of Soviet Jews to immigrate not only to Israel, but to the United States or anywhere else they might wish to go. UCSJ activists campaigned throughout the 1970s and 1980s to keep the gates of the U.S. open to Soviet Jewish refugees who chose not to go to Israel.

The UCSJ avidly supported those members of the Jewish movement within the Soviet Union, including Natan Sharansky in the years before his arrest by the KGB in 1977, who wanted to form working alliances with non-Jewish dissidents like Andrey Sakharov who were struggling for democratization within the Soviet Union. Naftalin noted that the UCSJ always referred to Jewish activists in prison or Siberian exile as "Prisoners of Conscience," abjuring the term "Prisoner of Zion," which was favored by the SSSJ as well as the Israelis and the Soviet Jewry establishment groups in the U.S. The UCSJ applied the term "Prisoner of Conscience" both to Jewish prisoners like Sharansky and to non-Jewish exiles like Sakharov, whose cause the UCSJ also championed.

According to Glenn Richter, these ideological differences precluded a merger between the UCSJ and SSSJ, but did not prevent the two organizations from forming an operational alliance. What brought the groups together was a common self-definition as activists, and a shared perception that both groups were being harried and undercut by the establishment groups. The SSSJ people repeatedly put their bodies on the line in demonstrations and acts of civil disobedience, often going to jail on behalf of Soviet Jews in well-publicized actions at Soviet institutions in New York, the kind of activities that members of the Jewish establishment groups rarely participated in. The UCSJ, for its part, provided an army of grassroots volunteers for the cause around the country and sent a large numbers of visitors to refuseniks in the USSR. Yet despite the undeniable contribution these two groups made to the movement, their leaders almost invariably found themselves being prevented by the establishment from participating in major movement events like the annual Solidarity Sunday rallies in New York.

Although occasionally given seats on the podium at Solidarity Sunday, leaders of the SSSJ and UCSJ and its constituent groups were almost never allowed to address the crowd at this mass event, which during the 1980s drew 100,000 or more marchers each year to Manhattan's Fifth Avenue and to Dag Hammarskjold Plaza in front of the United Nations. Solidarity Sunday was officially under the aegis of the GNYCSJ, but included the active participation of the NCSJ and its constituent groups. Leaders of the NCSJ and GNYCSJ addressed Solidarity Sunday year after year, leaving the distinct impression among the thousands of participants in the annual march and rally that the establishment groups represented the totality of the Soviet Jewry movement in the United States.

With the exception of Avital and Natan Sharansky, whose star quality made them too big to ignore, very few former refuseniks were permitted to address the Solidarity Sunday assemblages. Officially, the excuse offered by the GNYCSJ for the blackballing of ex-refuseniks and Prisoners of Zion from the speakers' platform was that more time had to be given at the rally to remarks by a myriad of local politicians, whose support was deemed vital to the movement.

There is reason to believe, however, that this near ban also was related to concern by the Jewish establishment leaders that ex-refuseniks might use the platform to make statements at variance with official movement policy. This fear was undoubtedly greatly magnified by events at Solidarity Sunday in May 1987, when Yosef Mendelevitch, one of those convicted at the Leningrad trials and since his arrival in Israel at the beginning of the 1980s a staunch advocate of the toughest possible line with the Soviets, seized the microphone at the rally and attacked the Soviet Jewry establishment. In particular, Mendelevitch savaged NCSJ president Morris Abram and World Jewish Congress president Edgar Bronfman for having flown to Moscow two months before and having reached understandings with the Soviet leadership, without having bothered to consult first with the leaders of the Jewish movement within the USSR. With Abram glowering from a few feet away in a seat on the speakers' platform, Mendelevitch shouted defiantly to the crowd, "I know you have your leaders. You elected them. But don't send them anymore to Moscow. They don't know how to deal with the Russians."[3]

Despite their pronounced differences, the UCSJ and SSSJ both fashioned tough lines regarding the Soviet regime. Both groups staunchly opposed any relaxation of the Jackson-Vanik amendment denying the Soviet Union most-favored-nation (MFN) trading status with the United States. The two activist groups remained vigilant in support of Jackson-Vanik even during periods like the late 1980s when the NCSJ began moving toward calling for a one-year waiver of Jackson-Vanik to reward the Gorbachev regime for liberalization of emigration. Some NCSJ-affiliated organizations like the American Jewish Congress called outright for such a waiver. The SSSJ and UCSJ insisted there should be no relaxation of Jackson-Vanik until 50,000 to 60,000 Jews a year were allowed to leave.

Both activist groups supported public protests against Soviet mistreatment of Jews even at times when the NCSJ and other Jewish establishment urged a toning down of such protests to give inside diplomacy a chance to work. Both groups viewed themselves as the voice of refuseniks in the West (or as Micah Naftalin put it, the "junior partners" of the refuseniks). Indeed, Naftalin said there was never a serious possibility of his group uniting with the NCSJ. Even in 1989, when two figures at the top of the NCSJ who evinced a personally confrontative attitude toward the UCSJ—Jerry Goodman and Morris Abram—had been replaced by the somewhat more conciliatory Martin Wenick and Shoshana Cardin as executive director and president of the NCSJ, a merger was not an option. According to Naftalin, when Cardin suggested the possibility, he responded that such a merger would be like merging General Motors and the United Auto Workers Union; both groups were in the same business, but approached their missions from very different perspectives. Originally pushed to the sidelines by the hostility of the Lishka and establishment groups, the UCSJ had by the 1980s come to feel secure in its outsider role, and was not willing to consider giving up the independence it had come to cherish.

As I look back at the American Soviet Jewry movement from 1970 onward, three episodes stand out as delineating the sometimes sharp policy and philosophical differences between the activist and establishment wings of the movement. Each was significant in creating among both American Jewish activists and members of the Jewish movement in the Soviet Union the sense that the establishment had an agenda fundamentally different than their own, and therefore could not be fully trusted to do the right thing for the refuseniks.

The first of these episodes, the adoption into law of the Jackson-Vanik amendment during the period 1973–75, featured the ardent support of the activist wing of the movement for Senator Henry Jackson's insistence on firmly linking Jewish emigration from the Soviet Union and U.S.-Soviet trade, and a far more equivocal attitude on the part of much of the American Jewish establishment.

The second such defining moment for the Soviet Jewry movement involved the sometimes hostile attitude of the Lishka toward Anatoly Sharansky in the mid-1970s because of his efforts to build close ties between the Jewish emigration movement and the pro-democracy dissidents in the Soviet Union. After Sharansky's arrest, Jewish establishment groups in the United States, apparently at the behest of the Lishka, sought to downplay subtly the importance of the Sharansky case in favor of supposedly "more Jewish" prisoners like Ida Nudel and Yosef Begun.

The third and final defining moment came in early 1987, when the two top leaders of American Jewry, Morris Abram, NCSJ president and chairman of the Conference of Presidents of Major American Jewish Organizations, and World Jewish Congress president Edgar Bronfman, flew to Moscow for meetings with Kremlin leaders concerning the fate of Soviet Jewry without bothering to consult beforehand with the leaders of the Jewish emigration movement. The Bronfman-Abram affair was the most spectacular of numerous incidents over the years in which the leaders of the American Jewish establishment exhibited an often callous disregard for the thinking of the people on whose behalf they were supposedly fighting. Yet because of its particularly flagrant nature, the incident precipitated an open revolt on the part of the refusenik leadership that deeply embarrassed the American Jewish establishment and exposed its longtime disregard for refusenik opinion.

Jackson-Vanik

The NCSJ exhibited its ambivalence early on to the idea of creating "linkage" between U.S.-Soviet trade and Soviet emigration policies. In

June 1972, NCSJ executive director Jerry Goodman warned U.S. Representative Thomas Rees that the NCSJ could not support his bill, a less stringent precursor to the Jackson-Vanik amendment authorizing the president to prohibit commodity exports or export of information to any nation that prohibited freedom of religion and emigration (*AM* 131). While the Rees amendment allowed the president to decide to permit trade to continue if he determined it to be in the national interest, the Jackson amendment, which emerged in the fall of 1972 after the failure of the Rees amendment, restricted presidential maneuvering on the point by requiring the president to file a report making a compelling case that the country in question was not in violation of the terms of the agreement.

After the Rees bill was defeated, Senator Jackson, urged on by then staffer Richard Perle, announced his intention of proposing an amendment to the Trade Reform Act denying the Soviet Union MFN status unless it liberalized its emigration policies. The NCSJ reversed its earlier opposition position and joined the activist groups in support of the Jackson amendment after a personal appeal at a September 1972 NCSJ emergency session by the senator, who enjoyed widespread support in the Jewish community (*AM* 133). Jackson formally introduced his amendment in the Senate on 4 October 1972, together with seventy-three co-sponsors. Soon thereafter, Representative Charles Vanik of Ohio offered a similar amendment in the House. Consideration of the Jackson and Vanik amendments began in earnest in Congress in the spring of 1973.

When then President Richard Nixon and Secretary of State Henry Kissinger found that they were unable to convince key senators to abandon support for Jackson-Vanik, the president gathered a group of American Jewish leaders, including three top GOP supporters, philanthropist Max Fisher, then president of the Jewish Agency board of governors; Jacob Stein, then chairman of the Presidents' Conference; and Charlotte Jacobson, head of the World Zionist Organization–American Section. The group issued a statement praising Nixon's efforts on behalf of Soviet Jewry, but omitted any mention of Jackson's role (*AM* 140). The embrace of Nixon by the Jewish leaders allowed the administration to claim that Jewish support for the Jackson amendment was less than solid.

In the wake of the presidential meeting, a firestorm of criticism erupted against Stein and Fisher. These attacks were encouraged by Perle, and included statements by the UCSJ, SSSJ, and GNYCSJ, among other groups, rebuking Stein and Fisher and strongly reaffirming their endorsement for Jackson-Vanik. A similar statement was issued by 105 leading Moscow Jewish activists. The NCSJ found itself in a more ambivalent position. The NCSJ executive committee resolved to reiterate its support for Jackson-Vanik, but the group could not take an official stand without the approval of the Presidents' Conference. Stein, fearing for his White House connections, resisted pressure to endorse Jackson-Vanik. Subsequently realizing that he was in a small minority within the Jewish community, Stein capitulated and agreed to endorse the amendment, but he, Fisher, and NCSJ president Richard Maass still tried to square the circle by issuing a statement applauding both Nixon and the Congress for their efforts on behalf of Soviet Jews (*AM* 141).

Stein and Fisher further alienated American Jewish opinion by attending a banquet for visiting Soviet leader Leonid Brezhnev on 18 June 1973 at the invitation of Nixon, who several days later declared in a reference to Soviet Jews that the United States "cannot make its policy hostage to any one group" (*AM* 142). But the strong stand taken by Jackson, combined with a letter of support for the Jackson amendment by the Soviet Union's leading dissident, Andrey Sakharov, appeared to cement mainstream Jewish opinion in support of Jackson-Vanik, a process undoubtedly helped along by a perception that Nixon had been greatly weakened by the exploding Watergate scandal.

The eruption of the Yom Kippur War in October 1973 momentarily changed the political calculus and gave the administration a chance to argue that forcing Jackson-Vanik through Congress might have disastrous consequences for Israel. Secretary of State Henry Kissinger, who was attempting to enlist Soviet support for a Mideast cease-fire, asked the House of Representatives to postpone consideration of the Trade Reform Act to which the Jackson-Vanik amendment had been attached.

Under renewed pressure from Stein and Fisher, Maas of the NCSJ, together with Charlotte Jacobson and Rabbi Arthur Hertzberg, president of the American Jewish Congress, met with U.S. Representative Al Ullman, chairman of the House Ways and Means Committee, and urged him to delay consideration of the bill. At a meeting with Jackson on 5 November, Maas relayed a message from Kissinger that passage of the Vanik amendment (the House version of Jackson-Vanik) would sever "the last thread between the U.S. and Soviet Union," and complicate Kissinger's negotiations. Stein asserted that Israel's safety was American Jewry's paramount concern, and Jews therefore had to defer to Kissinger's concerns (*AM* 146–47).

But if Maas and other top Jewish leaders were prepared to back away from linking Soviet trade and emigration under administration pressure, Jackson emphatically was not. He responded to Maas by accusing Nixon of exploiting the Jewish leaders, and reminding his audience that Congress, not the administration, had been Israel's staunchest friend. Jackson argued that only support of the amendment would ensure continued Jewish emigration, while abandoning it would betray Soviet Jews and dissidents like Sakharov (*AM* 147).

As the Yom Kippur War waned and Kissinger succeeded in negotiating separation-of-forces agreements among Israel, Egypt, and Syria, with Soviet acquiescence—and as Nixon slipped ever deeper into public disfavor—both Jewish and liberal opinion solidified in support of the amendment, which overwhelmingly passed the House in December 1973. In subsequent negotiations between the Senate and the administration, Kissinger reluctantly accepted the principle of linkage between U.S.-Soviet trade and Jewish emigration; the terms remained to be worked out over more than a year of torturous negotiation.

Finally, the Senate agreed on a measure that denied MFN status to the Soviet Union unless, among other terms, 60,000 people were allowed to emigrate annually, and the Soviet government ended harassment and punitive action against potential émigrés. Kissinger and the new president, Gerald Ford, finally accepted these conditions, although the Soviets rejected them, leading to the collapse of the 1972 U.S-Soviet trade agreement. The decisive Soviet *nyet* to Jackson-Vanik and the subsequent collapse of the U.S.-Soviet détente of the early and mid-1970s ensured the denial of MFN status to the Soviet Union for fifteen years, until the rapidly dissolving Soviet Union began allowing mass emigration in late 1989.

The American Soviet Jewry activist groups, who passionately supported Jackson-Vanik throughout the long and torturous period leading up to its passage by Congress, were left by that experience with the distinct impression that while Jackson remained steadfast in support of securing Jewish emigration through economic pressure on the Soviets, important sectors of the Jewish establishment, including the leadership of the Presidents' Conference and the NCSJ, had been prepared to accept limitations upon Soviet Jewish emigration in order to curry favor with Nixon and Kissinger.

The sense that the Jewish establishment had been ambivalent toward Jackson-Vanik all along was reinforced in the mid- to late 1980s with the advent of Mikhail Gorbachev and the beginnings of glasnost and perestroika. During that period, the activist groups suspected the NCSJ and other establishment groups of being ready to sanction a waiver of Jackson-Vanik in exchange for increased emigration (including direct flights to Israel) at much lower levels than the 60,000 a year that had become the benchmark of mass emigration. Indeed, by 1986, the NCSJ was already hinting in public statements that it could support a temporary waiver of Jackson-Vanik in response to the Soviets' allowing much higher levels of emigration, freeing prisoners of Zion and resolving most refusenik cases.

Finally, in June 1989, in the face of strong opposition from the SSSJ and UCSJ, the NCSJ board voted in favor of a yearlong waiver of Jackson-Vanik if the Soviets offered assurances of sustained high levels of emigration, the settling of outstanding refusenik cases, and the passage by the Soviet Union of a law that would regularize and rationalize emigration procedures. The activist groups accused the NCSJ of betraying

Soviet Jews, contending that the Soviets should be judged upon performance, not assurances.

The NCSJ stance gave the Bush administration the political cover it needed to grant the Soviets their long-sought waiver and much desired MFN status. Interestingly, however, that step did not come until December 1990, a year and a half after the NCSJ's green light, by which time Jewish emigration had reached nearly 200,000 a year. The administration was particularly unhappy with the Soviet parliament's failure to follow through on repeated assurances and pass its long-awaited emigration law.

Also, the administration insisted on limiting its waiver to periods of only six months, compared to the year period recommended by NCSJ. (The waiver for the Soviet Union and its successor states has been renewed every six months; although Jackson-Vanik remains on the books, the waiver could be revoked if free emigration is again sharply curtailed and human rights conditions deteriorate.) It is ironic that the business-oriented Bush administration proved less amenable to waiving trade restrictions on the Soviet Union than did the NCSJ, the organization that purportedly represented the interests of long-repressed Soviet Jewry.

Anatoly Sharansky

Today, looking back on the nearly thirty-year trajectory of the Soviet Jewry movement, there is a consensus among participants and observers that the struggle to free Anatoly Sharansky from the gulag was one of the most glorious chapters of the movement, and one in which the entire spectrum of the movement can take pride (Sharansky took the name Natan after his arrival in Israel). Thanks to Sharansky's eloquent and inspiring speech at his trial for espionage and treason in 1977, and the stirring worldwide campaign undertaken by his wife Avital on his behalf, the once-obscure Sharansky grew enormously in stature until he came to symbolize to Jews around the world (and many gentiles as well) the aspirations of all Soviet Jews to live full Jewish lives in their historic homeland.

Given Sharansky's unassailable "apple pie" status within the Soviet Jewry movement by the 1980s, it is often forgotten that he was considered a highly controversial figure by many supporters of Soviet Jewry in the West in the period leading up to and following his arrest. The Lishka, in particular, took a harshly critical view of Sharansky's close ties with Andrey Sakharov and other leaders of the human rights movement within the Soviet Union. In the wake of Sharansky's arrest by the KGB in March 1977, the Lishka appears to have discouraged groups like NCSJ and NJCRAC from highlighting Sharansky's case or involving themselves too closely in Avital's ongoing campaign in the United States on her husband's behalf. The position of the Israelis, often echoed in the 1970s by groups like the NCSJ and NJCRAC, was that the Jewish emigration movement in the Soviet Union should be kept completely separate from the human rights movement, and Jewish activists should not appear to be attempting to change the Soviet system.

After Sharansky's arrest, Irene Manekovsky, the longtime Washington representative of the UCSJ, became the prime mover in arranging meetings for Avital with congresspeople and representatives of the Carter administration, which was placing unprecedented emphasis on human rights issues. As a result, Manekovsky was summoned to the Israeli Embassy and told to cease her efforts on behalf of the dissident movement. Infuriated by the pressure, Manekovsky charged openly that Israeli officials had warned Avital that no one in the movement would help her if Anatoly were arrested because of her work with the dissidents.

Manekovsky and other activists also contended that the Lishka and establishment sought to downplay the Sharansky case in favor of refuseniks like Yosef Begun and Ida Nudel, who were not involved in the dissident movement and therefore were considered "more Jewish" (*AAS* 190–92). According to Glenn Richter of the SSSJ, "What came through from Jerusalem was an attitude that when Sharansky was arrested, he got what was coming to him" because he had not heeded Israeli warnings against linking the Jewish emigration movement with the Helsinki Watch Group (*AAS* 192). Harvard University law professor Alan Dershowitz, who served as one of the Sharanskys' main legal advocates in the West, recalls that the Israelis tried to discourage advocacy for Anatoly's case by withholding important information from key supporters (*AAS* 192–93). Dershowitz said, however, that he and other activists for Sharansky were able to secure reliable information through their own contacts among refuseniks in the Soviet Union, and through American authorities and other sources.

Leaders of the establishment groups denied that they were pressured by the Lishka to play down Sharansky, but acknowledged that the Israelis did express strong opposition to any link between the Jewish emigration movement and the dissident movement. Goodman of the NCSJ said that establishment groups pushed for more effort on behalf of other prominent Prisoners of Zion like Begun and Nudel in part because of "a nagging sense of concern that perhaps we were allowing Anatoly's strong personality and charisma" to eclipse the larger movement (*AAS* 193). Bayer of NJCRAC said that Levanon and other spokesmen of the Lishka "only expressed a viewpoint, one held by many of the refuseniks in Moscow, that they ought to stay within the Jewish sphere. People were warning Anatoly it was a dangerous path. The Jewish business is risky enough without getting involved in a cause that threatens the Soviet order" (*AAS* 193).

A key former member of the Lishka who had repeatedly clashed with the activists during the 1970s, when he represented the Office With No Name in the United States, told me in 1986, soon after Sharansky's liberation, that he still believed Sharansky had inadvertently harmed the Jewish emigration movement by linking it to Sakharov and other dissidents in the Helsinki Watch Group. It was a mistake, the source said, for American activist groups to have concentrated so heavily on the Sharansky case, as though it were the only one. The source argued that from a Jewish perspective, there were other cases that were more important, adding that Sharansky represented a "borderline case" because he was interested in both Jewish and dissident activities. The source asserted, however, that while the official Israeli position was that linking the two movements was extremely ill-advised, the Lishka "did not abandon Anatoly Sharansky or encourage others to do so" (*AAS* 193–94).

Perhaps so, but in the weeks following Anatoly's arrest in 1977, the hard-pressed refusenik leadership in Moscow in 1977 became concerned enough about ambivalent attitudes toward Sharansky in Western Soviet Jewry organizations that they decided to send a sharply worded appeal on his behalf. The message, signed by Mark Azbel, Alexander Lerner, Victor Brailovsky, Vladimir Slepak, Ilya Essas, and Ida Nudel stressed that Sharansky had been arrested because of his Jewish activism, and that although the Jewish problem in the USSR stood very much apart, it was essential for the Jewish and human rights movements to work together (*AAS* 195).

In the early 1980s, long after the Jewish establishment groups had embraced the Sharansky case as representative of the entire movement, these groups still had a somewhat prickly relationship with Avital Sharansky. There was considerable queasiness with her intense religiosity and alliance with Gush Emunim and other Israeli settlers' groups. More galling to the establishment was that on her frequent visits to America, Avital insisted on maintaining a close collaboration with Rabbi Avi Weiss, whose frequent attacks on the establishment as being too timid in confronting the Soviets infuriated these groups.

On his first trip to New York after his release, Natan Sharansky, reportedly acting at his wife's behest, angered the establishment groups by spending Shabbat at Weiss's synagogue in Riverdale instead of the Upper East Side shul of Rabbi Haskell Lookstein, then president of the GNYCSJ. Sharansky also upset the plans of Morris Abram, president of the NCSJ, to accompany the refusenik hero to a scheduled meeting with President Reagan at the White House. Sharansky insisted that if Abram were to come, Weiss and Morey Shapira of the UCSJ should also be invited. Rather than accept the humiliation of being placed on the same level as the gadfly Weiss, Abram decided that Sharansky should meet Reagan on his own.

Looking at the overall historic record, it is clear that both the Israelis and the Jewish establishment organizations in the United States were uncomfortable with the independence of Anatoly and Avital Sharansky. Indeed, at the time of Sharansky's greatest peril, both appeared reluctant, until their hands were forced by Sharansky's own eloquence, to highlight Sharansky's heroic stature and symbolic importance to the larger movement.

This ambivalence toward Sharansky, who was emerging during the mid-1970s as the most politically savvy and charismatic of the refusenik leaders, seems bizarre when viewed from the present. It becomes, perhaps, less mystifying when one considers that by refusing to back away from his stance that the Jewish emigration movement should work closely with that brave handful of individuals of disparate nationalities who had the courage to say no to the Soviet system, Sharansky was also asserting the right of the Soviet Jewish movement to follow its own agenda, regardless of the opinions of the Israelis or the American Jewish establishment.

Significantly, Sharansky has maintained the same independent stance since coming out of the gulag. Having reached the conclusion that the Israeli government has failed to keep its promises to the new immigrants (and, in the process is alienating thousands of ex-Soviet Jews already in Israel and hundreds of thousands more who have remained in the ex-Soviet Union), Sharansky has launched a new and independent movement that promises to transform itself in the next several months into a full-fledged political party. Proponents of a new "Russian" party hope the party can win five to ten Knesset seats in 1996, thereby establishing itself as the balance of power between Labor and Likud and allowing the Russian Jewish community to speak both to the Israeli government and world Jewry for the first time from a position of strength.

The Bronfman-Abram Visit

The third defining moment during which the American Jewish establishment made clear to the participants in the Jewish emigration movement in the Soviet Union that they would be given little say in deciding their own destinies came in March 1987, when the two ranking representatives of Diaspora Jewry flew to Moscow for meetings with Soviet officials on the subject of Soviet Jewry.

The two leaders were Morris Abram, president of the NCSJ and chairman of the Conference of Presidents of Major American Jewish Organizations, and Edgar Bronfman, president of the World Jewish Congress. To many observers, they seemed like something of an odd couple. Indeed, the decision of the two to form an alliance and work together was somewhat startling given that many of the American Jewish establishment organizations represented in the Presidents' Conference had been sniping for several years at the WJC.

In not for attribution comments, leaders of several establishment organizations portrayed the WJC as an upstart, shoot-from-the-hip outfit headed by a self-styled general secretary named Israel Singer, who brilliantly used the clout represented by Bronfman's immense personal fortune to create the illusion that the WJC, whose tiny staff operated out of cramped offices on Manhattan's Park Avenue South, somehow represented the Jews of the world. Still, there was no question in 1987 that the newly minted alliance of Bronfman and Abram represented a formidable marriage of Jewish money and political clout. Abram, a longtime southern Democratic progressive, who had supported Reagan in 1980 and served on the U.S. Civil Rights Commission in the early years of the Reagan administration, brought his access to the top figures of the administration when he became president of the NCSJ and, in 1986, chairman of the Presidents' Conference.

Despite his ardent (some would say obsequious) support for Reagan, and enormous pride in his friendship with figures like Secretary of State George Shultz, Abram resented suggestions in the Jewish media, upon his appointment as Presidents' Conference chairperson, that he had abandoned his traditional liberalism or commitment to the advancement of black America. Abram clearly considered himself to be the patriarch of American Jewry, and became infuriated at any criticism from within the Jewish community.

The World Jewish Congress had a reputation for appeasement of powerful gentiles going back to the days of Bronfman's predecessor, Nahum Goldmann. Bronfman's cultivation of the Soviet government made veteran refuseniks particularly uneasy about the growing dialogue between Bronfman and the Soviets. Indeed, they feared that Bronfman, president and chief executive officer of Seagrams, had another agenda in Moscow: to reach agreement with the Soviet government to market its vodka in the West or, perhaps, to sell Seagrams products in the Soviet Union.

Bronfman's almost complete inaccessibility—he rarely gave interviews and never talked to the Jewish press—and his growing tendency to parley with foreign leaders in the pose as a kind of "pope of the Jews," fanned the fears of many Jews in Moscow that they might get sold down the river on a flood tide of vodka. Indeed, Natan Sharansky used the occasion of his speech at Solidarity Sunday in New York in May 1986, his first address to the Jews of America, to criticize implicitly Bronfman for presuming to conduct "quiet diplomacy" with the Soviets on behalf of Soviet Jews. There should be no "quiet diplomacy" between Jews and the Kremlin, Sharansky stated. Let the U.S. president pursue a double policy alternating between quiet diplomacy and publicity; the Jews of America needed to be single-mindedly active and noisy in pursuit of their goal (*AAS* 280–81).

Another concern among refuseniks about Bronfman's involvement in Soviet Jewry issues related to the fact that during the months preceding the Bronfman-Abram visit, the WJC had closely allied itself with Eliyahu Essas, a former Prisoner of Zion and leader of the growing *ba'alei teshuva* (return to religious Judaism) movement among Jews in the Soviet Union. Since being allowed to leave on aliyah the previous year, Essas had advocated an increasingly accommodating position toward the Kremlin, apparently out of a calculation that the new Soviet regime would choose to tolerate a Jewish religious revival in the USSR. Essas had repeatedly stated in press interviews that the *ba'alei teshuva* movement had no fundamental conflict with Soviet power. The larger refusenik movement, which was more secular than Essas's devout followers and more interested in mass emigration than in nurturing Judaism on stony Russian soil, feared that Bronfman and Abram might sell out their interests to push Essas's agenda.

Upon arrival in Moscow, Abram and Bronfman went directly to the Kremlin for meetings with Soviet officials. Only at the end of two days of intensive meetings did the two American Jewish leaders gather representatives of the larger refusenik movement in their hotel room to report what had allegedly been accomplished in their behalf. According to several people who attended the meeting, Abram and Bronfman represented their meetings with Soviet leaders as having been highly successful, and said they had been assured that all refuseniks would be allowed to emigrate within one year except for "legitimate national security cases." It was also variously reported that Bronfman and Abram had been told that 10,000 to 12,000 Jews would be allowed to leave the Soviet Union, and that the Kremlin would allow the beginnings of Jewish cultural expression in the Soviet Union, including the opening of a kosher restaurant in Moscow.

There was widespread speculation among the refuseniks that Bronfman and Abram had held out the prospect of a waiver of Jackson-Vanik restrictions against the Soviet Union in exchange for direct flights of Soviet Jewish immigrants from Moscow to Tel Aviv. Both Abram and Bronfman had expressed support for the long-standing Israeli policy goal of arranging direct flights to staunch the "dropout" phenomenon. In the absence of such flights, tens of thousands of Soviet Jewish refugees left the USSR for Vienna and Rome on Israeli visas, allegedly for the goal of reunification with family members in Israel, and later exercised their option to settle instead in the United States, Canada, or other Western countries.

What became immediately evident was that nearly the entire refusenik community was infuriated by the Bronfman-Abram meetings with the Soviet officials. In a telephone conversation from Moscow several days later, Vladimir Slepak informed me that members of the Jewish movement were deeply offended and alarmed. According to Slepak, the refuseniks felt strongly that Bronfman and Abram had no right to negotiate on their behalf without consulting them first, and feared the two Jewish leaders might have made dangerous concessions that could badly damage the emigration movement.

Bronfman and Abram sought to convey the impression that whatever the comments of a Slepak, most refuseniks were more appreciative of what they had accomplished in Moscow. But Abram was deeply embarrassed at the annual Solidarity Sunday rally in early May, when Mendelevitch commandeered the microphone with the seeming connivance of Sharansky, who had just finished speaking and jumped back from the microphone when Mendelevitch approached. Mendelevitch then delivered his blistering tirade against Abram and Bronfman for allegedly having made dangerous concessions to the Soviets and having betrayed the Jewish emigration movement.

Two weeks later, when I arrived in Leningrad and Moscow for a ten-day visit, I found unanimity among refuseniks that the behavior of Bronfman and Abram in Moscow had been unforgivable. I was impressed at how this fury at Bronfman and Abram animated refuseniks of all ideological stripes, with the exception of Essas's deeply devout followers. Those who spoke out against Bronfman and Abram spanned the spectrum from Lev Elbert, a yarmulke-wearing militant Jewish nationalist who looked forward to making his home in a West Bank settlement, to Victor Brailovsky, a gentle cyberneticist who expressed distaste for Israeli expansionism.

Elbert spoke of the "disaster brought upon us by Bronfman and Abram," and asked rhetorically, "Can't Western Jewish leaders get it into their heads that we are intelligent people capable of speaking for ourselves? . . . The Soviets promised Bronfman and Abram that 12,000 Jews would get out and we would be given a kosher restaurant. In fact, since those meetings, there has been a sharp increase in anti-refusenik articles in the Soviet media, and 2,000 new people have been issued refusals." Elbert said he was worried that the Soviets might be preparing to sharply increase emigration, but to prevent most of the long-term refuseniks from emigrating. "If 50,000 Jews are let out, the West will forget the refuseniks," Elbert predicted. "Yet the accomplishments of the movement were made possible by these long-term refuseniks who gave their lives for the cause."[4]

Brailovsky called the behavior of Bronfman and Abram "extremely disappointing," and worried that their visit might portend a situation wherein Israel and the American Jewish community would take a lower profile in the struggle for Soviet Jewry in the hope that the Soviet Union would agree to allow the reopening of the long-closed Israeli embassy in

Moscow. "A low profile on Soviet Jewry is not worth an embassy," Brailovsky said emphatically.[5]

It can, and has, been argued that all of these disputes became irrelevant in the last years of the 1980s as the Soviet government in fact began moving, with some starts and stops, toward open emigration. Indeed, during the course of 1987, Slepak, Brailovsky, Nudel, Elbert, Yuli Edelstein, and many of the other top refusenik figures were allowed to emigrate. The numbers of legal emigrants from the Soviet Union soared from 914 in 1986 to 8,155 in 1987, and 18,965 in 1988, before shooting through the roof to 71,217 in 1989 and 213,042 in 1990.

A strong case could be made that the upsurge in emigration in 1987 and 1988, and the freeing of the very refuseniks who had so ardently criticized Bronfman and Abram proved that the two American Jewish leaders had been on the right course all along. Nevertheless, the Bronfman-Abram meeting with Soviet officials, like the ambivalence of the American Jewish establishment toward the Sharanskys and its mixed signals during 1972–73 toward the Jackson-Vanik amendment, left a residue of anger and mistrust on the part of many ex-Soviet Jews toward the American Jewish leadership.

All three incidents, and scores of others like them over the decades, convinced Soviet Jews that the American Jewish establishment, like its patrons in the Israeli government, viewed them essentially as a group of children who were unschooled both in Judaism and in the vicissitudes of international politics, and who needed powerful protectors to speak for them and channel the direction of their struggle.

Significantly, a similar attitude has been manifested toward ex-Soviet Jews even in the post-Soviet era by the Israeli-American establishment. As they have launched programming in the former Soviet republics, organizations like the Jewish Agency, the Joint Distribution Committee, and the Lishka have often spurned close cooperation with homegrown Soviet Jewish groups like the Va'ad (the umbrella group of Soviet Jewry founded in December 1989). Instead, these and other groups have insisted on running their own programs around the ex-Soviet Union, wasting in the process considerable amounts of money in duplication and fostering destructive turf wars.

While the Va'ad and its successor umbrella groups in the various republics of the former Soviet Union have never seemed to fulfill their early promise, ex-Soviet Jewry has in the past few years developed a plethora of community organizations focusing variously on religious life, Jewish culture, sports, business, and philanthropy. With anywhere from one to two million Jews still remaining in the former Soviet Union, ex-Soviet Jewry has begun to assume its place as a Diaspora community to be reckoned with, and is becoming more vocal in its demand that it be given a place at the world Jewish table consonant with its demographic weight.

Meanwhile, former Soviet Jews in Israel and the United States continue to evince a keen sense of resentment at what they perceive as the failure of both the Israeli government and the American Jewish community to treat them as equals. Ex-Soviets in Israel are particularly hurt and angry about what they see as the failure of their new country to take advantage of the enormous potential the highly educated and skilled ex-Soviet aliyah represents for the rapid development and modernization of the Jewish state. This growing anger portends a social and political rift that may, like the Ashkenazi-Sephardi chasm of the previous generation, define Israel for decades to come.

Ex-Soviet Jewry is now a world community. It has shown itself for more than a generation to be a vital, sometimes angry, but always creative force, with a crucial role to play in a hoped-for revival of Jewish identity during the twenty-first century. Indeed, if the purveyors of "Jewish continuity" in America hope to ignite their nascent and so far rather sluggish campaign with some of the dynamism, soul, and electric pride in Jewishness that has characterized the miraculous rebirth of Jewish identity in Russia in recent decades, they must acknowledge our ex-Soviet Jewish brothers and sisters as equals.

The truth is that the Jews of the former Soviet Union have as much or more to teach American Jewry as we have to contribute to them.

Notes

1. Jerusalem Post, *Anatoly and Avital Shcharansky: The Journey Home* (San Diego: Harcourt Brace Jovanovich, 1986), 192; hereafter cited in text as *AAS*.
2. William W. Orbach, *The American Movement to Aid Soviet Jews* (Amherst: University of Massachusetts Press, 1979), 79; hereafter cited in text as *AM*.
3. *American Jewish Year Book 1989* (New York: American Jewish Committee and Jewish Publication Society), 227.
4. *Long Island Jewish World,* "Moscow Jews: Do All Strategies Lead To Jerusalem?" 19–25 June 1987.
5. Ibid.

The Activist Movement

It is unimaginable that, scarcely a decade ago, the possession of a Hebrew book served as evidence for a three-year prison sentence. It was a time when the Soviets assigned the KGB to "tail" activists because they were teaching Hebrew, and broke up Jewish seminars and holiday celebrations in the forest. Even a Jewish nursery school for four- and five-year-olds was fair game for the fearsome Fifth Directorate of the KGB. It was not uncommon for Soviet officials to cut the home telephone lines of Jewish activists and plant drugs and guns in their apartments, leading to wildly outrageous accusations against Jewish refuseniks in the Soviet press, tactics reminiscent of the worst Nazi propaganda. Also, regrettably, it was not all that long ago that the world press was silent, and supporters of moral relativism equated the problems of Communism with the problems of a free democracy.

In response to this dire situation, the Union of Councils for Soviet Jews and others in the independent grassroots activist movement in the West, in full, nonpaternalistic partnership with our brethren in the USSR, conducted the struggle by a sustained effort to educate our legislatures, our governments, and the hearts and minds of the public of the need to pressure Soviet officials whenever and wherever we could find them. As Pamela Cohen, former UCSJ national president, has eloquently observed,

Our dream was inviolate and unshakable. We were defiant and unrelenting and stubborn, and we fought on every front: We fought when Jews were fired from their jobs after they applied to emigrate, and we fought when they were stripped of academic degrees in public humiliation. We fought when they were denied medical attention, and we fought for the rights of our people in the prisons and labor camps. We fought anti-Semitic article by anti-Semitic article and we knew that every battle was a skirmish that had to be won.

We understood that we had to demand the delivery of every letter, the successful completion of every phone and tourist contact, and the release of every refusenik and prisoner of conscience. We knew that our momentum and determination would eventually crescendo into a force that would ultimately rip open the gates.

It's fair to say that UCSJ always had access to factual information, to the evidence that could expose the Soviet's anti-Jewish exploits—and either the West's or the Jewish establishment's naïveté. And we stubbornly confronted the Soviets with their lies in front of their embassies and consulates, and whenever Soviets attended multilateral governmental meetings or tried to charm the world with their dancers, musicians, Olympic champions, scientists, and circus performers.

Our compulsion for accurate information came from our refusal to draw conclusions and create policy without broad and careful consultation with Jewish refusenik leadership. Our responsibility was to reveal that truth to the public, their governments, and the Jewish communities through the general media and Jewish press. All too frequently, the Jewish press depreciated pivotal conflicts of worldviews, including the differences between the Israeli government and the UCSJ and its refusenik partners, to that of petty organizational rivalry, thereby demeaning and even marginalizing the issues and their campaigns.

It is necessary to convey not only the historical facts of the grassroots activist branch of the Soviet Jewry movement, but also the unique emotional and political convictions—the style and passion—that distinguished the approach and behavior of activists from the "establishment" branch of the movement. What unified them was the sharing of a fundamental premise: that they were the voice, the mechanism for empowering the Jewish national movement, the activists themselves, inside the Soviet Union. For the activists in the West, it was the Soviet Jews' movement first and last, and not the movement of the Jewish establishment organizations of the Diaspora or the government of Israel.

What the general public perceived to be the "Soviet Jewry movement" had, in fact, many strands. Most important among these strands is the one consisting of tens of thousands of individuals—mostly American Jews—who raised their voices at home and made trips to the Soviet Union on behalf of the refuseniks. Their numbers, organized by activists and establishment personalities alike, knew little and cared less about "leadership issues" or "strategies." They constituted the magnificent strength of the movement in the West.

The policymaking strands comprised many venues, but can generally be divided into two camps: the establishment and the independent grassroots activists. From the 1940s through the mid-1990s, despite fundamental differences, all supporters of Soviet Jews were united under the banner, "Let My People Go." However, the activists had a second slogan, "Never Again," which referred to the almost total abandonment of the Jews during the Holocaust by Western governments (including the

United States and especially Great Britain), as well as the Jewish organizational establishment.

Whether or not the establishment players liked or admitted it, the movement was, in reality, pluralistic. Generally, the activists fought for pluralism while the establishment's attitude ranged from ambivalence to hostility. Both sides made vital contributions to the movement's success, which culminated in the late 1980s. By its very definition, the establishment side has been dominant in explaining the movement to the wider public. Activists fear that such explanations are increasingly trading in revisionist history.

While most chapters in this book have been prepared by establishment leaders, this section is an early attempt to raise the balancing considerations. It is hoped that, ultimately, historians will address this aspect of the movement and recount it as a remarkable, historic, and successful exercise in Jewish solidarity and self-defense. My goal here is to argue that questions of organizational turf played little or no important role in the issues of principle, strategy, and tactics that divided the two very different philosophies of the movement.

Born partly out of the fundamental Jewish need to ransom the captives and take responsibility one for another, and partly out of a sense of guilt that the Jews of the Holocaust had been abandoned, Jews worldwide banded together to pressure the Soviet Union to "Let Our People Go." The grassroots campaign began in Palestine, haltingly, even before the State of Israel was established; it spread to the United States, Canada, France and the U.K. during the 1960s; and, by the early 1970s, it was on its way to becoming the massive Soviet Jewry movement as we now know it.

The early roots of the movement in Palestine are described in a slim book that should be required reading for those who fail to understand the depths of Israeli governmental antagonism to the activist campaign: *A Matter of Priorities: Labor Zionism and the Plight of Soviet Jewry, 1917–1996*, introduction by Dr. Victor Polsky, former Soviet Jewish refusenik, and written by the transparently pseudonymous Dr. Geoffrey Martin and Natan Herzl. *Priorities* begins by tracing the passion for Russian communism by the early labor Zionists: "While still on the train taking him out of the USSR [in late 1923], Ben-Gurion was drawing up plans for reshaping Zionist attitudes toward the Soviet Union." The author wrote that his goal was "to immediately change the policy regarding Soviet Russia, to cease all attacks and provocations against the [Soviet] government and all the various slanders." He went on: "Bowing to grassroots pressure . . . from Palestine Jews who for years had been decrying the Labor Zionists' lack of interest in Soviet Jewry . . . the Labor Zionist leadership in early 1940 decided to recognize and cooperate with 'Magen' [shield], the Tel Aviv–based ad hoc committee to assist Soviet Jewry that had been operating informally since 1928."

When the Soviet Union unexpectedly decided, in 1947, to recognize the State of Israel, Magen leaders wrote to Foreign Minister Shertok, urging him to "seize the opportunity to press the Soviet government to free all the Prisoners of Zion and permit them to immigrate to Israel." But Shertok responded that "relations between Israel and the USSR are the relations of two states, and neither one may interfere in the other's internal affairs in any way." This was precisely the position the Soviets used in opposing the Soviet Jewry movement in the West.

In the early 1950s, Stalin's paranoia and rabid anti-Semitism reached their apogee with the infamous accusation of the existence of a "doctor's plot" to kill him and other Soviet leaders, followed by a "show" trial that led to internal exile and threatened pogroms. Yet World Jewish Congress president Nahum Goldmann, who once claimed that "the accusations of anti-Semitism made against the USSR have been very much exaggerated," not surprisingly opposed Magen's efforts in early 1953 to organize an emergency world conference on the plight of Soviet Jewry. The immediate need for an emergency conference faded when Stalin suddenly died.

By the mid-1950s, the Israeli government's grip on the subject was beginning to slip, due to domestic pressure from Magen and the stirrings of anti-Soviet criticism from so-called conservative American organizations like the American Jewish Committee, a special target at the time. In response, mainly in order to co-opt this growing opposition, the government initiated quiet discussions about the Soviet Jewry problem between its diplomats abroad and Diaspora Jewish leaders. The Israeli strategy of containment vis-à-vis the Diaspora organizations was set and described in a September 1995 letter to its embassies and consulates, written by Avraham Harman, the deputy director-general of the Foreign Ministry. Harman instructed Israeli diplomats "to intervene in local Soviet Jewry protests to keep their tone down."

Furthermore, Harman directed: "We must prevent all anti-Soviet sentiments from being expressed in such activities, whether by Israeli representatives or local Jewish sources. . . . We must act, lest the impression be created that we are interfering with the international effort toward détente, or are inciting against the Soviet Union. . . . [We must] pay special attention to [Diaspora] Jewish newspapers. We must prevent two dangers: writings that are inciteful, and anti-Soviet writings."

In America, the activist rescue movement arose in the 1960s in response to the Soviets' repression of Jews and their refusal to permit them to emigrate to Israel. The principal enduring organizations were Student Struggle for Soviet Jewry, founded by Jacob Birnbaum and led by him with Glenn Richter, and the Union of Councils for Soviet Jews, founded in 1970 by five local action committees that had been operating in the 1960s. (In the 1980s, Rabbi Avi Weiss joined the SSSJ leadership as its national chairman.)

Soviet Jews—refuseniks and Prisoners of Zion (a.k.a. Prisoners of Conscience)—ignited the sparks themselves. Fearful that these sparks would be fanned into an uncontrollable firestorm of public protest, the Labor-dominated government of Israel attempted to take control. By and large, the Israelis were successful at bottling up the grassroots' impulse to make noise throughout the 1950s and most of the 1960s. But by 1970, the genie of confrontational freedom demonstrations and activism was out and running.

I use "activists" to denote the grassroots Soviet Jewry leaders who were independent of the Jewish "establishment." The activists and the establishment were divided by questions of turf and control, to be sure, but primarily over matters of principle. They differed over their respective perceptions of who was the client they served above all other considerations: the Soviet Jews themselves or the State of Israel. They disagreed over questions of tactics and style: quiet diplomacy versus making noise. And they argued over many key policy issues, from the Jackson-Vanik amendment to the necessity of aliyah only (that is, only the right to emigrate from the USSR, as opposed to the freedom of choice to emigrate to wherever they chose), to the propriety of inclusion of broader human rights concerns and alliances.

Perhaps the ultimate distinction between the two camps was that the establishment preferred to work with, perhaps even to trust in, governmental leaders; the activists, believing that all governments put "national" interests ahead of "human" interests, put their trust in their partners among indigenous Soviet Jewish leaders. The activists' strategy gave validity to their claim that the establishment routinely patronized the Soviet Jews; the establishment countered that the activists were not subject to discipline. Such was the essence of the pluralistic movement.

But to the tens of thousands of Israeli and Western Jews (as well as many non-Jews) who stood in vigils, wrote letters and telegrams, and traveled (often covertly) to the USSR to meet with Soviet Jews, such distinctions were largely unknown. Everyone who participated was indeed an activist in his or her own right. Without these legions, the cause would surely have failed. In contrast to the Holocaust, our combined efforts had positive results in the raising of the Iron Curtain, and a miraculous exodus ensued. At various moments, Western human rights organizations and democratic governments lent their voices and diplomacy to this extraordinary movement. The UCSJ/congressional initiative to enact the Jackson-Vanik amendment, which denied most-favored-nation (MFN) trade status to Communist countries that denied their citizens the freedom of emigration, was America's finest hour in the international battle for human rights.

For for the most part, however, governments behaved like governments; it was "people power" that pressed for human rights and helped bring down the Soviet Union. In efforts to demoralize Anatoly Sharansky, the celebrated Jewish dissident, his KGB captors told him he would never leave prison because the world had forgotten him. Against the might of the Soviet state, he was told, his only supporters were "an army of students and housewives," a derisive reference to Student Struggle for Soviet Jewry and the Union of Councils for Soviet Jews. These captors clearly underestimated how much an army of students and housewives could alter international politics. Their underestimation was especially vivid in the case of Sharansky, who was not supported initially as a Prisoner of Zion by the Israelis or the Western Jewish establishment because he had been a political dissident.

By the late 1980s, virtually every Jew in America supported or had joined that army. And on the occasion of the first Reagan-Gorbachev summit meeting in Washington in 1987, some 250,000 Americans, mostly Jews, gathered on the National Mall for Freedom Sunday to send Gorbachev the message. It was a brief but satisfying union of all the strands of the Soviet Jewry movement called together at the behest and inspiration of the recently released Sharansky, now an aliyah Zionist.

Origin and History of the UCSJ

On 2 May 1968, in a memo to other local action councils, Dr. Louis Rosenblum, vice chairman of the Cleveland Council on Soviet Anti-Semitism (writing on behalf of the council's chairman, Dr. Herbert Caron), proposed a meeting to explore the establishment of a coordinating committee to "generate or support sustained community action on behalf of Soviet Jewry." Such a committee, preliminarily named the National Advisory Council on Soviet Jewry (NACSJ), "would [continue] to work within and through the existing Jewish organizational structure. . . . As a consequence of our efforts, we now are the de facto leaders on this issue in our communities. In view of our leadership role, and in light of the failure of the American Jewish Conference on Soviet Jewry (predecessor of today's National Conference for Soviet Jewry) to generate or support sustained community action on behalf of Soviet Jewry, it seems timely to seek ways of augmenting our local efforts, as well as ways to aid in the establishment of new councils of concern."

In March 1970, this new committee took permanent organizational form with the establishment of the Union of Councils for Soviet Jews. Dr. Lou Rosenblum was named its first president. At the outset, it consisted of five local councils: the Bay Area Council on Soviet Jewry in Northern California, the Southern California Council for Soviet Jews, the Cleveland Council on Soviet Anti-Semitism, the Washington (D.C.) Committee for Soviet Jewry, and the South Florida Conference on Soviet Jewry. California Students for Soviet Jews also participated in UCSJ's creation.

The ink was barely dry on the incorporation documents when Rosenblum found it necessary to raise with Israel's ambassador to Washington, Yitzhak Rabin, "the behavior of a member of the Israeli Diplomatic Service, Dr. Yoram Dinstein, in what appears to be an overzealous discharge of his instructions." In his letter to Rabin of 4 May 1970, after summarizing examples of "bullying tactics" aimed at the activists dating back to 1966—including threats such as "I shall see to it that my government destroys you"—Rosenblum said, "In addition to his intemperate speech, Dr. Dinstein has acted in a manner to suggest interference by your government in American Jewish affairs. . . . And, recently, it has come to our attention that Dr. Dinstein has fomented the discharge of Zev Yaroslavsky (chairman of California Students for Soviet Jewry) from his position with the Jewish Federation Council of Greater Los Angeles [due to his cooperation with UCSJ activists]. Dr. Dinstein's behavior is calculated to exacerbate the issue of Israeli control of American Jewish organizations."

By July 1971, UCSJ had expanded to comprise 11 local organizations, with new councils in Philadelphia, Chicago, Pittsburgh, and Montreal, as well as the Student Council for Soviet Jews in Ontario. To the dismay of the Israelis and the establishment leadership, public advocacy was being institutionalized. The following is from a status report publicly released by UCSJ on 12 July 1971:

> The UCSJ arranged and subsidized the visit of Luba Bershadskaya, a recent Jewish émigré from Russia, to major North American cities and campuses during February and March of this year. Co-sponsor of the tour was the B'nai B'rith Hillel Foundation.
> The People to People Greeting Card project of the UCSJ has provided, during the past two years, the vehicle for hundreds of thousands of North American Jews to communicate directly with Soviet Jews who signed petitions appealing for exit permits. Project coordinator Si Frumkin, director of the Southern California Council for Soviet Jews, estimated that in the most recent greeting-card mailing before Passover, more than 150,000 cards were distributed. . . .
> Member councils of the UCSJ produce materials for national distribution. "Let My People Go," a new documentary film, is distributed by the California Students for Soviet Jews, Los Angeles. A 125-page handbook for community action, planning and education, and "Before My Eyes," a film featuring Dr. [Rabbi] A. J Heschel, is produced by the Cleveland Council on Soviet Anti-Semitism. Other items produced by the councils range from bumper stickers to buttons and posters to protest seals.
> Member councils also provide the organization for action of national scope, as exemplified in the coordination by the Bay Area Council on Soviet Jews, San Francisco, of the constructive confrontations greeting the 1970 tour of the Moiseyev Dancers in cities across the country.

UCSJ's first national conference was held in Philadelphia on 4–6 September 1971. By then, the number of councils had risen by sixteen, with the additions of Norfolk, San Diego, Toronto, Long Island, and Wilmington. Twenty-five activists attended this historic meeting. At the

5 September Plenum, dues were fixed at $100/council/annum; a surtax of 5 cents per pack of cards and ½ cent per sheet of stamps was levied on the councils producing cards and stamps, the proceeds to go to the UCSJ treasury.

Morey Shapira, a past president of the Bay Area Council and UCSJ, cut his Soviet Jewry activism teeth in the 1970s as a student in Boston. In a paper reminiscing on the Soviet Jewry movement in Boston in the 1970s, he reviews first his early involvement in Student Struggle and the student Jewish newspaper *Genesis 2*, which he called "the main newspaper in which the topic of Soviet Jewry was raised, analyzed and debated. It wasn't that [it] was the only newspaper in existence, but the so-called Anglo-Jewish press reflected the apathy and disinterest of the Jewish leadership in Boston."

In Boston, according to Shapira, there was a galvanizing moment: "In March 1971, after the worldwide Brussels Conference on Soviet Jewry, the editorial staff of *Genesis 2* issued the following indictment in a lengthy editorial":

> There was a stench in the crisp Belgian air. It stank of opportunism, organizational self-aggrandizement, bureaucratic buck-passing, cowardice and cynicism. It was the smell of Jewish politics, as the world Jewish establishment bickered in the face of crisis. The world press recorded it all, and despite the hysteria in *Pravda* and *Izvestia*, no doubt the KGB recognized in the Brussels World Conference that same penchant for disunity that paralyzed world Jewry while six million died.

In three days in February, many of us, who had rejected the Radical Zionists on one hand and the Jewish Defense League on the other with their insistence that the Jewish establishment was too corrupt to be reformed, and who chose in the face of our friends' scorn to work within the system to deter Jewry from its death wish, were shown the futility of our delusions. The Brussels Conference was perhaps the most telling evidence of the moral bankruptcy of world Jewish leadership since the Holocaust.

In 1974, Shapira and other dedicated activists in the Boston area decided to make a break from the Jewish establishment, organizing Action for Soviet Jewry. Frustrated with the establishment's incessant bickering and ineffectiveness, Action for Soviet Jewry relied on grassroots campaigning to get the message across that Soviet Jews needed help. Council members spoke at synagogues and briefed tourists to the USSR; files were kept for individual refuseniks. Members briefed their representatives in Washington, including those who flew to the Soviet Union. They even sponsored an art exhibit, "Twelve from the Soviet Underground," that featured works from refusenik artists at Brandeis University. The resulting publicity elicited interest from the Boston Jewish community and brought funds to the council, allowing it to remain independent of establishment support.

Shapira's account is typical of UCSJ's local activists and councils, who made waves in their respective communities through popular outreach and mobilization. Over the years, the Bay Area Council, led by Harold Light and David Waksberg, provided the signal venue on the West Coast for demonstrations in front of the Soviet Consulate in San Francisco. In 1972, Light boasted in the *Jewish Post and Opinion* that grassroots activists had "almost single-handedly created the pressures" that made the Mack Truck Company withdraw its application to build the world's largest truck factory for the Soviet Union. Similarly, activists approached other American businesses to convince them not to invest in the Soviet Union. Light also trumpeted his organization's direct discussions and alliances with veterans' groups, labor groups, and influential politicians, as well its successful letter- and telegram-writing campaigns.

The Washington Committee's decades of weekly vigils in front of the Soviet Embassy, organized by Ruth Newman, served the same function. Similarly, demonstrations in New York were regularly undertaken, targeted at the Soviet Mission to the United Nations and the Aeroflot offices, by UCSJ's Long Island Committee for Soviet Jewry, chaired by Lynn Singer, and the SSSJ.

On 30 August 1990, the *Los Angeles Times* published a profile of Si Frumkin, UCSJ's third president (after Rosenblum and Harold Light), based on many interviews, including one from Zev Yaroslavsky, by then a Los Angeles city councilman. If there is one story that sums up Si Frumkin, however, Yaroslavsky would have to choose the one about the toilet plunger:

A Soviet freighter came into Los Angeles Harbor in the early 1970s. Yaroslavsky and Frumkin rented a motorboat and chugged out to the ship, intending to paint "Let the Jews Go" on the side. But how to stay in place once the engine was shut off? Frumkin solved the problem. They moored themselves to the freighter with a toilet plunger. "He's such a smart man," Yaroslavsky said, chuckling fondly. "He's so quick. His talents are so interchangeable. He'll be translating Russian one minute, fixing the refrigerator the next, figuring out the toilet plunger.

The activists found the Los Angeles Jewish Federation too conservative, cautious and bureaucratic. Whatever their ideas, they were always cautioned not to rock the boat. Frumkin split off from Federation, formed the council, teamed up with student leader Yaroslavsky and got going. Their modus operandi often bore the stamp of Frumkin's prankish wit. They hired a helicopter to fly over the Super Bowl with a banner: "Save Soviet Jewry." When Soviet Premier Leonid Brezhnev visited President Richard Nixon at San Clemente, they released five thousand helium-filled balloons imprinted with "Let My People Go." When the Bolshoi Ballet came, they distributed fake programs outside which said: "Enjoy the show, but . . ." They were accused of scare tactics, of intimidation in some of their boycott threats, such as their efforts to stop travel agents from promoting trips to the Soviet Union. "We found out there were other nuts like us across the country," Frumkin said. They teamed up to form the Union of Councils for Soviet Jews.

Just as the Doctors' Plot was a galvanizing moment for Jewish activists in then Palestine, the Leningrad trials in 1970 were perhaps the stimulant for the local councils to coalesce in forming UCSJ. One of the defendants, who had attempted to commandeer an airplane to take them to Israel, was Yosef Mendelevitch, whose religious passion was so beautifully described by coprisoner Natan Sharansky in *Fear No Evil*. Once released and allowed to emigrate to Israel, Mendelevich founded the Soviet Jewry grassroots organization, Soviet Jewry Education and Information Centre, with funds from many sources, including UCSJ. He was joined in the enterprise by Shmuel Azark, Yuri Shtern (currently a member of the Knesset), and others. The SJEIC later became the organizational platform upon which Sharansky founded the Soviet Jewry Zionist Forum, which led to the formation of the Israeli political party Bet Aliyah. In the early 1990s, UCSJ organized the first U.S. fund-raiser for the forum in Norfolk, Virginia.

In his introduction to *A Matter of Priorities*, Victor Polsky asserts that "Soviet Jews won their fight not because of the efforts of the Labor party establishment, but rather despite the establishment's apathy and even resistance." He refers to the book by Geoffrey Martin and Natan Herzl (pseudonyms) that "gives appropriate credit to the many activists who took part in the struggle to free the Prisoners of Zion in particular and Soviet Jewry in general. . . . Those activists in the free world who refused to buckle were the ones who earned respect from the Soviet Jews who were struggling against an oppressive regime." The authors document decades of Labor's enchantment with Communism and indifference to Soviet Jews, both before and after diplomatic relations were broken. They validate UCSJ's refusal to submit to the silence that Israeli governments attempted to impose on us.

The rapid rise of the Soviet Jewry protest movement in Israel and the West compelled the Labor government to at least pay lip service to the cause. In the United States, the Student Struggle for Soviet Jewry, the Union of Councils for Soviet Jews and the International League for the Repatriation of Russian Jews were stirring American Jewish consciousness. In what appeared to be a hopeless situation, a part of hope was ignited, thanks both to the courage and heroism of the Jews in the Soviet Union, first among them the Prisoners of Zion, and to the struggle waged by various Jewish activist organizations and individuals in the West. During those long years, every day, whether in the blistering heat of summer or the freezing temperatures of winter, on every street corner and outside of every Soviet office, activists for the cause of Soviet Jewry made their voices heard. Their stubbornness gladdened the hearts of all those who eventually saw the light of freedom.

In its first dozen years, UCSJ often employed a Washington representative, but its headquarters moved each year or two as its respective council-based presidents changed. In the early 1980s, under the presidencies of Robert Gordon (Boston Action) and then Lynn Singer (Long Island Committee), the Union planned and then established a permanent headquarters in Washington. (Under the rotating system, the temporary headquarters were previously located in Washington during the presidency of Irene Manekovsky, who spearheaded UCSJ's collaboration with Congress to enact the Jackson-Vanik amendment.)

By 1985, UCSJ was a 32-member council organization, with 50,000 grassroots members. By 1988, membership soared to nearly 100,000 (UCSJ and council membership combined), and UCSJ was affiliated with Soviet Jewry organizations in the United States, United Kingdom, Australia, Canada, France, Israel, and Moscow.

Throughout the 1970s and 1980s, UCSJ and its councils maintained extensive databases and telephone contacts, tracking the cases of thousands of refuseniks, Prisoners of Conscience and their families. The councils maintained a "real time" communications network via fax machines; e-mail and the UCSJ website (www.fsumonitor.com) are more recent additions to its communications efforts. The case information was at the heart of our ability to provide instantaneous public information about crisis situations, and to inform the administration, Congress, and nongovernmental organizations. UCSJ worked with scientists, attorneys, and medical professionals in exposing ethical violations against refuseniks and prisoners, including psychiatric abuse, illegal detention, and job discrimination and dismissals. Boston Action established the Medical Mobilization for Soviet Jewry, while UCSJ launched the International Physicians Commission (operating out of Chicago Action) and a Soviet Jewry Legal Advocacy Center, organized by law professor Donna Artz and housed initially within Boston Action.

UCSJ maintained a continuing interest and direct involvement in the Helsinki Human Rights Review Process. In 1980, for instance, it formed the Robert F. Drinan Human Rights Center at the Helsinki accords review meetings in Madrid, thus creating a focal point for disseminating information to conference delegates and the press, and providing a venue for human rights activists to publicize their concerns. Well into the 1990s, UCSJ leaders participated in every human rights conference. I represented the U.S. government as a public member of the delegation to the 1993 Warsaw review conference; Pamela Cohen had similarly represented the United States at the 1991 Geneva conference.

In 1988, three major refusenik groups in Russia became affiliated with UCSJ; the following year, UCSJ held its annual meeting in Moscow and Leningrad. UCSJ became the first Western nongovernmental organization to hold a public meeting on Soviet soil. Other firsts associated with these meetings were the first-ever public meeting of Soviet human rights dissidents, and the first public academic forum on anti-Semitism in Leningrad. (Shortly after the breakup of the Soviet Union, Pamela Cohen became the first human rights or Jewish leader to address a formal session of the Leningrad city council; immediately afterward, our delegation met with the chair and members of the Leningrad Soviet's human rights committee.)

In 1990, shortly after receiving permission to emigrate to America, Moscow refusenik leader Dr. Leonid Stonov established UCSJ's human rights bureau in the capital, the first Western human rights joint venture registered in the history of the Soviet Union. Since then, UCSJ has established bureaus that monitor anti-Semitism and human rights concerns. These bureaus are in Saint Petersburg (coordinated by the Bay Area Council), Kiev (later to become independent), Bishkek, Almaty, Minsk, Tbilisi, Lviv, and Riga, with plans to establish a monitoring post in Minsk. (Leaders of the National Conference for Soviet Jews and the Council of Jewish Federations publicly condemned UCSJ for establishing the Moscow bureau, claiming that the newly credentialed Israeli Consulate was fully capable of defending the rights of Soviet Jews.)

Throughout most of the 1970s and 1980s, UCSJ leaders were denied visas to enter the Soviet Union. Pamela Cohen, for instance, was denied entry for nine years following her 1978 trip. Our leaders maintained contact with our partners inside the USSR through phone calls that were routinely jammed and by proxy visitors not on the KGB watch lists. My first trip occurred in 1987 on the occasion of the first Moscow summit between Presidents Reagan and Gorbachev. After being denied a visa as usual, Pam and I traveled to Helsinki, where Reagan stopped on his way to Moscow. Avi Weiss and Glenn Richter of SSSJ accompanied us to the Finnish capital, and we conducted daily demonstrations that made the front pages of the European press. At the last moment—due in part to our theatrics and, more important, to the direct intervention of General Colin Powell, Reagan's national security adviser—we were permitted to enter Leningrad for the week of the summit and Moscow the following week.

One telephone call from outside our Leningrad hotel to Leningrad refusenik leader Edward Markov led to fourteen days of continuous meetings with Soviet Jewish activists. Merely by word of mouth, close to one thousand Soviet refuseniks traveled from as far as twelve time zones westward to express their gratitude to Pam and UCSJ, and to confer with us about their common situation and the strategies best calculated to achieve their freedom. Pam knew scores of them personally, and she had extensive knowledge of hundreds of specific cases. Beyond the sheer power of this universal response, I was struck most by a phenomenon of selflessness: in all the hundreds of interviews we conducted during those two weeks, not a single refusenik or prisoner's family member advocated on behalf of his or her own case. Such was their commitment to the unified cause.

Surely the bitterest issue that divided the grassroots activists from the establishment in the late 1980s was Israel's efforts to persuade the Soviets to permit Soviet Jews to fly directly from Moscow to Israel, in exchange for Israeli and American establishment promises to seek repeal of Jackson-Vanik. Israel had always defined the Soviet Jewry movement as exclusively an aliyah movement, a definition that ruled out the freedom to choose emigration to the United States and all other human rights considerations.

Earlier, Israeli diplomats had appealed to Washington to curtail the U.S. refugee program for Soviet Jews. The American Jewish establishment, joining UCSJ, opposed such an initiative. Thus, the Israelis developed the "direct flight" alternative. But in devising this scheme, Israel never consulted with the refusenik leadership, nor did representatives from the American Jewish establishment that promoted this new plan.

While recognizing the importance to Israel's security in receiving this important influx of Jews, we nonetheless publicly advocated the principle of freedom of choice and retaining the all-important Jackson-Vanik amendment. The reason was that we consulted with the refusenik leadership in the Soviet Union—our partners and clients—and this was the preferred approach of the overwhelming majority of them. As their voice in the West, we could take no other position. The rationale for their position was embedded in two strategic views, one principled and one pragmatic.

First, there was significant overlap between Jewish prisoners and refuseniks and human rights leaders (then called dissidents). The Jewish leadership believed that both their security and that of the dissidents were based in common causes. To them, aliyah and emigration to the West were indistinguishable components of the freedom to move to any country, as is guaranteed by the Helsinki Final Act and the Universal Declaration of Human Rights. To be limited to going to Israel undermined the international force of the broader human rights movement and thus undermined the strength of their dissident colleagues. Beyond this, they strongly believed in the human rights principle of freedom of movement and thus—even for many who were themselves planning to make aliyah—they could not sacrifice the rights of those who, despite Israel's needs and demands, chose to emigrate to the West, typically to be reunited with close family members.

Second, these Soviet Jewry activists had a practical concern as well. They saw their ultimate safety and rescue as depending upon pressure on the Soviets from the West, especially the United States, and not from Israel, which had little if any leverage on Soviet policy compared to her

Arab neighbors (who were in total opposition to expanding aliyah). The Soviet Jewish leaders feared that if the American refugee program and the emigration stream of Soviet Jews were to end, the U.S. government would withdraw and cede the issue to the advocacy of the Israelis. What's more, the pending Israeli plan would have shifted the transit point from Vienna to Romania, which, unlike the Soviet Union, actually had scheduled air service to Israel. Thus, they feared, the plan would push the entire Jewish emigration program out of the international spotlight and far from American influence and the monitoring capacity of human rights and Soviet Jewry organizations. As long as Soviet emigration policy limited even the small number of émigrés to Jews departing on Israeli documents, direct flights to Israel via Romania were extremely dangerous to the millions of Jews hoping to leave. Freedom of choice to travel via Vienna was thus essential.

The issue, which immediately escalated into a question of who has the right to speak on behalf of Soviet Jews, burst into explosive public discussion in April 1987. Rabbi Arthur Schneier, president of the Appeal of Conscience Foundation in New York, claimed to have negotiated a plan whereby the Soviets had agreed to establish a new transit procedure for future Jewish émigrés that would eliminate the phenomenon of Jews dropping out and going to the United States instead of Israel. There was no mention of the number of Jews allowed to leave. Morris Abram, chairman both of NCSJ and the Conference of Presidents of Major American Jewish Organizations, had previewed a similar plan earlier, based on his own trip to Romania the previous December. He told the press that Romania's success in getting a Jackson-Vanik waiver should encourage the Soviets to take the same tack.

With this as background, in late March, Abram and Edgar Bronfman, president of the World Jewish Congress, traveled from Israel to Moscow to meet with Soviet officials. Abram, in a statement upon his return to Israel, said his and Bronfman's aim "was to get the 'Jewish problem' off the table so as to remove it as an issue of contention." The deal involved direct flights to Israel and annual U.S. waivers of Jackson-Vanik for the Soviets, assuming at least ten to twelve thousand of the longest-held refuseniks were permitted to emigrate.

The activists in Moscow and the West expressed outrage, both on the merits and on procedure. UCSJ, then a member of the Conference of Presidents, was never made aware of the trip or its purpose: Abram had no right to negotiate in the name of his umbrella organization. Refusenik leaders and Prisoners of Zion in Moscow complained that there were neither prior consultations with them, nor a meaningful discussion after their consultations with Soviet leaders. Activists also complained that the offer lacked firm commitments of major emigration—on the order of fifty to sixty thousand people per year—as a basis for even a one-year waiver of Jackson-Vanik, and there were no discussions of the Soviets reversing a wide range of anti-Jewish behaviors. Activists also condemned the direct flight idea as running counter to international human rights guarantees of freedom of movement.

Of course, the Soviets agreed to no such deal. This episode underscored the fact that Jewish establishment leaders continued to have faith in secret meetings to negotiate for the rights of people whom they do not legitimately represent. This embarrassment provided the background for an important Soviet Jewry meeting a few weeks later in London. At the time, the Israelis convened annual meetings of the Soviet Jewry worldwide establishment. NCSJ was the official delegate to such meetings from the United States, and ordinarily UCSJ was not invited. In early June 1987, in the interest of détente with UCSJ, the Israeli Soviet Jewry office's envoy in Washington invited Pam and me to attend the three-day meeting in London, scheduled the last week in June. We accepted. However, a day or two before our arrival, the 18 June issue of the *New York Times* (and, subsequently, the *International Herald Tribune*) published our op-ed article entitled "Give Soviet Jews a Choice," and opposing the coercive elements of the Israeli direct-flight plan.

When we arrived at the London meeting of the Soviet Jewry "Praesidium," as it was then called, we faced a firestorm of organized anger and condemnation. If there had been an agenda for the three-day meeting, it was canceled in order to deal with us. For two and-a-half days, speaker after speaker, country after country, condemned us. On the third day, they finally let Pam speak. When she began, the leader of the French Soviet Jewry establishment organization interrupted her to announce that he would not remain in the room while she was speaking, and promptly left.

Perhaps the most effectively presented diatribe came from Morris Abram, purportedly the chief spokesperson for American Jewry. I recall vividly his main points: (1) Soviet Jews have no right to emigrate to America as persecuted refugees; their only goal is economic advantage; (2) the Soviet Jewry Movement is exclusively an aliyah movement, not a human rights movement—how dare we distort it.

In contrast, at the conclusion of the meetings, Abram was the principal spokesman. Here, in public, he made an eloquent and passionate speech about the importance of the meeting, about the desperate plight of Soviet Jews. Throughout his remarks to the press, he repeatedly referred to the Soviet Jewry movement as a human rights effort. We wondered if either he or the other assembled participants gathered around him noticed the incongruence.

A new chapter in Jewish history opened with the dissolution of the Soviet Union and the mass emigration of many of its Jews. While Israeli and U.S. policies with the fifteen successor republics understandably may still not reflect a primary concern for the Jews living there, altered conditions have created a new playing field. First, the situation in and regarding Israel has changed. Israel's direct relations with the FSU (former Soviet Union) republics obviate her former reliance on proxies in the Jewish establishment. This alone has largely resolved the conflicts between UCSJ and the Israeli-led Soviet Jewry establishment in the United States. Second, there has evolved a grassroots Soviet Jewry presence in Israel. This is an allusion to, of course, Natan Sharansky, Yuli Edelstein, and Yuri Shtern, who have now become part of the political establishment there. What effects the inevitable politics of compromise will have on Soviet Jews is unpredictable, but one cannot expect a cabinet minister to act as a Soviet Jewry grassroots activist. Third, as a result of American immigration policy, Israel has become, by default, the destination for the vast majority of Jews seeking refuge, and the center of Soviet Jewry advocacy has shifted from Washington to Jerusalem's multitiered relations with those former Soviet governments. The potential for quiet diplomacy between Israel and the republics, previously conducted even in the absence of official relations, are inherent in the nature of bilateral politics.

In such conditions, the potential for the Israeli government to become the exclusive "agent" for advocacy, or for it to develop a monopoly on information, raises concerns. This concern gives increased importance to the need for independent monitoring of anti-Semitism and neofascism in the FSU, distribution of information to train a protective spotlight of world attention on the physical and political jeopardy of FSU Jews, and to provide related advocacy—activities all but exclusively the province and mandate of UCSJ and its bureaus across the former Soviet Union.

Revolutionary changes in the American Jewish community will impact on UCSJ and its leadership. Two billion dollars are being transferred from the accounts of aging and recently deceased Jewish philanthropists to their children, who themselves are now the heads of corporations, foundations, charities, and other philanthropic institutions. The Jewish elders, if they were not Holocaust survivors themselves, carried within them the memory of the Shoah; strongly identified with the State of Israel that was born within their lifetime; and recognized the mitzvah of *tzedakah*: feeding the Jewish hungry, caring for the aged, and educating the young. The new Jewish leaders are further from the Holocaust; are more psychologically distanced from Israel; are less guided by a deep sense of Jewish responsibility; and seem more inclined to support secular institutions such as hospitals, universities, museums, symphonies, and opera companies than the needs of their brethren abroad.

There is more than a suggestion that American Jews are turning inward, away from the needs of Israel, certainly away from the issues of Soviet Jews, under the misconception that their problems were resolved with the emigration option. The massive needs for Yiddishkeit and Jewish education and to ensure post-Soviet Jews' physical and political security are tough sells to an American Jewish public increasingly concerned about being decimated through assimilation.

On top of these developments, there have transpired fundamental political and socioeconomic shifts in the former Soviet Union. Nearly a million Jews from this region have emigrated, and as many no longer confront the same state-imposed bars. Nor, for the most part, are they confronted by the harshest manifestations of government-sponsored anti-Semitism. One cannot, however, conclude that they now live in a post-Soviet utopia.

Although the conditions in the republics vary, anti-Semitism remains. Fires and explosions have destroyed or damaged more synagogues and other Jewish institutions since the fall of Communism than in all of post-Stalin communism. Jewish graves and cemeteries have been desecrated. Jewish property, expropriated under Communism, still has not been returned to many Jewish communities. Hate crimes against Jews and Jewish property often are not investigated; Jews are still subjected to arbitrary arrest and are denied visas on the pretext of state secrets. The language and rhetoric of nationalist extremism and the opposition to reform remain.

In September 1997, Russia enacted a discriminatory religion law, elevating the historically anti-Semitic Russian Orthodox Church to the de facto status of the state religion. A president who publicly expresses admiration for Adolf Hitler rules Belarus. The governor of the Krasnador region of Russia recently made a speech to a youth convention invoking such anti-Semitic epithets as kikes, kike-masons, and cosmopolitans no fewer than sixty-one times! And now, Russia faces a presidential succession crisis, with Russian nationalists such as General Lebed and Moscow mayor Lushkov the current front-runners. The result is that fear still stalks Jews in the FSU, especially those in the vast provinces far from the central cities of Moscow, Saint Petersburg, and Kiev.

The most effective way to combat anti-Semitism is through monitoring: recording and documenting individual and systematic abuses against Jews and making them known to Western policymakers and the general public. This is a particularly urgent need in the provincial areas of Russia and Ukraine, where the dearth of media attention has allowed anti-Semitic officials and neofascist groups to carry out their hateful campaigns with impunity. UCSJ has been at the forefront of such monitoring efforts, organizing a network of local monitors to report on the safety of these remote Jewish communities.

Decimated by high rates of intermarriage, Jews today are products of the systematic destruction of Jewish knowledge and Yiddishkeit and the cultivation of anti-Semitism that has bred Jewish self-hatred. It is in this context that Christian missionaries have flooded into Ukraine and Russia to harvest Jewish souls. In a corrupt society, the elderly and infirm are devastated by hunger, poverty, and lack of medicine, and scores of communities look to our partnership Project Yad L'Yad (Hand to Hand) for assistance. Today, seventy Yad L'Yad partnerships exist, organized chiefly through the efforts of cochairs Marillyn Tallman and Hinda Cantor, who also chair UCSJ's Chicago and South Florida councils, respectively.

The world's focus has shifted away from what was the Soviet Union, and so, too, has the interest of most of Western Jewry. But really, if we re-examine the past, it was ever so. Our sacred mission continues: to feed the hungry, educate the young, support emigration and aliyah, and combat anti-Semitism and neofascism through monitoring and advocacy. The Jewish future calls to us, in greater complexity, perhaps, but it is up to us, all of us, to meet it.

Note

I am indebted to Pamela B. Cohen for important contributions to this article.

Contributors

ALBERT D. CHERNIN is Executive Vice Chairman Emeritus of the Jewish Council for Public Affairs [formerly the National Jewish Community Relations Advisory Council]. As Executive of the American Jewish Conference on Soviet Jewry [now the National Conference on Soviet Jewry] he launched the American Campaign for Soviet Jewry. From 1975 to 1990 he served on the Presidium of the World Conference on Soviet Jewry.

MURRAY FRIEDMAN has served as Director of the Center for American Jewish History, Temple University, since 1990 and as Middle Atlantic States Director of the American Jewish Committee since 1959. He has published numerous works, including: *What Went Wrong: The Creation and Collapse of the Black-Jewish Alliance* (Free Press), *When Philadelphia Was the Capital of Jewish America* (Associated University Presses), and *The Tribal Basis of American Life: Racial, Religious, and Ethnic Groups in Conflict* (Greenwood).

DR. ZVI Y. GITELMAN is currently Professor of Political Science and Preston R. Tisch Professor of Judaic Studies at the University of Michigan. The most recent of his many books are *Developments in Soviet and Post-Soviet Politics* (co-editor, Macmillan, 1990, 1992, 1994), and *Bitter Legacy: Politics and the Holocaust in the USSR* (Indiana University Press, forthcoming).

MARSHALL I. GOLDMAN is the Kathryn Wasserman Davis Professor of Russian Economics at Wellesley College and Associate Director of the Davis Center for Russian Studies at Harvard University. His many books on the Soviet Union include: *Gorbachev's Challenge: Economic Reform in the Age of High Technology* (1987) and *Lost Opportunity: What Has Made Economic Reform in Russia So Difficult* (1996).

RABBI DOUGLAS KAHN is Executive Director of the Jewish Community Relations Council in San Francisco. His writings on community relations issues have been published in *American Jewish Yearbook, Journal of Jewish Communal Service,* and *Jewish Monthly.*

DR. WILLIAM KOREY is former Director of the Anti-Defamation League office in Washington, D.C., and Director of B'nai B'rith, UN office. His books include: *Glasnost & Anti-Semitism* (American Jewish Committee), and *Russian Anti-Semitism, Pamyat, and the Demonology of Zionism* (forthcoming).

NECHEMIA LEVANON was appointed by Golda Meir to head "Nativ" ("pathway"), the department in the Prime Minister's office that operated in 1969 behind the Iron Curtain to encourage and support the Jews in their struggle for their rights. As head of the department he worked directly under three prime ministers in unbroken sequence: Golda Meir, Itzhak Rabin, and Menachem Begin. In 1982 he retired from government service and has devoted his time to writing his memoirs, which are to be published soon.

MICAH H. NAFTALIN is the National Director of the Union of Councils for Soviet Jews in Washington, D.C. Previously he served as Chief Counsel of the U.S. House of Representatives Select Committee on Government Research and as senior policy analyst with the National Academy of Sciences. In 1990 he presided over the founding of the Russian-American Bureau on Human Rights in Moscow, the first Western human rights organization established in the Soviet Union.

WALTER RUBY has been a journalist in Israel, the United States, and the Soviet Union for over sixteen years. He has served as correspondent for the *Jerusalem Post*, the *London Jewish Chronicle*, and the *Long Island Jewish World*. His articles and op-ed pieces have appeared in the *New York Times*, the *Wall Street Journal*, the *Christian Science Monitor*, the *Village Voice,* and *USA Today*.

RICHARD SCHIFTER is Special Assistant to the President and Counselor on the staff of the National Security Council. His previous assignments have included Assistant Secretary of State for Human Rights and Humanitarian Affairs; Deputy United States Representative in the United Nations Security Council, with the rank of Ambassador; and United States Representative to the United Nations Human Rights Commission. In 1992 he was awarded the State Department's Distinguished Service Medal.

MYRNA SHINBAUM is Director of Media Relations and a spokesperson for the Anti-Defamation League, which she joined in 1991 as Director of Soviet and East European Affairs. In 1971 she joined the National Council on Soviet Jewry, and organized the Second and Third World Conferences on Soviet Jewry (Brussels 1976, Jerusalem 1983). She coordinated Freedom Sunday, the December 1987 Washington Mobilization in support of Soviet Jews on the eve of Summit II; and organized a human rights program in Helsinki, in advance of Summit IV in Moscow.

STEVEN F. WINDMUELLER is Director of the Irwin Daniels School of Jewish Communal Service of the Hebrew Union College. Before that, he was Executive Director of the Jewish Community Relations Committee of the Jewish Federation of Los Angeles. He has held academic positions at Rutgers, SUNY Albany, and Virginia Commonwealth University and is currently an associate member of the Jerusalem Center for Public Affairs.

Index

UNIVERSITY PRESS OF NEW ENGLAND
publishes books under its own imprint and is the publisher for
Brandeis University Press, Dartmouth College, Middlebury College
Press, University of New Hampshire, Tufts University, and Wesleyan
University Press.

Library of Congress Cataloging-in-Publication Data

A second exodus : the American movement to free Soviet Jews / Murray
    Friedman and Albert D. Chernin, editors.
        p.   cm. — (Brandeis series in American Jewish history,
    culture, and life)
        Includes bibliographical references and index.
        ISBN 0–87451–912–8 (cl : alk. paper). — ISBN 0–87451–913–6 (alk.
    paper)
        1. Jews—Soviet Union—Migrations—Public opinion.   2. Refuseniks.
    3. Public opinion—Jews.   4. Public opinion—United States.
    5. Jews—United States—Politics and government.   I. Friedman,
    Murray, 1926–   .   II. Chernin, Albert D.   III. Series.
    DS135.R92S38   1999
    305.8924047—dc21   98–54463